Semantic Under-Determinacy and Communication

Semantic Under-Determinacy and Communication

Delia Belleri
National Autonomous University of Mexico

© Delia Belleri 2014

All rights reserved. No reproduction, copy or transmission of this publication may be made without written permission.

No portion of this publication may be reproduced, copied or transmitted save with written permission or in accordance with the provisions of the Copyright, Designs and Patents Act 1988, or under the terms of any licence permitting limited copying issued by the Copyright Licensing Agency, Saffron House, 6–10 Kirby Street, London EC1N 8TS.

Any person who does any unauthorized act in relation to this publication may be liable to criminal prosecution and civil claims for damages.

The author has asserted her right to be identified as the author of this work in accordance with the Copyright, Designs and Patents Act 1988.

First published 2014 by
PALGRAVE MACMILLAN

Palgrave Macmillan in the UK is an imprint of Macmillan Publishers Limited, registered in England, company number 785998, of Houndmills, Basingstoke, Hampshire RG21 6XS.

Palgrave Macmillan in the US is a division of St Martin's Press LLC, 175 Fifth Avenue, New York, NY 10010.

Palgrave Macmillan is the global academic imprint of the above companies and has companies and representatives throughout the world.

Palgrave® and Macmillan® are registered trademarks in the United States, the United Kingdom, Europe and other countries.

ISBN 978–1–137–39843–7

This book is printed on paper suitable for recycling and made from fully managed and sustained forest sources. Logging, pulping and manufacturing processes are expected to conform to the environmental regulations of the country of origin.

A catalogue record for this book is available from the British Library.

Library of Congress Cataloging-in-Publication Data
Belleri, Delia, 1983–
Semantic under-determinacy and communication / Delia Belleri.
    pages cm
Summary: "This book investigates the phenomenon of semantic under-determinacy by exploring how under-determinacy can be explained, and how communication is possible despite it. Belleri argues that the comprehension of utterances of semantically under-determined sentences is made possible by our mastery of certain conceptual constraints, as well as the information we gain from the context which does not necessarily concern the intentions and beliefs of the speaker. Combining a fresh, previously unexplored view of the subject with a detailed overview of the past and ongoing philosophical discussion on the matter, the book asserts that semantic under-determinacy comes from nothing but a lack of words or under-articulation"— Provided by publisher.
    ISBN 978–1–137–39843–7 (hardback)
    1. Semantics, Comparative.   2. Contrastive linguistics.   3. Pragmatics.   4. Discourse analysis.   5. Speech acts (Linguistics)   6. Communication.   I. Title.
    P325.5.C6B45 2014
    401'.43—dc23   2014028142

Typeset by MPS Limited, Chennai, India.

Contents

List of Tables	vii
Preface and Acknowledgements	viii

Introduction		1
1	Preliminaries	1
2	Why semantic under-determinacy is problematic	3
3	Taking semantic under-determinacy seriously	6
4	From semantic under-determinacy to context-sensitivity	12
5	Understanding utterance comprehension	19

Part I On Semantic Under-Determinacy

1	Arguing for Semantic Under-Determinacy		25
	1.1	Arguments from Incompleteness	26
		1.1.1 Incompleteness as genericity	29
		1.1.2 The slippery slope of incompleteness arguments	33
	1.2	Arguments from context-shifts	36
		1.2.1 The slippery slope of Context-Shifting Arguments	39
		1.2.2 The objection from 'impoverishment'	42
		1.2.3 The meta-theoretical objection	46
		1.2.4 The 'many understandings' version of Context-Shifting Arguments is fallacious	47
	1.3	The Argument from Unclear Applications	48
		1.3.1 The Argument from Unclear Applications is fallacious	49
	Conclusion		50
2	The Peculiarity of Semantic Under-Determinacy		52
	2.1	The peculiarity of semantic under-determinacy	52
		2.1.1 Semantic under-determinacy is not ambiguity	53
		2.1.2 Semantic under-determinacy is not vagueness	55
		2.1.3 Semantic under-determinacy is not indexicality	56
		2.1.4 Semantic under-determinacy is not syntactic ellipsis	63
	2.2	The under-articulation view	65
		2.2.1 Under-articulation and Effability	67
		2.2.2 Ineffability and the 'gappy picture'	69

	2.2.3	Effable mental contents	72
	Conclusion		76

Part II Semantic Under-Determinacy and Communication

3 Semantic Under-Determinacy and the Debate on
Context-Sensitivity ... 81
   3.1 Extreme Contextualism ... 81
   3.2 Radical Contextualism ... 83
   3.3 Indexical Contextualism ... 90
   3.4 Minimalism ... 96
   3.5 Ultra-Minimalism ... 101
   3.6 Non-Indexical Contextualism ... 104
   Conclusion ... 111

4 Semantic Under-Determinacy and Conceptual Constraints ... 113
   4.1 A preference for a semantic (rather than pragmatic) account ... 113
   4.2 The plausibility of a semantic, non-syntactic account ... 118
      4.2.1 Semantic structure can be more complex than syntactic structure ... 119
   4.3 The Conceptual Constraints View ... 127
      4.3.1 Stating the view ... 127
      4.3.2 Conceptual constraints and the argument/adjunct distinction ... 129
      4.3.3 Conceptual constraints and their semantic effects ... 132
   4.4 Concepts and words: towards Molecularism ... 139
   Conclusion ... 145

5 Semantic Under-Determinacy, Comprehension and
Meta-Representation ... 147
   5.1 Inferential approaches: from Grice to Relevance Theory ... 148
   5.2 Non-inferential approaches ... 150
   5.3 Inferences, after all ... 152
   5.4 Reconsidering the role of meta-representation ... 154
   5.5 Conceptual constraints and non-meta-representational comprehension ... 158
   5.6 Advantages and objections ... 164
   5.7 Egocentric communicators ... 167
   Conclusion ... 170

Notes ... 173

Bibliography ... 181

Index ... 191

List of Tables

5.1 Comparing the Gricean, Relevance-Theoretic and
    Non-Meta accounts   163

Preface and Acknowledgements

The origins of this book lie in my doctoral thesis, which I defended in July 2012 at the University of Bologna. I started assembling the manuscript approximately one year after obtaining my PhD, while I was doing research at the COGITO Research Centre in Bologna as well as tutoring and teaching some classes at the University of Modena and Reggio Emilia. A few months later, I moved to Mexico City and started a post-doc at the Institute of Philosophical Investigations at the National Autonomous University of Mexico (UNAM).

I became interested in the topic of semantic under-determinacy, context-sensitivity and the semantics–pragmatics interface as a result of attending a series of seminars at COGITO (which I partly also organised) in the winter and spring of 2009. As I was beginning to work on an outline of the final thesis, I thought the topic of semantic under-determinacy with all its ramifications was worth exploring and clarifying, also in light of the massive amount of literature it had generated in the previous decades. Besides the topic of semantic under-determinacy per se, of what it consists in and how it can be defended, my interest became focused on providing an account of how semantic under-determinacy could be overcome in linguistic communication. I was somewhat dissatisfied with the views dominating the debate, which either explained the resolution of semantic under-determinacy in purely pragmatic or in rigorously syntactic terms. I also thought that other available alternatives, such as the Minimalist approach or the then emerging Relativist account, were either associated with implausible theses or could not constitute legitimate options. Whence my interest in a position that could account for the resolution of semantic under-determinacy in genuinely semantic terms; by this I mean in terms of specific features of the *meaning* of expressions (or features of the *concepts* or *concept-frames* associated with them), as opposed to pragmatic mechanisms or syntactically articulated forms. My attempt to develop such an account led me to think about linguistic comprehension and to whether the semantic account I was working on could provide a model of linguistic comprehension which would only minimally (if not at all) rely on meta-representation, thus offering a less sophisticated reconstruction of how linguistic comprehension is carried out. The structure of my thesis, thus, included some chapters centred on the nature of the phenomenon of semantic under-determinacy and whether we could reduce it to already familiar forms of semantic defectiveness, such as ambiguity, vagueness, indexicality or ellipsis; some chapters devoted to an account of the context-sensitivity associated with semantically under-determined expressions cashed out in semantic–conceptual terms; and a chapter dedicated to a model of linguistic comprehension that would rely on meta-representation as little as possible. All these contents naturally flowed into the book project, provided the re-elaboration and refinements that inevitably occurred in the process of revising the thesis with the aim of turning it into a monographic volume.

Many people have contributed in various and more or less direct ways to the writing of this book. My deepest gratitude goes, first of all, to my PhD supervisor Annalisa Coliva, who followed my work from its very beginning. She played an invaluable and irreplaceable role during my years as a PhD student, not only for the many discussions and her thorough and insightful comments, but also for her constant and unceasing support. She never failed to encourage me, to the point I became convinced she believed in me more than I myself did. This book would literally not have existed, had she been a little less confident in her reminding me I could make it. My co-supervisor Marco Santambrogio had a fundamental role in helping me find the right focus for my thesis, and I thank him for the endless meetings he endured at least in the first stages of the project. Paolo Leonardi deserves special thanks for having believed in me in the first place and for giving me the chance to join the PhD programme in Bologna, thanks to whose funding I was able to work with all comforts. I am also indebted to my external examiner Manuel García-Carpintero, who supervised my work during my visit to the LOGOS Group at the University of Barcelona in 2011, and who also never failed to support me in the first steps of my career as an academic philosopher. Finally, let me acknowledge the support of the Institute of Philosophical Investigations at UNAM and in particular of Mario Gómez-Torrente; work on this book was in part subsidised by the project CONACyT CCB 2011 166502, which he leads.

I have discussed my work with many people on many occasions, so let me express my gratitude to them as well. I owe a lot to Michele Palmira, who carefully read and sent me comments on substantial parts of the book; he never failed to keep my morale high and was always ready to share his thoughts and experiences. Thanks to all the COGITO members who heard my talks or read my material and provided me with helpful feedback: Giorgio Volpe, Sebastiano Moruzzi, Eugenio Orlandelli, Luca Zanetti, Raban Reichmann and Giovanni Galli. I am grateful to the members of the LOGOS group who attended my talks in Barcelona in 2011, among whom Max Kölbel, Dan Zeman, Adrian Briciu, David Rey and Giovanni Merlo. Special thanks go to the Northern Institute of Philosophy (NIP) at the University of Aberdeen, where I held a visiting fellowship in the summer of 2013. Parts of this book benefited from my discussions with NIP members or visitors, among whom Carl Baker, Paula Sweeney, Jonathan Jenkins Ichikawa, Filippo Ferrari, Giacomo Melis, Julia Zakkou, Alexander Dinges and Jeremy Wyatt. Palgrave Macmillan editors Elizabeth Forrest and Rebecca Brennan provided me with prompt professional assistance at each stage of the preparation of this volume.

Family and friends have always been and always will be my safe harbour. Their human contribution was priceless and no acknowledgement could really do justice to it. I thank my father, Giuseppe Belleri, and my mother, Maria Costanza Jaforte, for being such amazing parents. And of course I thank my partner, Mattia Filippini, for his loving presence in every circumstance of my life and for agreeing to share his own existence, projects and dreams with me.

Parts of the text are drawn from previous works that have already appeared in press. The subsection entitled 'Rigidity Effects' in section 2.1.3 contains ideas presented and developed in greater detail in 'Why Semantic Unspecificity Is not Indexicality', currently forthcoming in the *European Journal of Analytic Philosophy* (2014). Sections 2.2.1–2.2.3 develop ideas already published in 'On What is Effable', which appeared in 2013 on *Thought: a Journal of Philosophy*, 2 (4) (Dec.), pp. 341–49. Chapter 4 develops a proposal already advanced in 'Semantic Under-Determinacy and Conceptual Constraints (Towards a Proposal about Lexical Meaning)', published in an earlier version in 2013 in the *Rivista Italiana di Filosofia del Linguaggio*, 7 (3), pp. 109–24. Finally, Chapter 5 shares some excerpts with, and develops ideas already advocated in, 'Meta-Representation in Utterance Comprehension: the Case of Semantically Incomplete Expressions', which appeared in 2013 in the *Journal of Pragmatics* 57(C), pp. 158–69 (I thank Elsevier for allowing reproduction).

Introduction

1 Preliminaries

The topic of this book is the idea that the sentences that we use generally fail to express something that could determinately be true or false. Borrowing the term from Robyn Carston (2002a), I will refer to this phenomenon as *semantic under-determinacy*. The specific focus of this book are those sentences whose semantic content, even provided disambiguation, indexicality, ellipsis or vagueness resolution, is still incapable of determining a truth-condition for their utterances. Examples of semantic under-determinacy thus characterised abound, and we may encounter dozens of them every day. It may be useful to survey some examples.

Partially following Bach (2007, 2012), we may judge some sentences as semantically under-determined because they sound somehow *conceptually truncated* to us, that is they fail to articulate some information that we feel is conceptually important. A sentence like 'Jill is ready' is incomplete in that it fails to specify for what Jill is ready; 'It's raining' or 'It's snowing' are incomplete in that they fail to specify where the rain or the snow is falling; a sentence like 'Steel isn't strong enough' is incomplete too, for it fails to say for what steel is strong enough. 'Paracetamol is better' is incomplete because it fails to articulate with respect to what paracetamol is better; and finally, 'The leaves are green' fails to specify in what way or part the leaves in question are coloured green.

Some sentences may be semantically under-determined because they contain gradable expressions whose application depends on *standards or comparison classes*, but these aspects fail to be specified: in 'Naomi is rich', one could wonder 'By what standards?'; in 'Jamal is tall', one may be unsure with respect to whom Jamal is tall (Basketball players? Jockeys?) and so on.

Some other sentences contain expressions that are just greatly *unspecific*: for instance 'Peter's book is grey' is semantically under-determined because the genitive form 'Peter's book' fails to specify which relation holds between Peter and the book – is it the book owned by Peter?, is it the book written by Peter?, and so on. 'Jack got the virus' is under-determined to the extent that it is not clear in what sense Jack *got* the virus – did he catch it and came down with the flu, or did he find it out after a number of scientific experiments? In 'Bill cut the grass', we have semantic under-determinacy to the extent that 'cut' is not specific as to the manner in which the grass was cut – with a lawnmower, with a knife, with scissors?

Sentences that contain *adjective–noun phrases* as well, like 'red pen', 'red parrot', 'red watermelon', 'fast car', 'fast meal' and so on seem to exhibit semantic under-determinacy (Lahav, 1989): an utterance of the sentence 'I have bought a red pen' is semantically under-determined to the extent that it does not say in what way the pen is red: is it coloured red (but the ink is of another colour); does it contain red ink?, and so on.

Semantic under-determinacy might be generated by specific linguistic constructions as well, such as *negation*: for instance, Atlas (1977) and Kempson (1975) have argued that some negative sentences are 'sense general', that is they determine no truth-condition: for example, it is not clear whether 'The king of France is not bald' is true just in case there is a king of France and he is not bald, or it is true just in case there is no bald king of France. Also *definite descriptions* might be regarded as giving rise to semantic under-determinacy, and in more than one way. First of all, they might be *incomplete*: consider a sentence like 'The house is pretty'; to what does the definite description 'the house' refer? Presumably, in the relevant domain of discourse more than one house is present, and the description fails to pick out any single one. As a result, the sentence turns out as semantically under-determined. Moreover, a definite description could be seen as semantically under-determined in that it does not specify whether it should be given a *referential or attributive reading*. For example, it is not clear whether a sentence like 'The murderer of Smith is insane' is true just in case a specific individual (say Jones) is insane, or just in case whoever happens to be the murderer of Smith is insane.

In some cases, one may observe that a milder variety of semantic under-determinacy obtains: a sentence's semantic content does determine a truth-condition, but it fails to express *what the speaker means* with an utterance of it (Carston, 2002a, pp. 19–20). An example is provided by sentences that contain *unrestricted quantification*; these are capable of determining an evaluable proposition which almost never corresponds to what most speakers mean with utterances of these sentences. For example, in 'Everyone is going to Martha's wedding', it is not literally meant that every person in the universe is going to Martha's wedding, for this would be a blatant falsity, but that every person in a certain domain (for instance, the speaker's family or friends) is going to the wedding.

In a further array of cases, nothing more than a *lack of qualification* seems responsible for under-determinacy of what the speaker means: in the case of 'I've had breakfast', the sentence is literally true just in case the speaker has had breakfast at least once in her life, but it is usually uttered to mean that the speaker has had breakfast on the day of utterance; 'Jack and Jill are married' expresses a content which could be true even in a scenario in which Jack and Jill are married each to some distinct person, but it is usually employed to mean that Jack and Jill are married *to each other*. As one can see, these sentences may express truth-conditions, yet these may strike as much poorer than the content they are taken to express.

The central focus of this book will be the first kind of semantic under-determinacy characterised, whereby a sentence fails to determine a truth-condition for its utterances. The second kind of semantic under-determinacy illustrated seems less interesting in that it does not concern a failure to express something truth-conditional, but simply a failure to express what the speaker has in mind or intends to communicate. The problem does not seem to be one of semantic defectiveness, but rather one of pragmatic inadequacy of the content expressed by the sentence vis-à-vis the content intended by the speaker (see Borg, 2004). Be that as it may, we have no reason not to think that offering a solution to the first, and more serious kind of semantic under-determinacy will imply offering a solution also to the second and less serious kind. After all, it seems attractive and theoretically parsimonious to think that the mechanism by means of which the under-determinacy of truth-conditions is overcome is the same as the mechanism by means of which the under-determinacy of the speaker's content is overcome. In what follows, then, I will assume that the search for a solution to semantic under-determinacy in the first sense (as failure to express truth-conditions) will be indirectly also a search for a solution to semantic under-determinacy in the second sense (as failure to determine the speaker's content).

2 Why semantic under-determinacy is problematic

Semantic under-determinacy per se is the topic of the first part of this book, where I present and defend from recent criticisms the main arguments used to expose the phenomenon (Chapter 1), and defend the peculiarity of semantic under-determinacy as opposed to other kinds of semantic defectiveness (Chapter 2).

What I set out to do in this section is clarify the notion of semantic under-determinacy as I have defined it at the outset, in order to show exactly what its import is. Proponents of semantic under-determinacy have taken the phenomenon to be threatening for the project of a formal, truth-conditional semantics of natural language. In order to understand this threat, clarity on the terminology should be our first concern, in particular with respect to some of the core notions. Here is how I will use some of the basic terms that lie at the centre of the debate.

First of all I take *semantics* to be the study of the meaning that occurrences or tokenings of sentences have stably and by convention. It is not incompatible with context-dependency, as long as this is controlled and regulated by semantic factors. Semantics is compositional and what is subject to compositionality is occurrences or tokenings of sentences: the content of a sentence-token is determined by the content (in context) of its constituents and their syntactic arrangement. Moreover, semantics is truth-conditional: specifying the content of a sentence-token entails specifying in what conditions it is true.

By contrast, *pragmatics* I take to be the study of what speakers mean by using certain sentences, when this departs from their conventional meaning (in a context). Pragmatics studies the mechanisms through which speaker-meaning is generated, which involve exploiting knowledge of contextual facts, world knowledge and one's skills to recognise contextual clues as well as mind-reading skills.

The *meaning* of a sentence (type) is the content it has in virtue of linguistic conventions, independently of the context in which it is tokened. The meaning of a non-indexical sentence is determined by the meaning of its components and their syntactic combination: so for instance, the meaning of 'Snow is white' is *that snow is white*, as it results from the composition of the meaning of 'Snow', 'is' and 'white'. I will refer to this level of content also as 'literal meaning', 'strict meaning', 'austere meaning' and so on.

The *semantic content*, or simply *content*, of an occurrence of a sentence is its meaning in a context of utterance. It is determined by the standing meanings of non-context-sensitive terms and by the contents assigned to context-sensitive terms, such as ambiguous or indexical expressions. Thus, the semantic content of 'I am from Dublin' as uttered by James is that James is from Dublin; the semantic content of 'Claire went to the bank' as uttered by a speaker who is talking about the financial institution is that Claire went to the financial institution, and so on. I will interchangeably use also 'the content (of a sentence)', 'what is said (by the sentence)', 'what the sentence says', 'what the sentence expresses' in order to indicate this level of content.

The *content of an utterance* is what the speaker who utters a certain sentence means, what she wishes to communicate by saying what she says. Utterance content can coincide with a sentence's content whenever the speaker means exactly what the sentence says: for instance, when one utters 'The sun shines in Paris', one usually means exactly what the sentence says, namely that the sun shines in Paris. However, in some cases speakers utter a sentence and mean something more specific than or slightly different from what it says: for instance, when one utters 'Jack and Jill are married' one usually means that Jack and Jill are married *to each other*, not simply that Jack is married and Jill is married (which is what the sentence literally says). I will refer to this level of content also as 'utterance content', 'what the speaker means', 'what the speaker says', 'what is meant by the utterance', 'the utterance's truth-conditions' and so on.

Finally, *what is implicated* is the content that a speaker intends to communicate or suggest by uttering a certain sentence, over and beyond what the sentence says and even what is meant by the utterance. What is implicated is entirely independent, both conceptually and truth-conditionally, of both sentence content and utterance content. To illustrate, consider an utterance of 'Me and James are married' performed by Julie: its semantic content is that Julie and James are married; the utterance's content is (typically) that Julie and James are married to each other; finally, the implicature could be an entirely separate content, which the speaker may intend to convey by saying what she says: for instance, that she is not engaged any more, or that she and James are not siblings and so on. I will also refer to this level of content by using 'what is communicated', 'what is suggested', 'what is conveyed', and so on.

Once we have these notions at hand, we are in a position to understand more specifically in what way semantic under-determinacy is troublesome. The problem arises at the level of semantic content, that is the meaning that a sentence-token acquires in a context, after disambiguation and reference assignment to context-sensitive expressions (like indexicals). As it has been maintained, this level of content generally fails to determine a truth-condition for its utterances.

Why is this problematic? An important implicit assumption here is that the content of a sentence *should be* a truth-condition for an utterance of that sentence. This seems essential for a semantic theory to be successful: it is the distinctive task of a semantic theory to determine, given a sentence and a limited amount of contextual information, in which conditions an utterance of that sentence in that context is true. Yet the semantic content of a great number of sentences fails to provide such a truth-condition. For instance, a sentence like 'I am tall' uttered by Jamal expresses the content that Jamal is tall. This content by itself does not provide a truth-condition for the utterance, in that it fails to provide some information that would be needed to this end – namely the standard or comparison class with respect to which Jamal is tall. Unless this information is provided, the bare content that Jamal is tall *tout court* cannot receive an evaluation. The same argument could be replicated for countless other sentences, if not for all sentences in a language. This ensues in the thesis of semantic under-determinacy, which may be spelled out as a general statement as follows:

[Semantic Under-determinacy]
The semantic content of sentences generally fails to determine a truth-condition for their utterances.

The thesis of semantic under-determinacy is often also formulated in terms of the semantic content of sentences failing to determine a *proposition*. Many authors regard sentences as generally expressing a less-than-propositional entity, which Bach calls 'propositional radical' (1994a, b), Sperber and Wilson (1986, pp. 72–5, 179–92, 231–7, 252–3) indicate as 'non-propositional logical forms', Neale (2004) dubs 'blueprints', 'templates', 'schematic' or 'skeletal' representations and Soames (2004) labels 'matrices'. These contents are described as representations which bear *some* semantic properties but ultimately lack one or more of the components that would be needed in order for them to qualify as full-blown propositions and be evaluable.

3 Taking semantic under-determinacy seriously

Semantic under-determinacy seems to strike at the very heart of a popular conception of the semantics of natural languages. It threatens the long-standing idea that the semantics of a sentence (supplemented by a minimal amount of contextual information) could be enough in order to obtain the truth-conditions of the utterances that language users commonly make. At this point, adherents to the traditional picture face various options. One thing they could do is try to *deny* that there is anything like semantic under-determinacy. This could be accomplished by either criticising those very arguments purported to show that there are semantically under-determined sentences, or by trying to show that semantic under-determinacy is nothing fancy, really: it is just a version of some already familiar kind of semantic defectiveness, such as ambiguity, vagueness, indexicality or ellipsis. In Part I of the book I will engage with these kinds of objections in the attempt to resist them and show that semantic under-determinacy should be taken seriously.

Chapter 1 focuses on two important arguments that have been offered to show that language suffers from semantic under-determinacy. The first is known as the *Argument from Incompleteness*: this kind of argument consists in eliciting intuitions concerning the extent to which the semantic content of certain sentences is in various ways incomplete, and thus fails to determine a truth-condition for its utterances. This is indeed the very argument with which I opened this book: when introducing examples of semantic under-determinacy, I relied on the reader's intuition that it was impossible to say in which conditions a sentence like 'Jill is ready' is true (because the sentence does not say for what Jill is ready), or that it was impossible to say in which conditions a sentence like 'It's raining' is true (because the sentence does not say where it's raining). This kind of argument relies heavily on incompleteness intuitions being clear and shared, however it is always possible to resist these intuitions. A very easy way to do this is to say that sentences like 'Jill is ready' and 'It's raining' do have determinate truth-conditions. For example, a (token of) the sentence 'Jill is ready' is true just in case Jill is ready for something (Borg, 2004). Or even, (occurrences of) 'Jill is ready' are true iff Jill is ready *tout court*. After all, there is something like being ready *tout court*: it is what all the things that are ready for this or that particular thing share (Cappelen and Lepore, 2005).

These intuitions indicate that, if we adopt a coarse-grained enough conception of truth-conditions, we could say that sentences like 'Jill is ready' and 'It's raining' do have a truth-condition. The issue therefore seems to be the following: how fine-grained should truth-conditions be? This granularity question is best treated within a framework in which the truth-conditions of a sentence help to partition possible worlds. I will show that the right answer lies between the two extremes of a too loose conception and a too strict conception of the granularity of truth-conditions. The too loose conception has it that truth-conditions should be able to partition worlds into those where an occurrence of the sentence is true and those where an occurrence of the sentence is false: this conception is too loose because it makes nearly no sentence semantically under-determined. While the too strict conception has it that truth-conditions should, given a particular possible world or set thereof, enable one to determine whether an occurrence of the sentence is true in that world (or at that set of worlds): this is too strong, because I argue it would result in too many semantically under-determined sentences. The in-between option I will advocate is that truth-conditions should be non-generic as much as possible: they should characterise a *particular state of affairs*, that is a configuration of particular objects and properties. The problem with sentences like 'Jill is ready' or 'It's raining' is that they provide at best generic truth-conditions: at best, the former sentence is true iff Jill is ready for something and the latter sentence is true iff it's raining somewhere. These conditions could not be found at any particular possible world, where, if Jill is ready, she is not just ready for something, but she is ready for a specific aim or activity; or if it is raining, it is not just raining somewhere, but it is raining in a particular location. What we require from these sentences is that they characterise as much as possible a particular state of affairs: this would allow us to avoid the too loose partitioning of possible worlds, which would result in no semantic under-determinacy, as well as the too strict demand on sentential contents, which would result in too much semantic under-determinacy.

The second argument I will analyse is known as the *Context-Shifting Argument*: it consists in presenting a context C1 where a certain uttered sentence S turns out true, and a relevantly different context C2 where the same sentence S turns out false. Since, it is argued, S contains no recognised context-sensitivity, ambiguity, vagueness or ellipsis, and the way the world is does not change between C1 and C2, the best way to explain the change in truth-value of S is that of regarding it as semantically under-determined (Travis, 1985, 1997, 2002; Bezuidenhout, 2002). A famous example due to Travis consists in presenting a scenario in which Pia paints green the russet leaves of her Japanese maple; talking with a photographer friend, she utters 'The leaves are green' and she speaks truly; talking with a botanist friend, she utters again 'The leaves are green' but this time she speaks falsely. Since the sentence seems to present no obvious indexicality, vagueness or ellipsis, and the way the leaves are does not change between the two conversations, it is concluded that the sentence is just semantically under-determined.

This argument could be resisted in various ways. Cappelen and Lepore have protested, among other things, that the argument 'works too well', to an extent that it could be repeated with virtually any expression. This consequence may be problematic to accept for Moderate Contextualists, who wish to keep a moderate amount of semantic under-determinacy in language. My proposal to defy this objection is to distinguish between different typologies of context-shifting arguments, only one of which would produce results interesting for the Moderate Contextualist. On the one hand, some context-shifting arguments present a sentence which is true if uttered in context C1 and false if uttered in context C2 because it is completed in some way, as a result of either syntactic or semantic mechanisms. These kinds of arguments I call *completive context-shifts*. On the other hand, some other context-shifting arguments present a sentence which is true if uttered in context C1 and false if uttered in context C2 because some background assumptions change the way some terms that occur in it are applied. These I call *meaning-manipulative* context-shifts. The Moderate Contextualist could argue that only completive context-shifting arguments will be interesting for her purposes, especially if there is clear evidence for a syntactic or semantic account of the completive mechanisms. As to meaning-manipulative context-shifts, the moderate theorist could argue that the only thing they show is that our background assumptions could affect the way we use and evaluate sentences, but that this is not interesting as long as there is no independent evidence of a semantically or syntactically implemented context-sensitivity.

A second way to resist the Context-Shifting Argument is that of denying one of its premises, namely the one to the effect that the sentence at issue contains no familiar context-sensitivity (for instance, indexicality), or ambiguity, or vagueness, or ellipsis. Chapter 2 purports to contrast exactly this objection, by highlighting the differences between semantic under-determinacy and these phenomena and by advocating its *sui generis* nature.

To begin with, it seems rather easy to argue that semantic under-determinacy is not ambiguity. Ambiguous words like 'bank' are different from semantically under-determined words like 'ready' or 'green'. A word like 'bank' has more than one meaning (to be more precise, it is the common graphic realisation of a number of different lexemes, each with its own meaning); by contrast, a word like 'ready' or 'green' seems to have one single meaning but make different contributions to the content of the utterances it occurs in. Moreover, a word like 'bank' has a well-defined amount of meanings (to be more precise, it graphically realises a well-defined number of lexemes), while the contents that a word like 'ready' or 'green' could have in different contexts of utterance are indefinitely many (because there are indefinitely many things to be ready for, and indefinitely many ways in which something might be green).

Secondly, it does not look like semantic under-determinacy could be reduced to vagueness either. Sure, many semantically under-determined words are *also* vague, in the sense that they sometimes have unclear conditions of application, as a result of which the sentences in which they occur have no clear truth-value. Yet it seems that, in order to judge whether a sentence that contains one of these words is or is not vague, we have to resolve its semantic under-determinacy first. Consider 'The leaves are green' uttered concerning leaves that are naturally russet, but painted with a colour in between yellow and green. Before judging that the sentence has no clear truth-value, we would have to decide in what way the leaves are green – as their natural colour or as a result of painting. The vagueness and the semantic under-determinacy of the predicate are clearly separate, so the latter cannot be reduced to the former.

Thirdly, semantic under-determinacy is hardly reducible to indexicality understood as sensitivity to one or more contextual parameters, despite the fact that several theorists have argued for a reduction of semantic under-determinacy to *hidden indexicality* (Stanley, 2000, 2002a, 2005a; Szabó, 2001; Stanley and Szabó, 2000; King and Stanley, 2005; Rothschild and Segal, 2009). Many authors have emphasised the disanalogies between semantically under-determined and indexical expressions: Neale (2007) notes how indexicals express a perspectival aspect, while the alleged hidden indexicality of semantically under-determined expressions exhibits no such feature; Cappelen and Lepore (2002) point out that indexicals enter into anaphoric relations and give rise to a priori knowable truths, while nothing of the sort happens with purported hidden indexicals; Recanati (2010) and Hall (2008) argue that supposed hidden indexicals can give rise to indefinite readings (for instance, we can read 'It's raining' as 'It's raining *somewhere*') while we get no indefinite reading of indexicals ('He is a photographer' cannot be read as '*Some male* is a photographer'). Finally, I note that indexicals give rise to rigidity effects when embedded in modal contexts, while nothing similar happens with presumed hidden indexicals. For instance, suppose you are in Paris, where it does not rain. Still, you utter 'It could be raining here': your utterance would be true just in case there is a possible world where it rains *in the actual place of utterance* (Paris). If, instead, you were to utter 'It could be raining', supposing that the embedded sentence contains a hidden indexical element, the utterance could be true even in a possible world where it rains in a place *different* from the actual place of utterance. The many disanalogies between familiar indexicals and purported hidden indexicals give us good reasons to discard the view that semantic under-determinacy could be reduced to this kind of phenomenon.

Finally, it could be argued that semantic under-determinacy is a form of ellipsis. It seems reasonable to rule out that it could be reduced to syntactic ellipsis, for semantically under-determined sentences bear very few resemblances to syntactically elliptical ones. For instance, syntactically elliptical sentences could not be felicitously uttered if no sentence were articulated prior to them; by contrast, semantically under-determined sentences could be felicitously articulated even if no other sentence had been uttered before.

Perhaps, as Stanley (2005a) has already noted, the concept of ellipsis at play here is not a syntactic, but a semantic one. That is, the sentences that we call semantically under-determined are elliptical at the level of the content they express, in that they determine something incomplete or truncated (see e.g. Quine, 1940, Sellars, 1954, and Neale, 1990 on incomplete definite descriptions). The idea of semantic ellipsis may be cashed out in terms of what I will call 'under-articulation', where the advantage of the notion of under-articulation is that of not employing cross-categorial talk such as that of *semantic ellipsis* while being less syntactically informed than the linguist's notion of ellipsis. One could therefore say that semantic ellipsis obtains whenever a certain sentence S, whose literal content is q and is used to mean the richer content that p, is 'under-articulated' with respect to a longer sentence S´ which could have been used to fully express the same content that p. For instance 'Jill is ready', which says simply that Jill is ready and is used to mean that Jill is ready to ski, is under-articulated with respect to 'Jill is ready to ski'.

The first thing to notice with regard to under-articulation is that, even if we accounted for semantic under-determinacy in these terms, the account would be utterly non-explanatory (see also Stanley, 2005a on semantic ellipsis): if the explanandum is the fact that some sentences fail to express a truth-condition, it is not particularly helpful to say that these sentences are under-articulated with respect to longer sentences. This seems a mere redescription of the phenomenon.

An additional problem of under-articulation is under-determination: a sentence S could be under-articulated with respect to sentences S´, S˝, S‴ and there could be no principled way of selecting one rather than the other. Also trivialisation would beset the view: for instance, 'It's raining' could be trivially under-articulated with respect to 'It's raining and it's raining'. Moreover, the under-articulation idea could suggest that, if more linguistic material were added to a sentence, its semantic under-determinacy could be resolved. It is easy to show that things are quite different: the more linguistic material one articulates, the more potential semantic under-determinacy one creates.

Thus, we have many reasons to claim that semantic under-determinacy is a *sui generis* phenomenon, not reducible to other familiar kinds of semantic defectiveness. This should prompt us to take seriously both semantic under-determinacy and the arguments in favour of it: with semantic under-determinacy, we are facing a genuine semantic phenomenon. Our task, at this point, is to explore the question of how linguistic communication is possible, given sematic under-determinacy.

4 From semantic under-determinacy to context-sensitivity

The idea of semantic under-determinacy often goes hand in hand with the thought that the sentences at issue involve a form of *context-sensitivity*, meaning that the truth-conditions of their utterances are sensitive to one or more aspects of the context of the speaking. A motivation for this could be spelled out as follows: the content of sentences as determined by their linguistic constituents and the way they are syntactically arranged (relative to a context) is insufficient to render the truth-conditions of (most) utterances of these sentences; nevertheless, utterances of these sentences are understood by hearers, this meaning that their truth-conditions are grasped; if hearers manage to grasp the truth-conditions of these utterances, there must be something that supplements sentence content so as to make the utterance's truth-conditions exhaustive; what makes this supplementation possible is, most plausibly, contextual clues. If this is so, an utterance's truth-conditions in some sense *depend on* or *are sensitive to* contextual clues (see Searle, 1980).

The idea that the truth-conditions of our utterances display some kind of context-sensitivity has had huge success in recent decades and has fuelled a still ongoing debate, which has produced a range of significantly diversified positions. In Chapter 3, I review and criticise the main accounts in today's discussion; the ultimate aim of my criticisms is that of showing that there is room for a yet under-noticed and underestimated alternative, which I develop in the subsequent chapter.

The positions currently defended in the debate may be viewed as falling under two main headings, that of *Contextualism* and that of *Minimalism*. Contextualist theories have it that context-sensitivity pervades language and massively affects the contents of our utterances. Minimalist views, by contrast, try to limit as much as possible the impact of context-sensitivity in language and seek to explain the fact that the contents of our utterances seem to depend on context in alternative ways.

The most hard-line position on the contextualist side may be identified with *Extreme Contextualism*, that is the view that the *meaning itself* of words and sentences is sensitive to context. The position could be read in two ways and thus suffers from a certain instability: on one reading, it is the use of a word in a specific context that determines its meaning, so words do not have a meaning independently of their particular uses. This approach is characteristically averse to any attempt to work out a theory of meaning, but it also clashes with the presence of what may be called 'semantic constancies' that could reasonably make up or at least inform meaning. On another reading, it states that meaning could either be defined or explicated in terms of use, in which case the view becomes compatible with semantic constancies, but then it is not that extreme any longer.

A less unstable position is what may be called *Radical Contextualism*. This view admits that words and sentences bear certain context-invariant meanings, yet argues that these semantic features do not suffice to determine a proposition, a content that is truth-conditional and amenable to evaluation. To obviate this under-determinacy, Radical Contextualists argue that the content of a sentence gets 'fleshed out' with the help of contextual information in ways that depart from standard indexicality. These processes of content supplementation are not linguistically controlled but are rather 'free enrichments', which do not take place in compliance with semantic or syntactic rules, but are executed for pragmatic reasons, to enhance the relevance, informativeness, clarity or perspicuity of a certain utterance. Radical Contextualists see themselves as opposing the tradition of formal semantics according to which the content of a sentence, provided the resolution of ambiguity and indexicality, determines a truth-condition. In their view, what determines a truth-condition is rather the content of a sentence thus characterised *plus* a number of pragmatic processes of free enrichment. The main weakness of Radical Contextualism lies in its not being able to rule out, with independent arguments, that alleged processes of free enrichment are really semantically controlled processes, or processes that are pragmatic through and through but that do not affect sentence content. Radical Contextualism is exposed to what I call a 'divide and conquer' strategy, whereby the opponent could take any example cited by the Radical Contextualist as a case of free pragmatic process and give a suitable account of it in terms of purely semantic processes, or in terms of pragmatic processes that do not have an impact on what the sentence says. For instance, one could suggest that, in 'I've had breakfast', the time span within which the speaker has had breakfast results not from free pragmatic enrichment, but from filling in a variable introduced by tense; with 'Geena likes to wear rabbit', one could speculate that the rabbit-fur sense is not the result of a pragmatic process of adjustment, but of a selection between different meanings of the polysemous 'rabbit'; finally, with 'Susan got married and had a baby', one could argue that 'and' acquires a sense of temporal succession not through free enrichment, but as a result of a generalised conversational implicature generated by the Gricean sub-maxim 'Be orderly'.

A less radical variety of Contextualism compatible with the 'divide and conquer' manoeuvre is *Indexical Contextualism*, which is typically identified with the view that all context-sensitivity could be traced to the logical form of expressions. Sentences, like 'It's raining', 'Everybody is happy', 'Jill is tall', often carry within their syntax some hidden positions occupied by variables, which are assigned a reference according to context: in the case of weather predicates, the variable ranges over locations; with quantifiers, it ranges over domains; while with gradable adjectives, it ranges over comparison classes. Indexical Contextualism differs from Radical Contextualism precisely in its contention that the context-sensitivity of these sentences is syntactically (and thus semantically) controlled, and that there are no mechanisms of free enrichment, or completions of utterance content with constituents that are not articulated in syntax. I highlight one great limit of Indexical Contextualism: the main argument that has been used to support it, known as the Binding Argument, hardly shows that its central claim is true. Moreover, the commitments at the level of syntax that the Indexical Contextualist is ready to make seem to be motivated by a need to preserve compositionality and systematicity in semantics. However, I argue that the same features could be preserved even without making any special syntactic commitments, but simply by positing that the context-sensitivity of certain sentences is controlled by their semantics (for instance, by the lexical features of words). This way, we can avoid recourse to non-orthodox, pragmatically guided free enrichments by at the same time maintaining a compositional, systematic semantic account for the content of the utterances of sentences.

The family of Minimalists encompasses at least three views, all sharing a conservative approach to some of the mechanisms of truth-conditional semantics. Plain *Minimalism* refuses both the idea of semantic under-determinacy and that of context-sensitivity: as already mentioned, the content of a sentence like 'Jill is ready' is a proposition, more precisely the minimal proposition to the effect that Jill is ready *tout court* (Cappelen and Lepore, 2005); or, at least, the proposition to the effect that Jill is ready *for something* (Borg, 2004). The notion of minimal proposition has been questioned with what I have called the 'at-which-worlds' challenge (see MacFarlane, 2007): at which world, or set of worlds, is the proposition to the effect that Jill is ready (or even that Jill is ready for something) true? Minimalists seem to accept that, as long as the content expressed by the sentence enables one to partition worlds into those where Jill is ready (for something) and those where Jill is not ready (for something), then the sentence expresses a proposition, while their opponents think this is not enough, for there may be worlds where, for instance, Jill is ready for one thing and not ready for another, in which case the possible worlds partitioning would leave a lack of determinacy. Based on what I have argued in Chapter 1, I suspect that what opponents of Minimalism ask with the 'at-which-worlds' challenge is that propositions specify a particular state of affairs (a configuration of particular objects and properties), even though not a maximal state of affairs: this would suffice to successfully meet the 'at-which worlds' question. Be that as it may, even granting that there is something like minimal propositions, and in light of the fact that these are very rarely what speakers mean, one could ask what their role is. Since the role they are taken to play by Minimalists – acting as the shared content of distinct speech acts; illuminating our linguistic competence – could be fulfilled even by non-propositional objects, based on parsimony considerations minimal propositions would turn out as dispensable.

Ultra Minimalism, unlike plain Minimalism, does not countenance anything like minimal propositions, but instead maintains that sentence content generally expresses sub-propositional contents, named by Bach (1994a, b) 'propositional radicals'. Plus, it has a very austere vision of what counts as semantic content, which only admits the contribution of context-insensitive terms and automatic indexicals, excluding demonstratives and in general expressions whose content is fixed through speakers' intentions. Pragmatic mechanisms determine a third layer of meaning called 'impliciture', which is distinct from a sentence's strict and literal content. Ultra Minimalism closely resembles Radical Contextualism and many of the differences between the views look merely terminological, or at best differences between different broadly construed meta-theoretical views of the semantics–pragmatic interface. Just like Radical Contextualism, I argue that Ultra Minimalism is exposed to a 'divide and conquer strategy'.

Finally, *Non-Indexical Contextualism* aims at preserving a minimal amount of context-sensitivity, while attempting to explain context-shifting cases (whereby one and the same sentence S is true in context C1 and false in context C2) by appealing to a relativity of truth-value to features of a sentence's index of the *circumstances of evaluation*. The basic move of the Non-Indexical Contextualist consists in adding one or more parameters to the index of the circumstances of evaluation. With semantically under-determined sentences, it has been proposed that – for instance – 'The leaves are green' be true iff the leaves in question are green relative to <w, c>, that is relative to a possible world w and a 'counts-as' parameter c (MacFarlane, 2009; for proposals in a similar spirit, see Predelli, 2005a; Corazza and Dokic, 2007, 2010; Barba, 2007; Gauker, 2012). I note that Non-Indexical Contextualism could be considered nothing but a notational variant of Indexical Contextualism (see also Stojanovic, 2007) and Radical Contextualism, but that contrary to what its proponents allege, choosing the Non-Indexical Contextualist option does not bring any real advantages. For one thing, Non-Indexical Contextualism cannot account for semantic under-determinacy as incompleteness of content, and thus has to see intuitions of incompleteness as misguided; secondly, it cannot account for utterance comprehension as a process of 'fleshing out' a defective content, for there is no *content* defectiveness in its view; finally, its allegiance to semantic orthodoxy is to be traded with a non-orthodox view of truth. All things considered, it does not seem like Non-Indexical Contextualism is really an interesting option in the Minimalism–Contextualism landscape, so I suggest casting it aside.

Having reviewed critically the main positions currently defended in the debate, in Chapter 4 I move to an articulation and defence of the main proposal of the book, which may be called the *Conceptual Constraints View*. The proposal could be thus enunciated:

The Conceptual Constraints View
The context-sensitivity of semantically under-determined sentences such as 'It's raining', 'Jill is ready', 'The leaves are green' and so on is to be traced to a number of *conceptual constraints* associated with these expressions.

The proposal, in a nutshell, is that the content of these sentences is completed or fleshed out as a result of conceptual/semantic instructions. For instance, the content of 'It's raining' is supplemented with a location as a result of what may be viewed as a conceptually or semantically derived tenet, to the effect that if it rains, it rains *somewhere*. Similarly, the content of 'Jill is ready' is completed with a purpose or activity in compliance with another conceptually or semantically derived tenet, to the effect that if Jill is ready, she is ready for *something*. Finally, the content of 'The leaves are green' is completed with a part or aspect in which the leaves are green in accordance with the semantically or conceptually derived tenet to the effect that if the leaves are green, they are green in *some part, respect or way*.

The central idea of the proposal is that conceptual constraints are ways in which thought and discourse about certain matters are structured and organised. Thought and discourse about rain are organised so as to include information about times, locations, perhaps degrees of intensity of the phenomenon, and so on. Thought and discourse about being ready are organised so as to encompass the activities or purposes for which things or individuals may be ready. Thought and discourse about being green are organised so as to include parts or respects in which things are green, and so on and so forth. The picture may be cashed out also in terms of *frames* or *schemata*, familiar to cognitive psychologists and semanticists. Frames could be portrayed as structured configurations which comprise various 'slots' or 'dimensions' (see Minsky, 1975; Rumelhart, 1980). For instance, the rain-frame shall contain a slot for times, one for locations, one for degrees of intensity and so on; the being ready-frame shall contain a slot for individuals (or objects), a slot for activities (or purposes), and presumably also slots for times, places, manners. Similarly, the being green-frame shall include a slot for objects, a slot for parts or aspects, perhaps a slot for comparison classes, and presumably a time, location and manner slot.

In this framework, the proposal is that conceptual constraints (as they arise from the relevant frames) *control and guide the processes of completion of semantically under-determined sentences*. Provided a language user masters the conceptual frames associated with terms such as 'to rain', 'being green' or 'being ready', all she needs in order to flesh out the content of the previously cited sentences is to correctly apply the attendant conceptual constraints. The proposal thus regards the context-sensitivity of these sentences as an *entirely semantic* matter – to the extent that conceptual constraints play a key role in fixing the semantic features of these linguistic expressions.

The proposal diverges in a non-trivial way from the positions currently dominating the debate. Firstly, it diverges from Radical Contextualism, in that it ascribes the resolution of semantic under-determinacy to semantically controlled processes, rather than pragmatically controlled processes. This does not imply that admitting conceptual constraints entails banning altogether pragmatic effects on semantic content. If, upon scrutiny, it emerged that the most plausible account of how a certain content is enriched is pragmatic, then surely one should go for the pragmatic option. However, all things considered, I am inclined to think that *if a semantic explanation of content enrichment is available, this should be favoured* over a purely pragmatic explanation. This policy is clearly in contrast with the methodology of Radical Contextualism, which sees semantic content as pragmatic through and through and does not seem to be concerned with containing the impact of pragmatics over semantics.

Secondly, the Conceptual Constraints View diverges from Indexical Contextualism, at least in the version defended by Stanley (2000), Stanley and Szabó (2000) and Szabó (2001). This version of Indexical Contextualism clearly traces the context-sensitivity of sentences like 'It's raining' to their *syntax* understood as Chomskyan Logical Form (LF). This counts as a claim concerning the real structure of these sentences, and implies a commitment as to the existence of articulated items in the sentence's syntax, which needs to be substantiated with syntactic evidence. Yet, some authors have objected that Stanley's main argument for his view, known as the Binding Argument, only provides semantic considerations and no genuine syntactic proofs for the claim he wishes to defend (Neale, 2007; Pupa and Troseth, 2011; Collins, 2007). Moreover, the Binding Argument rests on what Stanley calls the Binding Assumption, which states that binding as a semantic phenomenon co-occurs with binding as a syntactic phenomenon. By helping himself to this assumption, Stanley is in a position to conclude that there are elements in the syntactic structure of 'It's raining', 'Cats are small', 'Every student answered every question' and so on, which explain and govern the context-sensitivity of these expressions. Drawing from considerations made by Neale, Pupa and Troseth and Collins, I argue that this assumption needs not be avowed in view of the fact that semantic and syntactic binding often do not coincide, and there is no evidence that syntactic binding should take place in the specific examples Stanley considers. If the Binding Assumption need not be avowed, then there is space for an account of Stanley's favourite cases in which binding is an exclusively semantic phenomenon, determined by interpretive aspects and not by syntactically articulated positions. For example, a sentence like 'Whenever John lights a cigarette, it rains' would be such that the bound reading to the effect that whenever John lights a cigarette at x, it rains at x, is instantiated only at the semantic level (that is, at the level of the formal or semi-formal rendition of the semantic interpretation of the uttered sentence), and not also at the level of the sentence's syntax. This view is in sync with the Conceptual Constraints proposal, according to which context-sensitivity is a matter of applying certain conceptual constraints at the purely semantic level, with no commitment as to the expression's syntactic form. Thus, the main difference is that the Conceptual Constraints View traces context-sensitivity to semantics (with no special commitment as to syntax), while Indexical Contextualism explicitly traces context-sensitivity to syntax.

Finally, the Conceptual Constraints View diverges from Minimalism (at least the version proposed by Cappelen and Lepore) in that it admits forms of context-sensitivity that are controlled and guided by conceptual constraints and which, as a consequence, go beyond the 'basic set' of obvious indexicals and demonstratives. It diverges from Minimalism also in its *not* marrying semantic Atomism (Borg, 2012): the Conceptual Constraints View sees concepts and lexical meanings as internally structured, and not, as the minimalist does, as punctuate or atomistic. This is related with the fact that the Conceptual Constraints View takes semantic under-determinacy seriously, as it were; that is, it acknowledges it and regards the semantic content of sentences like 'It's raining', 'The leaves are green', 'Jill is ready' as 'awaiting completion', where completion is to be effected under the guidance of conceptual constraints. By contrast, Minimalism does not admit semantic under-determinacy and has to see the content of these sentences as fully determinate and in need of no completion, an idea that becomes acceptable only if one construes meaning atomistically. The idea that concepts and lexical meanings are internally structured is exposed to the threat of Holism (see Fodor and Lepore, 1992), however I will argue that this threat can be thwarted and collapse into Holism can be avoided. Rejection of Atomism and Holism will bring me to conclude that the most reasonable option for the Conceptual Constraints View is to embrace a Molecularism on concepts and lexical meanings.

5 Understanding utterance comprehension

The Conceptual Constraints View provides the resources to deal with another issue on which philosophers seem to be divided: the nature of *processes of utterance comprehension*. In Chapter 5, I tackle the issue of how utterance comprehension is possible, given semantic under-determinacy. Two main positions may be identified concerning utterance comprehension: the first could be called Inferentialism, in that it pictures utterance comprehension as a matter of inference; the second may be called Anti-Inferentialism, in that it regards these processes as guided by mechanisms different from inference, such as translational or transfer mechanisms.

The roots of Inferentialism may be found in Grice's account of how implicatures are worked out. Two elements especially characterise

Gricean inferences: the first is their having the structure of inferences to the best explanation, which start from the hearer's recognition that the speaker has said so-and-so and go on to infer what the speaker means as a way of explaining her conversational move. The second is that the inference is meta-representational through and through: it relies on the hearer's capacity to represent other subjects' mental states, through belief- or intention-attributions of the form 'The speaker believes that p', 'The speaker intends that p' and so on. Relevance Theory authors, like Sperber (2000), Wilson (2000), Sperber and Wilson (2002) and Carston (2002b), have proposed a re-elaboration of Grice's model, where the inference is carried out by a dedicated mental module: this means that the process is subpersonal, fast and painless. Moreover, especially in Sperber's (2000) view, the inference that underlies utterance comprehension need not have any meta-representational premises (since, I take it, it is taken care of by the module), even though the conclusion is ultimately meta-representational. In this way, Sperber claims, we gain an account of utterance comprehension which does not demand too sophisticated capacities from the hearer.

Although I share Sperber's interest in reaching a less sophisticated account of utterance comprehension, I do not see how claiming that the conclusion of the comprehension process *is meta-representational* makes it accessible even to a less sophisticated reasoner. My proposal is therefore to maintain that utterance comprehension is inferential (perhaps in a subpersonal way), but that the conclusion of the inference need not be meta-representational *at least at an explicit cognitive level*. I am ready to grant that the notion of meta-representation (representation of the speaker's beliefs or intentions) is part and parcel of the *concept* of utterance comprehension and that anyone who masters this concept should have at least an implicit or dispositional appreciation of this conceptual role. However, I argue that comprehension as a cognitive process need not strictly speaking culminate in a meta-representation.

The Conceptual Constraints View sits particularly well with an attempt to construe utterance comprehension in an inferential, though not meta-representational fashion. The comprehension of utterances of semantically under-determined sentences will serve as an interesting case study for a broader proposal concerning utterance comprehension. As argued in Chapter 4, conceptual constraints are ways in which thought and discourse about certain matters are organised; these constraints can arguably guide utterance comprehension for the subject who masters them. This gives us good prospects for elaborating an account of utterance comprehension in which the role of meta-representation is significantly reconsidered: I shall dub it the *Non-Meta Account*.

In the case of semantically under-determined expressions, the Non-Meta Account has it that all the subject needs in order to understand an utterance of, for instance, 'It's raining', is mastery of the concept To Rain and its conceptual constraints, *plus* contextual information. Note that this does not require that the subject entertains any meta-representational premises of the form 'X means that *p*' or 'X believes that *p*'. This is a reconstruction of the potential process the hearer may go through in elaborating the content of an utterance of 'It's raining': first of all, she computes the meaning of the sentence, being simply that it is raining *tout court*; as a result of the conceptual constraint to the effect that if it is raining, it is raining somewhere, a semantic 'slot' may open itself in the semantic structure of the sentence; if the hearer can gather information about the location of rain from the context, she will complete the sentence's content accordingly ('It's raining in Paris'); if, by contrast, she can get hold of no contextual information, she may opt for existential quantification over places ('It's raining somewhere'). Of course, there may be cases in which the hearer who is trying to understand the utterance also entertains a meta-representation; for example, the hearer may include in the inference a premise to the effect that, for example, the speaker is talking about, or referring to, Paris. This, however, does not imply that the conclusion of the whole comprehension inference need be a meta-representation, as Sperber maintains. Meta-representational premises may have the role of specifying aspects of the utterance's background, which provide support for one or more premises in the inference, but from this there is no reason to conclude that the upshot of a comprehension process will invariably be meta-representational.

Thus, the Conceptual Constraints View provides the resources to work out a view of utterance comprehension which is still Inferentialist but which assigns a more limited role to meta-representation. This view takes a step in the direction of offering an account of utterance comprehension which is relatively more simple than the account suggested in Grice and by Relevance Theorists.

Part I
On Semantic Under-Determinacy

1
Arguing for Semantic Under-Determinacy

The idea that sentence meaning is semantically under-determined has been introduced by its proponents in order to counter a general approach to the semantics of natural language, that traces back to Frege, Russell, Carnap and the Formal Semantics initiated by Montague and Davidson. The picture promulgated by these authors is one where words are endowed with a stable meaning, and the meaning of a sentence is determined compositionally by the meanings of its constituents and by the way they are syntactically arranged. Sentence meaning is conceived in terms of truth-conditions, so the theory commits to the idea that, given a sentence *S*, it is possible to derive its truth-condition, for example in the form of a T-sentence ('*S* is true if and only if *p*') by applying the rules of compositionality to the meanings of the components of the sentence.

Semantic under-determinacy (and the attendant idea of pervasive context-sensitivity) is a threat to the idea of meaning as truth-conditional, because it shows that often meaning (even provided contextual resolution of indexicality and ambiguity) fails to express a truth-condition. Moreover, it threatens compositionality to the extent that, if so-called 'unarticulated constituents' (that is, propositional components that are not the semantic value of any articulated sentence part) need to be introduced, then the content of an utterance is not determined only by the meanings of the components of the sentence and their syntactic arrangement, but also by other, non-linguistically provided elements.

There are two main varieties of arguments that have been purported to shed light on semantic under-determinacy: *Arguments from Incompleteness* and *Arguments from Context-Shifts*. I will present these arguments respectively in sections 1.1 and 1.2. My intent is to clarify the way in which they show that there is something like semantic under-determinacy, by at the same time resisting the idea that they generate an inevitable slippery slope (as some authors have contended). My aim is that of showing that semantic under-determinacy is a genuine phenomenon by at the same time containing the seemingly universal application of these arguments, which generates confusion and needlessly muddies waters. In section 1.3, I will also briefly consider and discuss the methodological import of a third type of argument, which I will refer to as the *Argument from Unclear Applications*.

1.1 Arguments from Incompleteness

Some arguments purport directly to attract attention on semantic under-determinacy by triggering intuitions as to the 'incompleteness' of the sentences in question. The strategy consists in drawing a conclusion on semantic under-determinacy based on some 'intuitions' or 'feelings', or anyway pre-theoretical impressions. These arguments exhibit the structure of an inference to the best explanation. They usually present a certain sentence, S, as expressing a certain semantic content p. They subsequently show how p is not evaluable, or at least that we as normal speakers feel at a loss with respect to judging whether it is true or false; this is taken to be explained by the idea that p is not a proposition, and hence that S does not express a proposition, or truth-condition.

Up to this point, the upshot of the argument is that of exposing semantic under-determinacy. By adding to it the extra premise to the effect that an evaluable content is obtained only through the addition of further constituents directly in the proposition, it is possible to make a case for the context-sensitivity of these contents. These contents are supplemented with elements drawn from context that are not the value of any articulated component of the sentence, neither at the superficial or at the deep, covert level: these are so-called *unarticulated constituents* (Perry, 1986; Crimmins and Perry, 1989; Crimmins, 1992). Arguments from Incompleteness most naturally occur together with considerations as to how content must be 'fleshed out' in various ways, often with the use of unarticulated constituents. Here are some examples of sentences whose semantic content has been considered semantically under-determined, and in need of completion through so-called unarticulated constituents.

'It's raining'

John and George plan to play tennis on Saturday, but on that day it happens to be raining where they live, in Palo Alto. George utters 'It's raining', so John goes back to sleep. In the sentence 'It's raining', the predicate 'to rain' provides a dyadic relation *rain(t, l)*, while the tensed auxiliary 'is' provides a time, *t*. The resulting semantic content is that *it is raining at t*, where no specific location is supplied. This content is, as it stands, unevaluable, for it could be raining anywhere and a place is needed in order to determine to what exactly the predicate 'to rain' is correctly applied. So the content *that it's raining* is semantically under-determined. There is, however, a place that is salient in the context of the utterance, namely Palo Alto. That utterance of 'It's raining' is true precisely because it is raining in Palo Alto. So, Palo Alto is in some sense part of the proposition or truth-condition expressed by the utterance, even though it is not the value of any component of the sentence: it is an unarticulated constituent of it. So, it turns out that the semantic content of 'It's raining' is sensitive to and dependent on some aspect of the context – namely, a salient place (the example is inspired by Perry, 1986, p. 138. See also Perry, 1998, pp. 6–7; Korta and Perry, 2011, Ch. 9).

'Jill is ready'

The sentence expresses the proposition *that Jill is ready*, where the component corresponding to the purpose, or activity, for which Jill is ready, is missing. As a result, the content of the sentence is not evaluable: it does not amount to a proposition. So, it is semantically under-determined. It could express a proposition if the element corresponding to Jill's purpose were added to the content, yet since the latter would not be the semantic value of any component of the sentence, it would be an unarticulated constituent (see Bach, 1994a, pp. 127–8; 1994b).

'Steel isn't strong enough'

The content expressed by this sentence is that steel is not strong enough. However, one may wonder 'for what' steel is not strong enough. Without this piece of information the semantic content of the sentence is unevaluable. So, the sentence suffers from semantic under-determinacy. Plus, the content of the sentence could become evaluable if it were supplemented with the purpose for which steel fails to be strong enough. The latter not corresponding to any element of the sentence, it would be an unarticulated constituent (Bach, 1994a, p. 128).

'Jamal is tall'

The semantic content of the sentence is that Jamal is tall. However, by itself this content cannot be evaluated as true or false, because it fails to specify the comparison class relative to which Jamal is to be ascribed the property of being tall. So, the sentence is semantically under-determined. If such a comparison class were supplemented in the content, then the latter would express a full-fledged proposition. So, the content is sensitive to or dependent on the specification of such a class, which however would act as an unarticulated constituent (Bach, 2012, pp. 171–2). Similar observations hold for other gradable expressions such as 'small'and 'big' (Sperber and Wilson, 1986, p. 188).

'The leaves are green'

The content of this sentence is that the leaves are green. However, it may be pointed out that there are many respects in which a leaf can be green. It can be green because that is its natural colour, because it has been painted green, because a green light shines on it. The semantic content fails to specify in which respect the leaf is green, and is therefore strictly speaking unevaluable. So, it is semantically under-determined. The content could be made evaluable if it were supplemented with a 'respect' component, so it is context-sensitive to such an aspect in a way. However, the component would be an unarticulated constituent, in that it would not correspond to any element in the sentence (see Travis, 1997, p. 90; Lahav, 1989, p. 263).[1]

Other sentences trigger intuitions of incompleteness on account of exhibiting a different form of defectiveness, which pertains to the sentence *as a whole* being incapable of nailing down a truth-condition. These sentences do not seem to lack any specific component and yet their semantic content fails to express a truth-condition. The following are some of the most cited examples.

'Peter's book is grey'

The semantic content of this sentence is that *the book which bears some relation with Peter is grey*, however which specific relation should be instantiated in order for an utterance of this sentence to be true is not specified; consequently, it is not possible to judge whether an utterance of it is true or false. So, the sentence suffers from semantic under-determinacy (see Sperber and Wilson, 1986, p. 188).

'Bill cut the grass'

The semantic content of this sentence is simply *that Bill cut the grass*. As it stands, this content could be true in a variety of more or less far-fetched situations, for instance one in which Bill mows the grass with a regular lawnmower but also one in which Bill slices each leaf of grass with a knife and a fork. Nothing in the semantic content of the sentence enables the hearer to sort which situation is the one in which the utterance is true, so the sentence turns out as semantically under-determined (see Searle, 1980, p. 221).

Incompleteness, and intuitions thereof, is taken to reveal semantic under-determinacy. Yet so far we have been content with an intuitive grasp of the kind of incompleteness that afflicts the above sentences. As I will explain in the next section, it is important, for the Argument from Incompleteness to succeed and resist objections, that the task of sustaining the case for semantic under-determinacy is not left to our intuitions only, and that the notion of incompleteness be spelled out in clearer, theoretically more rigorous terms.

1.1.1 Incompleteness as genericity

The arguments just reviewed aim at establishing semantic under-determinacy through intuitions of incompleteness. With sentences like 'It's raining', 'Jill is ready' and so on, there is a 'felt' need to supplement them (Taylor, 2001, p. 53) – and that is what grounds our judgement of incompleteness. Incompleteness can be represented in a Russellian framework, which conceives of propositions as structured n-tuples of objects and properties: in such a framework, the contents of incomplete sentences may be regarded as featuring a 'gap', an unsaturated slot which calls for filling. For instance, the content expressed by 'It's raining' may be represented as an n-tuple with structure $<R, t, \_>$ containing the property of raining R, the time t, but only a gap in the location slot. Russellian propositions are a useful representational tool, provided that the intuition that the content is incomplete is shared by everyone (or nearly everyone) in the first place. Importantly, this may not be the case. Presented with a sentence like 'Jill is ready', one could in fact 'feel' that its content is just complete enough. So how is the contrast settled? What we need is a criterion independent of intuitions that helps us spell out precisely in what way these sentences are incomplete.

Incomplete sentences seem to fail to determine a truth-condition. But what does this mean exactly? One may suppose that 'determining a truth-condition' implies 'sorting the possible worlds where the utterance is true' from 'the possible worlds where the utterance is false'. If this is so, then the semantic content of incomplete sentences does not seem to fail to do *that*. The semantic content of 'Jill is ready' seems to succeed in sorting the worlds where an utterance of the sentence is true from those where it is false. The former will be all the worlds where Jill is ready to do something (and there is nothing for which she is not ready), while the latter will be all those worlds in which there is nothing she is ready for. So there is at least a sense in which the semantic content of one of the attended sentences does not fail to provide a truth-condition, as Cappelen and Lepore (2005, p. 158) and Borg (2004, pp. 231–2; 2012, p. 108) insist. In order for the incompleteness argument to show something, a stronger sense of 'determining a truth-condition' should be adopted.

One could understand 'determining a truth-condition' as 'determining in which particular world, or set of worlds, a specific utterance of the sentence is to be evaluated as true or false': for instance, whether the speaker's utterance of 'Jill is ready' is to be evaluated as true or false in w_1, where Jill is ready for skiing; or in w_2, where Jill is ready to get married. If this is what determining a truth-condition amounts to, then it is clear that the semantic contents of 'Jill is ready' or 'The leaves are green' do *not* succeed in doing this. Merely based on the content of the sentence to the effect *that Jill is ready*, there is no way of determining in which particular world w_1, w_2, w_3 ... w_n the utterance is to be evaluated, because the semantic content does not feed us with enough information to narrow down the conditions in which Jill is ready to conditions of being ready *for a specific thing*.

Yet the doubt remains that this may be too strong a requirement for any semantic content. It seems that other sentences would suffer from the same problem, yet we would not list them among cases of obvious semantic under-determinacy. One example is provided by the sentence 'Lisa is happy' (cf. Borg, 2004, pp. 232–4 for similar observations). The semantic content of this sentence, by itself, does not enable the hearer to know in which particular world the utterance is to be evaluated. This is because there are countless differently arranged worlds where Lisa is happy: in w_1 she is happy because she has just got married; in w_2 she is happy because she has won the lottery; in w_n she is happy because she has been able to eat lasagne, and so on. The mere content to the effect *that Lisa is happy* does not determine whether the utterance is to be evaluated at any of w_1, w_2 ... w_n, for the simple reason that it supplies no information as to the reason for which Lisa is happy. Due to this failure, we would have to list 'Lisa is happy' among cases of semantic under-determinacy even though it does not immediately strike as such an example. Moreover, even longer sentences, which supposedly provide more information as to how the world should look like, may wind up as semantically under-determined because they may fail to determine in which particular world, or set of worlds, they should be evaluated for truth or falsity. To illustrate, consider the sentence 'Jill is ready because she has won the lottery': there are a number of possible worlds where this obtains, but matters are arranged slightly differently. In w_1 Jill is happy because she has won the lottery with ticket no. 3000321, while in w_2 she is happy because she has won the lottery with ticket no. 3000322, while in w_3 she is happy because she has won the lottery with ticket no. 3000323 and so on. Given the semantic content of the sentence, namely that Jill is happy because she has won the lottery, there is no way to determine in which particular world, w_1, w_2 and w_3 the utterance should be evaluated. So again, a sentence like 'Jill is happy because she has won the lottery' would have to be regarded as semantically under-determined even though it does not seem so at first sight.

This prompts an attempt to reformulate the sense in which a semantically incomplete sentence 'fails to determine a truth-condition', such that it is not as weak as 'sorting out worlds' but not as strong as 'determining in which particular world, or set of worlds, the utterance should be evaluated' either. In order to do this, it might be useful to observe that sentences like 'It's raining', 'Jill is ready', 'The leaves are green', and so on, can all be taken to express *generic truth-conditions* for their utterances. For instance, 'An utterance of "It's raining" is true iff it's raining (somewhere)', 'An utterance of "Jill is ready" is true if Jill is ready (for something)', 'An utterance of "The leaves are green" is true iff the leaves are green (in some respect)', and so on. These T-sentences point at very generic conditions that could not obtain in any possible world. After all, in any possible world in which it is raining (somewhere), it is raining in a particular place; in any possible world in which she is ready (for something), Jill is ready for this or that particular thing; in any possible world where the leaves are green (in some respect), they are green in this or that particular respect. So one sense in which we could be dissatisfied with these T-sentences is that they only provide a generic truth-condition, failing to provide a *particular* truth-condition.

I suggest that the sentences that we intuitively judge as incomplete are such to the extent that they are *generic*, that is, they fail to determine a *particular* truth-condition. Providing a particular truth-condition would mean offering a condition that points to a *particular state of affairs*, such as it raining in Paris, or London, or Bogotá; or Jill being ready to ski, or to hike, or to eat sushi; or the leaves being green on the outer surface, as their natural colour, and so on. Here 'particular state of affairs' means a way for particular objects and properties to be arranged within a possible world: the contrast here is between generic conditions, that do not tie down the world to any configuration of objects and properties, and conditions that do point to such configurations. It seems clear that 'It's raining', 'The leaves are green', 'Bill cut the cake' do not point to any specific configuration of objects and properties unless some further information is provided, for instance as to the location where it is raining,[2] the respect in which the leaves are green or the way in which Bill cut the cake.

Specifying a particular truth-condition rather than a generic one has, among other things, the following advantage: suppose there is a world w_4 where Jill is *both* ready for skiing *and* not ready for her Spanish exam. In such a circumstance, it is not clear whether an utterance of 'Jill is ready' is true or false in w_4. The genericity of the truth-conditions of the sentence does not allow us to establish whether the sentence describes a state of affairs that obtains (that Jill is ready for skiing) rather than a state of affairs that does not (that Jill is ready for her Spanish exam). By contrast, if the sentence were to specify a specific state of affairs between the two just mentioned, it would be possible to evaluate it as true or false.

Specifying a particular state of affairs does not mean specifying a maximal state of affairs. For instance, the content of 'Lisa is happy' *does* determine a specific state of affairs. Yet, it does not specify for what reason she is happy, how long she has been happy, and so on. So, it certainly does not specify *every* aspect of how a world has to be in order for an utterance of that sentence to be true – even though it points to a particular state of affairs. This is because, I take it, a *particular* state of affairs is not a *maximal* state of affairs, such that it specifies all that is the case in a possible world. Precisely for this reason, a sentence whose content points to a particular state of affairs is not thereby capable of determining in which possible world, or set of worlds, the utterance is to be evaluated as true or false, since it would presumably leave out a lot of details needed in order to decide this. This explains why 'Lisa is happy' and also 'Lisa is happy because she has won the lottery', although they point to a particular state of affairs, are still not capable of determining in which possible world, or set of worlds, their utterances are to be evaluated. Yet, as we have seen, that these sentences are capable of determining in which particular world, or set of worlds, an utterance should be evaluated may be too demanding a condition (more on this topic will be said in section 3.4).

In this section I have been engaged with providing a characterisation of the notion of semantic incompleteness which informs arguments for semantic under-determinacy. I have ruled out that incompleteness amounts to a failure to 'sort possible worlds' into those where the sentence is true from those where it is false, for this seems too weak a condition. I have also ruled out that it amounts to determining in which possible world, or set of worlds, the utterance is to be evaluated as true or false, for this proves too strong a condition. I have proposed to regard it as a failure to provide truth-conditions that point to *particular* states of affairs, where these are possible configurations of particular objects and properties, which are to be distinguished from maximal states of affairs.

1.1.2 The slippery slope of incompleteness arguments

Against incompleteness arguments, Cappelen and Lepore have argued that the strategy leads us down a slippery slope and thus generalises in a vicious way in that, if the incompleteness argument applies to a sentence S, it applies to all sentences (see Cappelen and Lepore, 2005, pp. 59–64). In particular, what should worry its proponents is that, if the argument works for a supposedly incomplete sentence like 'Jill is ready', it will work for its completion 'Jill is ready for the exam' too. Cappelen and Lepore emphasise how the argument relies on nothing but *intuitions*: one decides whether a sentence is incomplete on the basis of one's intuitions or 'feelings' as to the deficiency of the content or truth-conditions of the sentence. Unfortunately, though, the same intuitions or 'feelings' could be replicated for those sentences that are allegedly complete. Ultimately, all sentences could be shown to be incomplete and, what is more, there seems to be no principled way to draw the line between different ways in which these might be deemed incomplete – perhaps in a 'more serious' as opposed to a 'less serious' way.

It is worth noting that this objection is bad news only for part of the Contextualist community. Radical Contextualists, who have it that all expressions in language are semantically under-determined and context-sensitive, would be perfectly happy with the conclusion established by Cappelen and Lepore's objection. Moreover, as Recanati (2006, p. 23) notes, Cappelen and Lepore's argument has force only for someone who *already rejects* the Radical Contextualist conclusion. The neutral, unbiased theorist may remain unmoved by the prospects of a slippery slope, insofar as Cappelen and Lepore do not give reasons why generalising Contextualism to all language would be a bad thing.

If anyone should be upset by this criticism it would be, Cappelen and Lepore think, 'Moderate Contextualists', who embrace Contextualism only locally, that is, for a limited number of expressions. Their objection would imply that incompleteness cannot be attributed only to some expressions, as the Moderate Contextualist would want, since once one acknowledges the problem for a sentence like 'Jill is ready', one has to acknowledge it for any other sentence. As a result, Moderate Contextualism would collapse into Radical Contextualism.

Let me remark first that it is not clear whether the latter objection hits any target, since it is not clear to me whether in the debate there are any self-confessed Moderate Contextualists in Cappelen and Lepore's sense. Many authors have written on the semantics of specific sets of expressions (for instance, epistemic predicates, moral predicates and so on) not because, it seems to me, they wish to defend Contextualism *only* with respect to that single class, but because that was their interest at the time. With regard to whether their account could apply to all the rest of language, their attitude would expectedly be one of openness or at worst lack of commitment, rather than one of intransigent restriction. In fact, some authors seem inclined to the view that the context-sensitivity they posit for a certain group of expressions *does* characterise many other expressions in language: even a cursory reading of authors like Stanley or Szabó is enough to gather that they are perfectly open to the idea that their approach applies to a great deal of expressions (provided there are good enough reasons to apply it),[3] including colour predicates, weather predicates, nominals, comparative adjectives and so on. As to Contextualists about 'know' (like Keith DeRose and Stewart Cohen) and about 'ought' or 'wrong' (like Gilbert Harman and James Dreier), it is plausible that they be either open or uncommittal about the issue, but not that they positively oppose an extension of their account to the rest of language. Therefore, it is not clear who should be unsettled by this critique of Cappelen and Lepore.

Be that as it may, it is certainly true that anyone who does not have sympathies for Radical Contextualism and is nevertheless willing to acknowledge some degree of semantic incompleteness in language may have an interest in trying to prevent or at least contain a potential incompleteness flood. One strategy that may be adopted is to admit that incompleteness intuitions apply potentially to all sentences in a language, but try to argue, on grounds independent of those very intuitions, that only some cases of intuited incompleteness deserve a theorist's attention.

When we speak of intuitions, here, we speak of *psychological states* a subject is in when she tries to work out the truth-conditions of a certain sentence. In the specific example of intuitions of incompleteness, we could describe the phenomenon as an impression or seeming that some information is missing, but this need not be more than a pro-tanto characterisation, good for operative purposes.[4] The point I wish to make is that these psychological seemings or impressions may be reliable, in the sense that they may detect some sort of incompleteness, however they may be *too coarse-grained* and fail to distinguish between different kinds or degrees of incompleteness – only some of which are worthy of philosophical consideration. It would therefore be good to have an independent, principled way of setting these incompletenesses apart.

One first datum that should be taken into account in pursuing this task is that there is a (yet again) intuitive difference between the incompleteness of 'Jill is ready' and 'Jill is ready for the exam' or 'Jill is ready to play'. How could this difference be spelt out? In the last section I proposed an answer along the following lines: the content of 'Jill is ready' is true if there is something for which Jill is ready, however this condition will never obtain in a possible world, for in any world in which Jill is ready for something, she is ready for *this or that* particular thing. The truth-conditions of 'Jill is ready' suffer from *genericity*, in that they point to no particular state of affairs in which their utterance could be true, such as being ready for the (salient) exam, being ready to play, and so on. By contrast, the truth-conditions of 'Jill is ready to take the exam', 'Jill is ready to play', and so on, do point to some particular state of affairs, understood as a configuration of particular objects and properties. The opponent to Radical Contextualism could say that those contents which are judged intuitively incomplete *and* have generic truth-conditions are those that suffer from a philosophically interesting incompleteness.

It could be pointed out that even those sentences whose truth-conditions seem to point to particular states of affairs suffer from genericity: for instance 'Jill is ready for the exam' is true iff Jill is ready for the only exam *in some domain*. However, in every world in which Jill is ready for the only exam *in some domain*, she is ready for the only exam in *this* or *that* particular domain. For instance, for the only exam she will have on 9 October 2013, or for the only exam that will start in ten minutes from the time of utterance and so on. This difficulty seems to depend on the fact that sentences could contain a number of expressions that in turn generate genericity, such as the incomplete definite description 'the exam'.

The objection is well taken, however, two observations are in point: first, since every sentence could be somehow generic, one may think that in order to be semantically determined a sentence should be *maximally* specific. But this is to demand too much of language and of our capacities to describe the world linguistically.

Secondly, one could accept that every sentence could harbour some amount of genericity, and yet maintain that some cases are more problematic than others. Certain degrees of genericity may be accepted and even go unnoticed for the purposes of fast and effective communication;

others may hinder communication and trigger the requirement for more specificity. So, genericity (and the semantic under-determinacy that follows from it) is a problem *when it goes beyond a certain threshold*. A sentence like 'Jill is ready' is far beyond this threshold, and probably even a sentence like 'Jill is ready for the exam' is too. However, a sentence like 'Jill is ready for the exam she will have on 9 October 2013' might count as specific enough for the purpose of describing the situation in which Jill is, even though it probably fails to specify a number of other aspects of the possible world in which the sentence is true (What is the topic of the exam? At what time does she have it? What will the venue be?).

The aim of this section was that of responding to Cappelen and Lepore's charge that intuitions of incompleteness launch us down a slippery slope, giving us no means to set apart 'serious' from 'less serious' cases of incompleteness. I have proposed that philosophically 'serious' incompleteness is detected by intuitions of incompleteness *plus* ascertaining that the sentence at issue has truth-conditions that suffer from (a suitable degree of) genericity, that is a failure to point to particular states of affairs.

1.2 Arguments from context-shifts

Probably the most employed argumentative strategy to show that sentence meaning (even relative to context) suffers from semantic under-determinacy is what Cappelen and Lepore (2005) have called the 'Context-Shifting Argument' (CSA). This argument presents the reader with at least two different scenarios, call them C1 and C2, in which the same sentence, S, is being used, and asks to evaluate each utterance of the sentence in the appropriate scene. Once again, it relies on *pre-theoretical* intuitions as to whether the uttered sentence is true or false; it does not ask the reader to tell what exactly in the utterance is true or false – whether its semantic content, the utterance's content and so on: it just confines itself to recording variations in intuitions as to truth and falsity. Here are some examples.

'The leaves are green'
Pia's Japanese maple has russet leaves, but one day she decides to paint them green. Shortly after, a photographer friend phones her, asking whether she has any green-coloured object he could use for a photo shoot. Pia is happy to give him her freshly painted Japanese maple because, as she states, 'The leaves are green'. In this case, she speaks

truly. Later on, a botanist friend calls her, asking for some samples of green-leaved plants. Again, she states: 'The leaves are green', but this time she speaks falsely (the example is inspired by Travis, 1997, p. 89, but see also Travis, 2008, pp. 25–6).

'Jill is ready'

Jill is studying for her Spanish exam, but she is horribly behind with grammar exercises and feels like she would need more time to be fully prepared. In the evening, her friend Carol picks her up at her house on their way to a concert. Jill is about to step out of the door, so Carol phones Charles and says 'Jill is ready': in this case, she speaks truly. Later on, when Charles asks her how Jill is doing with her preparation for the Spanish exam, she utters 'Jill is ready': this time, she speaks falsely (the example is inspired by Gauker, 2012).

'Jamal is tall'

Jamal is a basketball player. His mother always boasts with her friends saying: 'Jamal is tall'. In this case, she seems to speak truly, because Jamal really is taller than the average. Yet, when his mother talks to Jamal's basketball coach, who knows Jamal is average tall as a basketball player, her utterance of 'Jamal is tall' seems false.

'There is milk in the fridge'

The fridge in Laura's house is completely empty, except for a small puddle of milk on the bottom shelf. Laura's friend is worried that the fridge is completely empty and clean, so they open it for a check. Seeing the milk puddle, Laura utters 'There's milk in the fridge'. She seems to speak truly. When Sam comes to visit and asks for something to put in his coffee, Laura says: 'There's milk in the fridge'. In this case, it seems she speaks falsely (again the example is inspired by Travis, 2002, pp. 18–19).

'Smith weighs 79 kilos'

Smith weighs 79 kilos whenever he weighs himself in the morning, without his clothes on. Yet as soon as he puts on his trousers, a shirt and a pullover, when he steps on the scale, it reads 81 kilos. Suppose Odile is taking part in a conversation where the weights of people enrolled for an amateur football championship are discussed: each member should be at least 80 kilos in order to qualify. Odile utters 'Smith weighs 79 kilos' and seems to speak truly – so Smith is ruled out. Later on, she discusses who can step on a very old and unsafe bridge, where one cannot be more than 80 kilos. She utters 'Smith weighs 79 kilos' and, this time, she seems to speak falsely (this example also comes from Travis, 2002, pp. 19–20).

Context-Shifting Arguments follow a common schema: as already mentioned, the first premise has it that a certain sentence, S, is uttered in context C1, where it turns out true; the second premise has it that S is uttered in context C2, where it turns out false.

Two further premises need to be added in order for the argument to go through (for an opinionated analysis of the argument, see Predelli, 2005a, pp. 125–36). Firstly, that the expressions at hand are not examples of either ambiguity, vagueness, indexicality or sentential ellipsis. This premise is hugely important: it is vital to make sure one is not faced with an unexpected manifestation of any of these phenomena, which are also a hurdle to determining a truth-condition for their utterances (unless they are appropriately taken care of). This certainly holds for ambiguous sentences like 'Sam goes to the bank': an utterance of this sentence expresses no truth-condition unless the meaning of 'bank' is disambiguated. Vague expressions also suffer from a semantic deficiency: the meaning of 'red' for instance, is not carved up sharply enough to tell us whether the predicate does or does not apply in borderline cases – and hence whether a sentence like 'This is red' is true of them. Furthermore, indexical expressions too may be an obstacle to determining the truth-conditions for utterances in which they occur. Unless a context of utterance is disclosed where a referent could be assigned to the occurrence of 'I', a sentence like 'I wear glasses' expresses no definite truth-condition. Finally, elliptical sentences could impede determining the truth-conditions of an utterance for syntactic reasons, namely their failing to articulate enough words. In Chapter 2, I will pause to consider in greater detail on which basis authors argue that semantic under-determinacy cannot be reduced to either ambiguity, vagueness, indexicality or ellipsis. For the time being, it shall suffice to grant – for the sake of the argument – that context-shifting cases do not prima facie involve the kinds of semantic defectiveness just mentioned.

An additional premise has it that, between the first and second utterance in the context-shifting scenario, no relevant change in the way things are occurs: that is, for instance, the Japanese maple's leaves remain painted green; Jamal's height remains constant and nothing changes about the contents of the attended fridge.

Thus, we seem to have the following set of premises [1]–[4]:

[1] Sentence S is uttered within a context C1, where it turns out true;

[2] Sentence S is uttered in a second context C2, where it turns out false;

[3] There is no prima facie reason to think that S contains any indexical, ambiguous or vague components, nor that it involves sentential ellipsis;

[4] Between the first and second utterance, no relevant change in the way the world is has occurred;

whose conclusion is

[5] The meaning of S semantically under-determines the truth-conditions of its utterances.

The argument really has the structure of an inference to the best explanation. The question might be put this way: in light of the conjunction of [1]–[4], how is the truth-value shift of S to be explained? The answer could be thus spelt out: if the truth-value of S varies across contexts, even though how the world is does not change, and there is no reason to suppose that S exhibits any form of indexicality, ambiguity, vagueness, ellipsis and so on, this means that the linguistic/semantic content of S is not semantically determined enough. What those words mean does not determine a fixed set of conditions in which that sentence is true or false. This point of view is explicitly endorsed by Travis (1996, pp. 454–5), but also by Carston (2002a, pp. 19–20) and Recanati (2004, p. 91).

Context-Shifting Arguments may also be run in another version, whose two initial premises differ from those I have presented in that they do not concern a shift in truth-value but rather a shift in the *content understood* (Travis, 2002; Bezuidenhout, 2002). So, the argument goes, a sentence like 'The leaves are green' can be understood in context C1 as saying that the leaves are green *on the outer surface*, while in context C2 it can be interpreted as saying that the leaves are green *under the surface*. Together with the premises that there is prima facie no indexicality, ambiguity, and so on, and that the external circumstances (namely, the leaves being painted green) are held constant, they have been taken to lead to the same conclusion to the effect that what the sentence says in context is under-determined – in that it does not contribute any one content that can be the object of a hearer's interpretation in both contexts. For the present purposes, I will treat this version as equivalent to the one in terms of truth-value shifts and consider it a mere variant of the same argument.

1.2.1 The slippery slope of Context-Shifting Arguments

Cappelen and Lepore (2005, p. 40) protest that, exactly like Incompleteness Arguments, Context-Shifting Arguments cannot be run locally; once you endorse them for some expressions, you are forced to endorse them for all. This once again entails that Moderate Contextualism would collapse into Radical Contextualism, which is the view that all (or nearly all) language is context-sensitive.

To illustrate this, Cappelen and Lepore devise context-shifting cases for sentences that, at least prima facie, exhibit no under-determinacy or context-sensitivity (2005, pp. 44–7). Consider for instance 'Jill didn't have fish for dinner'; uttered in a context where Jill ordered fish, ate only the vegetables in the plate and then came down with food poisoning, it seems true. But the same sentence would not be true in the case she did not want to pay for her order just because she did not touch the fish that was in the dish. The sentence 'Justine destroyed those shoes' would be true in a context in which Justine spray-painted Mary's shoes yellow just before going out for a fancy dinner; it would be false if Mary had to wear those shoes in the jungle and be as visible as possible to fellow excursionists. 'That dog is dangerous' would be true if the dog's tendency to bite people were discussed and the dog were aggressive – but not if the dog were kind and loving, but unhealthy; it would be false if the dog were very small and lightweight and one were to consider the consequences of being jumped over by it. Since in all these and other cases, where no obvious under-determinacy or context-sensitivity is manifested, a Context-Shifting Argument can be reproduced, then semantic under-determinacy and context-sensitivity could potentially be shown to affect the entire language, thus giving way to Radical Contextualism.

The first thing to note is, once again, that this is an objection only to part of the Contextualist community. For many Radical Contextualists, including Travis, Bezuidenhout, Carston, Sperber and Wilson and Recanati, this is not an objection at all, indeed it is a welcome result. Moreover, and as already mentioned, it is not clear to me that there are any Moderate Contextualists in Cappelen and Lepore's sense, since these theorists should all be open or at least uncommittal on the possibility that greater portions of language than those they survey (if not all language) are context-sensitive.

Be that as it may, a Moderate Contextualist might want to block the alleged slippery slope on the account that, were she to give way to it, the amount of context-dependence she would have to postulate would be improbably high. For instance, Szabó (2006) agrees that 'cheap' postulation of context-sensitivity is to be avoided; his strategy for resisting the slippery slope to Radical Contextualism is then to discard, one by one, the examples invoked by Cappelen and Lepore. About the locution 'have dinner' in 'Jill didn't have fish for dinner', he claims it to be a case of ambiguity; concerning the word 'dangerous', he affirms that he does not share the intuitions fostered by Cappelen and Lepore: if the dog's biting tendencies were under discussion, saying that the dog is dangerous on account of its illness would be misleading but not false; finally, he admits that 'destroy' could mean 'make unsuitable for some purpose' and thus be context-sensitive, but that this is hardly a demonstration of the slippery slope towards Radical Contextualism. Finally, in some cases, context-shifting intuitions just do not suffice to show context-sensitivity, because vagueness and unspecificity could affect our way of judging the examples.

Szabó's strategy might be useful to contain the slippery slope argument as it is formulated by Cappelen and Lepore, however nothing prevents a stubborn opponent from searching for other, perhaps better examples with the purpose to launch a further attack. What the Moderate Contextualist needs is a principled criterion that could be used to distinguish between 'interesting' and 'non-interesting' cases of context-shifts, on the basis of which to draw the line between cases that deserve attention from the Moderate Contextualist from cases that do not. Ideally, what is called for is a way of telling how cases like 'It's raining', 'Jill is ready', 'The leaves are green' are different from Cappelen and Lepore's 'Justine destroyed those shoes', 'That dog is dangerous'.

An attempt to deal with this issue could be the following. In a range of context-shifting cases, it is arguable that contextual shifts mark a variation in the value of some parameter that can be traced at some syntactic or semantic level, perhaps as a free variable in the logical form of the sentence, or a slot in the lexical structure of a term.[5] This may well apply to expressions like 'to rain', 'being ready', 'being green', 'being tall', each of which seems to call for some completion at least at the semantic (if not at the syntactic) level. So, for instance, it seems that no use of the predicate 'to rain' could be correct unless locational information is provided, so that one could reasonably suppose that the locational aspect might be encoded either at some syntactic level in the sentence (as a free variable in its logical form), or as an argument at the lexical level (as a slot in the lexical or conceptual structure of the predicate). Where it is reasonable to suppose that context-shifts act on such elements, we could call them *completive context-shifts*.

On the other hand, some context-shifts do not, at first sight, provide any completive ingredients, but they alter some background assumptions, thus affecting the way in which the predicate is applied. This is what seems to hold for 'dangerous': in a scenario in which a dog's biting tendencies are at stake, being dangerous might depend on how easily the dog bites people – so the truth or falsity of a statement of 'That dog is dangerous' might depend on these facts; if a dog's likelihood to hurt a person with the weight of its body is discussed, then being dangerous will vary with the dog's size – and so will the evaluation of a dangerousness statement. Thus, depending on the conversational background, different criteria for ascribing the predicate 'being dangerous' and evaluating utterances of 'This dog is dangerous' will hold. Yet, the word 'dangerous' seems to always retain the same meaning ('threatening', 'unsafe'), and the criteria on the basis of which the property of being dangerous could be ascribed do not seem part of the syntactic or lexical structure of the predicate 'being dangerous'. The context-shift does not seem to consist in a shift of value of some argument slot or parameter, but rather in a shift of background assumptions which has repercussions on how the expression is applied: in this case, one could speak of *meaning-manipulative* context-shifts.

A strategy available to the Moderate Contextualist is that of restricting her attention to completive context-shifts and argue that *these* delimit her area of interest, to the extent that there are *independent reasons* to think that they act on slots in the semantic or syntactic structure of the expressions. Meaning-manipulative cases, by contrast, indicate that the way we use words and evaluate sentences can be sensitive to our background assumptions, but that by itself does not prove that the expression at interest is semantically under-determined, nor that its context-sensitivity can be traced to syntax or semantics. In fact, the expression could be semantically determined but sensitive to background aspects because there are multiple criteria for applying one single meaning (as in the case of 'dangerous'), or the word exhibits some sort of ambiguity, polysemy, vagueness or non-literality.[6]

Thus, Cappelen and Lepore's slippery slope could be blocked by saying that the Moderate Contextualist will take seriously only those instances that she will judge as *completive* cases of context-shifts. All other seemingly analogous context-shifts which will not be deemed completive will not be taken as revealing any under-determinacy or context-sensitivity worthwhile of interest to the Moderate Contextualist.

1.2.2 The objection from 'impoverishment'

Another criticism mooted by Cappelen and Lepore to Context-Shifting Arguments has it that these are, as they say, 'impoverished' (2005, p. 107; 2003, p. 30). An impoverished Context-Shifting Argument is one where at least three different contexts are involved: first is the 'Storytelling' context, where the philosopher speaks and asks us to imagine at least two further 'Target' contexts, T1 and T2. A sentence *S* is imagined to be uttered in T1 in such-and-such conditions, where *S* turns out true; the same sentence *S* is imagined to be uttered in T2 in relevantly different conditions, where *S* turns out false. Now this set-up is problematic, in the authors' view, because it does not allow the philosopher to *use* S, but only to *mention* it (or at least use it but only through indirect quotation).

Furthermore, 'Impoverished' Context-Shifting Arguments seem convincing to their proponents because, when running them, one has the impression of introducing a shifted interpretation of *S* in T1 and T2 respectively, but this would be accomplished in an ungrammatical way, Cappelen and Lepore say, namely by illicitly using operators which are compared to Kaplanian 'monsters', that is, operators that shift the interpretation of context-sensitive words (such as 'I', 'now') to the semantic value these would acquire in a context different from the context of utterance. The proponent of Context-Shifting Arguments expects to be able to form sentences like: 'In context T1, the leaves are green; while in context T2, the leaves are not green', thus forcing two different interpretations of 'green' by embedding the word under the two monster-operators 'In context T1' and 'In context T2'. The problem is, Cappelen and Lepore urge, that monsters do not exist in English, so the argument is undermined by this grammatical irregularity (2005, pp. 117–21; 2003, pp. 39–42).

Cappelen and Lepore propose a 'Real' Context-Shifting Argument (2005, pp. 106–8; 2003, pp. 30–1), where the expression is *both* grammatically used and mentioned in the Storytelling context. The argument is supposed to result in a judgement that contains *both* use and mention, which sounds as follows: 'There can be false utterances of "*S*" even though it is the case that *S*'. 'Real' Context-Shifting Arguments squarely apply to well-known indexicals, in that they issue the following results:

- There can be false utterances of 'I am Italian' even though I am Italian. (This is correct as long as the sentence could be uttered by another speaker.)
- There can be false utterances of 'Tom is leaving now' even though Tom is leaving now. (This is correct as long as the sentence could be uttered in another moment.)
- There can be false utterances of 'That is nice' even though that is nice. (This is correct as long as the sentence could be uttered while referring to another object.)

As opposed to this, it seems that the same judgements could not be issued relative to semantically under-determinate sentences like 'The leaves are green' or 'Jill is ready' and similar others (Cappelen and Lepore, 2005, pp. 109–12; 2003, pp. 32–4):

- There can be false utterances of 'The leaves are green' even though the leaves are green.
- There can be false utterances of 'Jill is ready' even though Jill is ready.

Cappelen and Lepore's objection to 'Impoverished' Context-Shifting Arguments and their defence of 'Real' Context-Shifting Arguments strike me as weak and tendentious.

With regard to the illegitimacy of 'Impoverished' Context-Shifting Arguments, it is not clear that Context-Shifting Arguments are only about mention and not use. These arguments usually require an imaginative effort which does not entail the use of quotation. The reader may be invited to imagine two target contexts T1 and T2 in which the expressions are genuinely *used*. For instance:

> T1: Pia has painted green the leaves of her russet Japanese maple. Now that the leaves are green, she can give the plant to her photographer friend, who needs some green subjects for a photo shoot.

> T2: Pia has painted green the leaves of her russet Japanese maple. Yet, since the leaves are not (strictly speaking) green, her botanist friend refuses to take them as samples for an experiment on green-leaved plants.

After these two imaginative exercises, the philosopher could ascend at the metalinguistic level, so to speak, and run the Context-Shifting Argument thus: 'Since in T1 an utterance of "The leaves are green" would be true and in T2 an utterance of "The leaves are green" would be false, we have reasons to think that the semantic content of a sentence like "The leaves are green" is semantically under-determined and/or context-sensitive.' Here the argument is admittedly run from a different context (the 'Storytelling' or the philosopher's context) and it involves only mention of the sentence 'The leaves are green'. However, the argument would be *based* on genuine (albeit imaginary) uses of the predicate at issue. Since these are definitely possible uses, their status should not be seen as inferior to that of actual uses of the predicate, so these imaginary cases should count the same as any other past, present or future use of 'green' by actual speakers. These cases constitute the *evidence* from which Context-Shifting Arguments draw; sure, these arguments cannot but be run from a 'third' philosophical context in which quotation is used, however I do not see anything intrinsically problematic in this, as long as the data underlying the argument are made up of genuine uses.

Moreover, it is not clear at all that Context-Shifting Arguments need to use monsters. Now that we have established the legitimacy of Context-Shifting Arguments which are run in terms of mentionings but are *based on uses*, it becomes unproblematic to use the perfectly grammatical and monsters-free conjunction: 'In T1, an utterance of "The leaves are green" would be true and, in T2, an utterance of "The leaves are green" would be false', where the phrases 'In T1' and 'In T2' act as simple modifiers and do not shift the interpretation of any expression in either the uttered or mentioned sentences.

As to the success of 'Real' Context-Shifting Arguments, I think Cappelen and Lepore's argument is tendentious in that it takes advantage of the fact that recognised indexicals are associated with a contextual parameter, which makes it easy to see *how* a sentence like 'I am Italian' could have false utterances even though, as a matter of fact, I am Italian. One only has to imagine that the speaker-parameter shifts its value, that is, that someone different than the actual speaker/writer (me) utters that same sentence. Analogous considerations apply to sentences that contain occurrences of 'now', 'today', and so on.

Conversely, it is not equally easy to figure out how sentences like 'The leaves are green' or 'Jill is ready' could have false utterances even though the leaves are green and Jill is ready. Cappelen and Lepore certainly register a difficulty in getting our intuitions straight with this kind of sentence; however, from this it does not follow that there is no semantic under-determinacy or even context-sensitivity here. For our initially unclear intuitions could be 'educated' with some reflection so as to make the semantic under-determinacy (and putative context-sensitivity) apparent. Note that our intuitions are equally 'educated' in the case of indexicals, in the sense that they presuppose a prior understanding of the semantics of these expressions as determining a function from some contextual parameter to a content. So, it is not the case that intuitions in the indexicals case are more pre-theoretical and immediate than those which may be elicited by cases involving 'green' or 'ready'. Both cases need some theory in the background (no matter how informal) and require a little reflection in order to have some intuitive appeal.

The main difficulty associated with 'green' or 'ready' cases seems that of figuring out exactly what parameter or aspect of the context could shift in order for utterances of a sentence like 'The leaves are green' to become false.[7] One needs to conceive of a situation in which the same sentence is uttered, but some clearly identified aspect of the context is shifted. But this is certainly conceivable: one could envisage a different context in which the *respect* in which the leaves should count as green changes (even though all worldly conditions are held constant). This allows us to construct consistent 'Real' Context-Shifting cases such as the following:

> *[Real Context-Shifting Argument for 'The leaves are green']*
> Pia has just painted green the russet leaves of her Japanese maple, so now the leaves are green. Yet in different circumstances, had the natural colour of the leaves been at issue, the sentence 'The leaves are green' would have been false.

Perhaps the passage would sound better if one replaced 'the leaves are green' with 'the leaves *count* as green' and 'would have been false' with 'would have *counted as* false'. This need not change anything at the level of semantics, that is, what is evaluated as true or false in the context of an utterance: it suffices for our purposes that some aspect of what it is to be green can be shifted from one context to another, so as to affect the understanding and evaluation of the first and second occurrence of 'The leaves are green'.

What I take myself to have shown so far is that 'Real' Context-Shifting Arguments could work for 'green' and 'ready' too, once our intuitions have been informed with and 'educated' by some theoretical considerations.[8,9] If these observations are correct, then Cappelen and Lepore's argument that 'Real' Context-Shifting arguments only reveal the context-sensitivity of 'official' indexicals fails.

1.2.3 The meta-theoretical objection

Finally, Cappelen and Lepore criticise an assumption that can be glimpsed behind Context-Shifting Arguments, which they call the 'Mistaken Assumption' (MA), to the effect that semantics should take account of the intuitions of speakers as to what utterances say in theorising about their semantic content (see for instance Recanati's 'Availability Principle' in his 1989, pp. 309–10; 1993, p. 248; 2004, 2010). This implies that, if Context-Shifting Arguments result in the conclusion that an utterance u of a sentence S expresses content p, then an adequate semantics should assign p as the semantic content of u (2005, pp. 53–4). This, Cappelen and Lepore say, is contentious. Speakers' intuitions often have nothing to do with semantics – they are contaminated with intuitions as to what the speaker means or what information is conveyed by the fact that an utterance is performed, which might obviously go beyond what a sentence says in a minimal way (see Cappelen and Lepore, 1997).

Although I am inclined to think that Cappelen and Lepore have a point when emphasising the heterogeneity of our semantic intuitions, by advancing this objection they move the debate to a further level which I would regard as 'meta-semantical'. The controversy becomes one between different visions about semantics, its task and its goals, where Contextualists take it to be the task of semantics to capture untutored speakers' intuitions, while Minimalists protest that semantics should simply be concerned with invariant meanings and compositionality, leaving out speakers' intuitions.

When such ample and foundational issues are at stake, the debate becomes highly complex and, given that we seem to have no theory-neutral criterion to assess the reasons of each party, the disagreement becomes difficult to settle, to an extent that it is not even clear that any sustainable contrast obtains. It might be that at the meta-semantical level, proponents of a 'Minimal' approach and proponents of Contextualism may have to *agree to disagree*. If this were so, Cappelen and Lepore's criticism would be sound, though dialectically ineffective in that it would move the debate to a level where the parties are in a condition of 'dialectical stalemate'.[10]

1.2.4 The 'many understandings' version of Context-Shifting Arguments is fallacious

Context-Shifting Arguments, especially in their version featuring different ways of *understanding* a sentence in different contexts, have been criticised as fallacious by Montminy (2010, pp. 321–2): as he contends, from the fact that a sentence in different contexts can have different interpretations, it does not follow that it does not express a truth-condition. There could be cases in which a sentence is understood in different ways in different contexts of utterance and yet it *does* have a truth-condition: for instance, the sentence 'John owns a vehicle' could be understood as saying that John owns a car, a bicycle or a shopping trolley depending on the context, yet this does not entail that the sentence expresses no truth-condition. So, the objection goes, Context-Shifting Arguments that draw on different understandings of the same sentence in different occasions of utterance fail to generalise.

Context-Shifting Arguments may offer support for sentences which are, by Montminy's lights, *properly* under-determined because they suffer from some clearly identified incompleteness: cases in point are

'Jamal is tall', 'Jill is ready' and so on (see ibid., pp. 225–8). However, in a whole range of other cases, where Montminy claims that sentences are merely afflicted by *unspecificity*, Context-Shifting Arguments do not convincingly establish semantic under-determinacy.

Unspecificity implies, in Montminy's view, that a sentence *does* express a truth-condition, however this is not specific enough for capturing what speakers could mean in each single context: an example is 'Bill cut the grass', which fails to specify *with what* Bill cut the grass. Montminy (2010, pp. 324–5) insists that it would be a mistake to infer that the contents of these sentences are semantically under-determined (non-propositional) just because they are unspecific with respect to what speakers usually mean. For instance, it would be a mistake to infer that 'Bill cuts the grass' expresses no proposition just because hearers usually understand utterances of this sentence as stating that Bill cut the grass *with a lawnmower*. All that could be inferred is that the content of the utterance is typically more specific than the content of the sentence, not that the content of the sentence is less than propositional.

Montminy seems to assume that an unspecific content could be propositional and hence determine a truth-condition, however it is not clear how he understands this requisite. If expressing a truth-condition means 'sorting worlds where the sentence is true from those where it is false', then an unspecific content succeeds in this. Yet this requirement is so loose that almost any sentence could be taken to express a proposition in this sense. Even sentences that in Montminy's view suffer from incompleteness and thus express no proposition, such as 'Jill is ready', may allow one to sort worlds in this fashion. So, this way of understanding talk of 'expressing a truth-condition' overreaches. Yet strengthening the requirement as being 'determining in which particular world, or set of worlds, the utterance is to be evaluated as true or false' or even just 'determining a particular state of affairs' seems to clash with the unspecificity of the content and thus seems to rule it out automatically.

Ultimately, it is not clear whether Montminy's notion of 'unspecific proposition' is in any way joint-carving or even coherent. Therefore, his objection to the effect that, through Context-Shifting Arguments, we can infer that some contents are unspecific, but not semantically under-determined, seems to have hardly any bite.

1.3 The Argument from Unclear Applications

The Argument from Unclear Applications is premised upon the possibility that a sentence is uttered and evaluated in some 'special' or 'borderline' circumstances. In these cases, it is said, the semantic content of the sentence does not allow us to tell whether the sentence is true or false in those circumstances. This is taken to imply that the content of the sentence is under-determined. An example of this argument may be the following.

'The cat is on the mat'
The semantic content of this sentence is *that the cat is on the mat*. Although it may seem to have some univocal truth-conditions, it is not difficult to picture a number of non-conventional scenarios with respect to which one may have to evaluate it: for example, the cat in question is floating in space together with the mat, or the cat has only one paw on the mat, and so on. What is peculiar about these scenarios is that we do not know whether the sentence 'The cat is on the mat' would be true in them; the semantic content of the sentence reveals nothing in this direction, in that it selects no specific set of truth-conditions for its utterances. So, the sentence is semantically under-determined (the example is inspired by Searle, 1978, p. 211).

1.3.1 The Argument from Unclear Applications is fallacious

Montminy (2010, pp. 329–30) argues that, from the fact that sentential content may not allow us to predict whether some possible or actual utterances of a sentence in unusual circumstances are correct or incorrect, one cannot derive that that sentence has under-determinate truth-conditions, or has only context-dependent truth-conditions. This would imply that sentences which contain vague predicates would have no context-independent truth-conditions, but nothing compels us to think that this is so.[11] For instance, it could be the case that the sentence 'Carl is bald' had determinate truth-conditions, while these truth-conditions fail to settle for each single scenario in which Carl is deprived of one hair, whether Carl is bald or not. In other words, the fact that there are 'borderline' cases, in which sentence content does not help us to decide whether it does or does not apply to a certain setting, need not imply that the sentence expresses no truth-condition. That sentence *could* have determinate truth-conditions that correctly or incorrectly apply in a range of clear cases – for instance, when Carl has zero hairs, one hair, … one hundred thousand hairs; and which do not clearly correctly or non-correctly apply in a range or other, borderline cases – when Carl has forty-nine, fifty thousand hairs and so on.

Thus, Montminy argues, it would be fallacious to conclude that 'The cat is on the mat' suffers from semantic under-determinacy based on the fact that there could be 'strange cases' like that of the cat floating in space with the mat, in which it is not clear whether the sentence would be true or false. As long as the sentence is clearly true or false in the majority of cases, the sentence may be ascribed semantically determined truth-conditions.

These points appear entirely reasonable to me, and they induce some considerations concerning the methodology of arguments from under-determinacy. A lesson that we could draw is that arguments aimed at displaying the phenomenon of semantic under-determinacy should concern cases in which, for instance, a predicate applies (or does not apply) in a *clear* manner. The point may perhaps be seen more clearly with colour cases. If we take Pia's green-painted maple leaves, in order to effectively argue for the semantic under-determinacy of 'The leaves are green', we should stipulate in advance that the predicate 'green' clearly applies to the leaves at issue in C1 (where external appearance is at issue), and clearly does *not* apply to the leaves in C2 (where colour under the paint matters). The resulting Context-Shifting Argument would thus show that, since the predicate 'green' sharply applies in C1 or does not apply in C2 in the same worldly circumstances (the leaves being painted green), there may be no determined condition of application imposed by the content of 'green'.

We may thus see the range of applications of a predicate like 'green' as a spectrum which includes a region of clear positive applications, a 'grey' area of unclear applications and a region of clear negative applications. That there are unclear applications suffices for establishing that the term suffers from vagueness. However, the fact that a clear positive application could (in appropriate circumstances) turn into a clear negative one could be revealing of the semantic under-determinacy of the expression.

Conclusion

In this chapter, the main arguments in favour of semantic under-determinacy have been reviewed. Some considerations have emerged from an analysis of these arguments, which I will succinctly recall in this conclusive section.

The *Argument from Incompleteness* deploys intuitions as to the semantic or conceptual 'truncation' (Bach, 2012) of certain sentences in order to draw attention to their under-determinacy. But what does such an incompleteness amount to? A sentence might be said to be semantically incomplete just in case it fails to sort worlds into those in which the sentence is true and those in which the sentence is false; but as we have seen, semantically incomplete sentences succeed in doing that. Semantic incompleteness could amount to a failure to determine in which possible world, or set of worlds, the utterance is to be evaluated as true or false. Semantically incomplete sentences clearly fail this task, but so do allegedly complete sentences: so the requirement might be an excessively strong one. I have proposed that incompleteness correspond to a failure to determine a *particular* truth-condition, understood as a configuration of particular objects and properties: so for instance, a sentence like 'It's raining' fails to indicate a *particular* state of affairs (it raining in Paris, London, Bogotá) and rather indicates only a *generic* state of affairs (it raining somewhere, or it raining, *punkt*). Note that determining a particular state of affairs is not at all equivalent to determining a *maximal* state of affairs.

The *Argument from Context-Shifts* is based on a single sentence which turns out as true in one, first scenario and turns out false in another, second scenario, where no recognisable context-sensitivity is present and worldly conditions remain constant. Context-shifting cases are not all the same: some of them are such that the context-shift arguably marks a change in some *parameter* – whether articulated syntactically or lexically. This parameter is there to be filled, and simply gets filled differently in each scenario. These I call *completive* context-shifting arguments. By contrast, other context-shifting arguments are such that the context-shift marks a change in background assumptions or presuppositions, thus altering the conditions of application of the sentence. I call these *meaning-manipulative* context-shifts. The distinction between completive and meaning-manipulative context-shifts could be invoked in order to delimit interesting cases of semantic under-determinacy: in particular, the Moderate Contextualist could urge that her range of interest covers only those expressions for which there are reasons to think that they undergo completive context-shifts.

Finally, *Arguments from Unclear Applications* proved fallacious, in that from the fact that a sentence (or predicate) has unclear applications it does not follow that it is semantically under-determinate. Yet these cases taught us a methodological lesson: when mounting an argument for semantic under-determinacy, make sure that the cases you focus on are cases of clear as opposed to borderline applications of a predicate (for instance, clear cases of greenness, fatness and so on).

2
The Peculiarity of Semantic Under-Determinacy

In this chapter, I will firstly delve further into the notion of semantic under-determinacy, emphasising that it is a *sui generis* phenomenon not to be conflated with other kinds of semantic defectiveness, such as those generated by ambiguity, vagueness, indexicality or syntactic ellipsis (section 2.1). The difference between semantic under-determinacy and indexicality will receive special attention, in light of the fact that some theorists have tried precisely to trace the former down to the latter. In section 2.2 I will then concentrate on a potential way in which semantic under-determinacy could be accounted for, that is, in terms of 'semantic ellipsis' or 'under-articulation' (that is, lack of words used by the speaker to express what she means). I will argue why an under-articulation account would not be recommendable. One prominent reason is that it is usually accompanied by the idea that propositions can be expressed through further articulation (Effability), when evidence suggests that the opposite is true: propositions are in general ineffable (Ineffability). I will close the chapter by trying to resist the idea, propounded by some ineffabilist theorists, to the effect that our thoughts are ineffable to the extent that they are propositional.

2.1 The peculiarity of semantic under-determinacy

As I already mentioned in section 1.2, language could be defective in many ways, displaying phenomena that range from ambiguity, vagueness and indexicality to ellipsis. In this section of the chapter, I will argue that semantic under-determinacy is not reducible to any of these phenomena. Special attention will be devoted to distinguishing semantic under-determinacy from indexicality.

2.1.1 Semantic under-determinacy is not ambiguity

Ambiguity obtains whenever a single linguistic form is associated with more than one meaning. There is *lexical* ambiguity, whereby words can have more than one meaning: the classic example is the word 'bank', which means both 'financial institution' and 'river side'. There is phrasal ambiguity, such as that shown in 'additional vitamin source', which means both 'additional source of vitamin' and 'source of additional vitamin'. And there is sentential ambiguity, as for instance in 'Every woman loves a sailor', which means both 'There is a sailor which is loved by every woman' and 'For every woman, there is a sailor which that woman loves' (here the ambiguity specifically concerns the *scope* of quantifying expressions 'every' and 'a').

Let us confine our attention to lexical ambiguity for the moment[1] and let us define a word as ambiguous iff it is associated with more than one meaning by the dictionary;[2] or, in more formal terms, iff the lexicon assigns to a single lexical entry ('bank'), more than one 'lexical address', to be written as $bank_1$ and $bank_2$ (see Gillon, 1990).

A *cognitive* argument to rule out that semantic under-determinacy is ambiguity may be the following. Let us assume that ambiguity responds to the definition just stated and that, importantly, although the number of meanings or 'lexical addresses' can increase or decrease over time, it has to be definite, for reasons connected to language acquisition and memory. Let us then consider a word like 'ready' and let us say that the lexical entry 'ready' could be associated with indefinitely many meanings, $ready_1$, $ready_2$, $ready_3$ ... $ready_n$, to be selected each according to the context of utterance. So, the word 'ready' will have to be ambiguous between indefinitely many meanings. This, however, goes against the requirement that the meanings of ambiguous terms be definitely many. Therefore, there is reason to believe that semantic under-determinacy is not ambiguity.[3]

Tests could also be deployed to rule out that 'ready' is ambiguous. The first could be called the 'conjunction test' (see Searle, 1980, p. 224 and Zwicky and Sadock, 1975, pp. 17–18): take a typically ambiguous word like 'bank'. If Sam goes to the bank (in the sense of a financial institution) and Sal goes to the bank (in the sense of river side), then, once 'bank' is disambiguated in context, it is false to say 'Sam and Sal both went to the bank'. This, however, would not seem to happen with 'ready'. Suppose Jill were ready for her Spanish exam, while Bill were ready to eat sushi. Even in light of these differences between the activities for which Jill and Bill are ready, it would seem correct to state 'Jill and Bill are ready'. This asymmetry gives us reasons to believe that the semantic under-determinacy of 'ready' is not ambiguity.

A second test could be dubbed the 'affirmation and denial test' (see Zwicky and Sadock, 1975, pp. 7–8): suppose that yesterday Jim went to the financial institution but not on the river side. Once the word 'bank' is disambiguated in context, a sentence like 'Jim went to the bank and he didn't go to the bank' does not sound like a contradiction. This does not seem to apply to 'ready': suppose one wishes to describe Jill, who is ready for the Spanish exam but unready to get married, by uttering: 'Jill is ready and is not ready'. Even though one could interpret each occurrence of 'ready' differently in light of the described scenario, the latter sentence sounds much more infelicitous to utter than its bank counterpart. This would at least show that 'ready' is not obviously ambiguous as 'bank' is.

Finally, inter-linguistic considerations could be advanced: as Zwicky and Sadock (1975) argue, a good test to verify whether a word in a certain language is ambiguous is to see whether other languages overtly articulate the different meanings assigned to that single lexical entry. In the case of 'bank', this can be easily ascertained, for example with the two different words used in Italian for financial institution ('banca') and river side ('sponda', 'riva'). The same does not seem to apply to 'ready': assuming that in Jill's case there is an ambiguity between 'being ready for the exam' and 'being ready to get married', this difference in meaning is not plausibly articulated in other languages (and for sure not in Italian).

Recently, a case has been made by Kennedy and McNally (2010) for the idea that 'green' and colour adjectives in general are ambiguous between a gradable and non-gradable reading. Gradable readings correspond to the simple property of manifesting a colour, something which could obtain to different degrees (as in 'This leaf is too green', 'This leaf is greener than that', and so on). In the case of non-gradable, or classificatory readings, colour is attributed in order to categorise a certain item, whose colour properties are non-accidentally correlated to other (non-chromatic) properties: for instance, 'green apple', 'red wine' and so on. It is this ambiguity that can explain the context-shift in Travis' (1997) Pia case: in her dialogue with the photographer friend, an utterance of 'The leaves are green' is true in virtue of 'green' meaning 'appearing green', while in her dialogue with the botanist friend an utterance of 'The leaves are green' is false because 'green' is classificatory and means 'naturally/genetically green'. If this is the case, Kennedy and McNally say, then Travis' argument is undermined: there is no semantic under-determinacy in 'The leaves are green' – at best, there is ambiguity.

I will not discuss Kennedy and McNally's arguments here, but I think their case has very little bite against Travis' argument. Travis could concede that the mentioned readings obtain, and thus that the example was ill-conceived, however he could propose another example in which, provided 'green' is determinedly assigned one of the two readings, the truth-value of a sentence like 'The leaves are green' shifts as the context changes relevantly. A case in point could be the following:

> Suppose Pia has a white vase in her living room, on which a green light shines, making its surface appear green. Her son arrives with a pair of glasses that switch colours. He asks for something green to look at, just to see what colour it changes into. She points at the vase and says: 'The vase is green'; she speaks truly. Later on her daughter comes up, searching for a green object to bring to a St. Patrick's day party. Pia utters 'The vase is green', but this time she speaks falsely.

In this example, we could hold the reading of 'green' fixed as being the gradable 'appears green'; this notwithstanding, a context-shifting case can be constructed. This shows that – even acknowledging Kennedy and McNally's ambiguity – semantic under-determinacy still can affect the predicate 'green'.

In conclusion, a number of considerations, including a cognitive argument, the tests from conjunction and from affirmation-and-denial and inter-linguistic observations, suggest that 'ready' and similar predicates are not ambiguous. Moreover, we could concede that predicates like 'green' display some ambiguity, but as long as context-shifting arguments could be run by holding one single reading fixed, we can still show that these predicates are affected by semantic under-determinacy.

2.1.2 Semantic under-determinacy is not vagueness

Even though the matter of what vagueness is is itself controversial, let us assume, in line with the standard conception, that a necessary feature of vagueness is the obtaining of borderline, or unclear cases. We can see how vagueness generates unclarity by observing how it defies the principle of bivalence according to which every statement is either true or false (Williamson, 1994). Take the question whether Rembrandt is old: there must have been a time in Rembrandt's life, perhaps when he was middle-aged, when it was unclear whether it was true or false that Rembrandt was old (or whether the sentence 'Rembrandt is old' was true or false at that time; or, whether the predicate 'is old' correctly applied to him). As a consequence, it was unclear whether he was old or not old.

Here I will argue that the under-determinacy of terms like 'green' has nothing to do with their vagueness. One should of course concede that an expression like 'green' does give rise to borderline or unclear cases – this is relatively easy to ascertain. However the particular defectiveness that makes 'green' semantically under-determined is arguably not connected with its being vague. To illustrate, consider an utterance of 'The leaves are green' which one assesses as not determinately true or false (suppose the leaves are of an intermediate shade between green and yellow); in order for one to be able to say that the utterance does not have a definite evaluation in the first place, one needs to *already* have figured out in which respect the salient leaves are to be said green – on the outside, underneath the surface, and so on. That is, in order to judge about the vagueness of a statement of 'The leaves are green' one must previously resolve the semantic under-determinacy of the content of the sentence as to the respect in which the leaves are green. (The same, of course, also holds for cases in which an utterance of 'The leaves are green' has a definite truth-value. So, any judgement concerning truth-value requires a prior resolution of semantic under-determinacy.)

This seems to make a case for the idea that semantic under-determinacy is not reducible to vagueness, on the account that acknowledging vagueness implies, at least in some cases, resolving precisely semantic under-determinacy (see also Travis, 1997, p. 91; Bezuidenhout, 2002, p. 115).

2.1.3 Semantic under-determinacy is not indexicality

Surely indexicality is a paradigm of context-sensitivity: expressions such as 'I', 'here', 'now', 'this', 'today' are indexical to the extent that they shift their reference according to the context in which they are uttered. *Plus*, at least since Kaplan (1989), they are taken to have a twofold meaning: a context-invariant character, which contains an instruction about how to fix reference; and a context-variable content, or reference.

More than one theorist has tried to trace the context-sensitivity of expressions that generate semantic under-determinacy ('to rain', 'being ready', 'being green', 'being enough') to some form of indexicality. There are a number of ways in which this can be done. One can suppose that expressions like 'green' are simply indexed to the context of utterance, having a content-invariant character 'green$_x$' which means roughly 'being green in some contextually salient way x' and which picks out different properties depending on context ('being green on the outside', 'being green under the paint') (Rothschild and Segal, 2009). Alternatively, one can suppose that 'being green' features an extra argument-place in its syntactic structure, whose value varies relative to contexts; Szabó (2001) is a proponent of this view, according to which 'being green' has logical form *green(C, P)*, in which *C* stands for a comparison class and *P* stands for a part in which the object is green. Finally, one could propose, following Stanley (2000), that 'green' co-occurs with a contextual index in the logical form of the sentence, which acquires different values when context differs relevantly. What these approaches all have in common is an indexing of the meaning of the word 'green' with respect to a certain contextual parameter, be it a 'catch-all' contextual parameter *x* (as in Rothschild and Segal or in the Stanley-style proposal), or a parameter aimed at some specific contextual feature (as in Szabó). This indexing should be enough to ensure that the expression behaves like an indexical, changing its content in context according to some specific feature. So it seems semantically under-determined expressions could be sensibly compared with and made to behave like indexicals. But what about what someone may indicate as *other essential features* of indexicals? Do these forms of 'hidden', 'implicit' or 'covert' indexicality live up to the comparison with the other features of recognised indexicals? Relying on arguments that have been offered by some authors in the debate *plus* some original observations, I will argue that hidden indexicals bear too few similarities to genuine indexicals and that, therefore, we have reasons to rule out that semantic under-determinacy and the context-sensitivity that seems to arise from it are reducible to (hidden) indexicality.

(i) Perspectivality

A fundamental mark of indexicality is, according to Stephen Neale (2007), *perspective*. Words like 'here'/'this' and 'there'/'that' express a *proximal* and *distal spatial* perspective respectively; 'now' and 'then' express a proximal and distal *temporal* perspective respectively. Using an indexical like 'I' signals what Neale calls the 'perfectly proximal perspective' from which the speaker may be performing a certain predication – namely the *self* perspective; while using an indexical like 'you' marks a 'second-order perfectly proximal' perspective from which a certain predication could be effected – which we could cash out as 'the most proximal perspective after the self perspective'.

Neale wonders if the aphonic, syntactically hidden contextual indexes posited in the logical form of, for instance, 'It's raining', can be described as having such a perspectival character, too. Take for example the aphonic index on location, call it *loc*, which Stanley postulates as figuring in the logical form of 'to rain'. Its function is that of referring to different objects in different contexts: but does it do so in a perspectival way? Neale observes that the perspective involved cannot be the same as that expressed by 'here' or 'there': for suppose I am in Paris, talking on the phone with Carlos, who is in the same room with Juan. Juan asks Carlos to ask me what the weather is in Paris. I utter 'It's raining'; Carlos in turn utters 'It's raining' to Juan. The hidden indexical *loc* cannot be equivalent to 'here', otherwise Carlos could not have repeated my utterance the way he did; nor can it be equivalent to 'there', for this would make my utterance absurd. So *loc* lacks an intrinsic perspectival character. Is then *loc* synonymous with some definite description or proper name, like 'Paris' or 'where Delia is'? Obviously not, because the sentence 'It's raining' could have been used to say that it's raining in some place other than Paris, as well as in some place other than where I am at a certain moment.

So, *loc* is expected to behave like an indexical, which is though *aphonic* and *aperspectival*. The only function performed by *loc* is that of referring to whatever location is salient at any stage of the conversation. But then, what is the communicative utility of such an item? Suppose *loc* had a phonic counterpart, call it *loke*. Anybody who wished to say that it is raining in some particular place – whether the place of the utterance or any other salient place – could utter 'It's raining *loke*'. But then, do we really need the contribution of *loke* in order to explain the fact that the proposition expressed by 'It's raining' is about a certain particular place? Could we not just say, for example, that 'to rain' *lexically* incorporates locations as playing a constant role in the interpretation of any occurrence of 'rain'? This would be enough to explain why an occurrence of 'It's raining' demands provision of a place, in order to express a proposition (see Neale, 2007 and Taylor, 2001 for this suggestion). Here is another reason to regard *loke* as syntactically superfluous: suppose that someone utters 'It's raining here in Paris'. If one is talking about Paris and one is indeed in Paris, then by uttering 'here' and 'in Paris' one is referring to the same place, even though with two different 'modes of presentation': 'here' presents Paris as the place of the utterance, while 'in Paris' presents the place of the utterance as being Paris. Suppose one now added to the previous sentence an occurrence of *loke*: 'It's raining *loke* here in Paris'. What is the contribution of *loke* to the information conveyed by the utterance? Neale's answer is: none. There would be no informational loss if one dropped the occurrence of *loke*, because *loke* has no communicative role: it just refers to whatever one wishes it to refer to. From a methodological point of view, then, there is no good enough reason to recognise *loke* as an expression with a bona fide role in one's syntax, because even though the idea of such an expression is not incoherent, it does not make any difference at the communicative level. Now remember that, in Stanley's discussion, no such thing as a phonic location parameter is at stake, for all that Stanley discusses is the presence of an *aphonic* locational parameter, *loc*. So let us go back to *loc*: since *loc* has no phonic realisation and no communicative role, is there any reason for positing it besides that its presence is not incoherent with the rest of our syntactic posits? Neale thinks there is not: in his view, positing these hidden indexicals just because it does not seem syntactically incoherent is not enough to justify the proposal.

(ii) Anaphoric relations

A characteristic feature of indexicals highlighted by Cappelen and Lepore (2002), which hidden indexes seem to lack, is that *indexicals can enter into anaphoric relations*: that is, their reference can be picked up by a pronominal element that occurs after them in a sentence. For example, consider an utterance of 'That is a duck and *it* is my favourite animal'. Here the pronoun 'it' is anaphoric for 'that'. Now Cappelen and Lepore surmise that, if hidden indexes are genuine indexicals, they will be able to generate anaphoric relations, too. Consider a sentence like 'It's raining'. The real structure of the sentence is, by hypothesis, such that it contains a variable for locations. If this is the case, then the indexical element *l* should be able to generate anaphoric readings. But this is not the case. The sentence 'It's raining and it is a big location' has no anaphoric reading, despite the prediction. So the Indexicalist view fails to satisfy the prediction that hidden indexes, just like overt indexicals, should be able to generate anaphoras.

(iii) A priori truths

Indexicals also give rise to a priori knowable truths. For example, the sentence 'I am the person who is uttering this sentence' is going to be a priori true. The character of 'I' is such that it imposes on any occurrence of 'I' the requirement that its referent be the speaker of the utterance: only knowledge of the word's character is required in order to derive that the sentence 'I am the person who is speaking' is true (indeed, logically true). Now Cappelen and Lepore surmise that, if hidden indexes are indexicals, then they will give rise to a priori truths, too. They therefore consider an occurrence of 'Everyone': suppose that the real logical form of the phrase is 'Everyone *in domain D*', where D is to be saturated with a contextually salient domain. If the domain index is an indexical, then the following sentence should be a priori true: 'Everyone is in the contextually salient domain'. This sentence should be known as true only in virtue of the fact that 'everyone' is associated with an element ranging on contextually salient domains. However, this sentence is not an a priori truth, because it does not seem part of the meaning of 'everyone' that it (even implicitly) points to any contextually salient domain. If this is the case, then the proponents of hidden indexicality should at least explain and defend this departure from the predictions released by the paradigm account of the semantics of genuine indexicals (Cappelen and Lepore, 2002, p. 279).

(iv) Indefinite readings

A further asymmetry that has been noted between expressions that theorists like Stanley have associated with hidden indexes and true indexicals is that the former, but not the latter, can give rise to *indefinite* readings (see Recanati, 2002a, 2010; Martí, 2006; Hall, 2008). For instance, we can assign to an occurrence of a sentence like 'It's raining' the content that it's raining *somewhere*. Indeed, it is not difficult to imagine a scenario in which this could be the favoured reading. Recanati (2002a, 2010) has envisaged a situation in which rain on Earth has become extremely rare; the planet's weather is monitored from a weather station, so when rain is spotted, the person in charge could felicitously utter 'It's raining!' where this should be interpreted as meaning that it's raining *somewhere* (on Earth). Similarly, we could find situations in which one could read an occurrence of 'The leaves are green' as meaning that the leaves are green *in some respect;* and the same goes for 'Jill is ready'. However, it is not the case that we can read an occurrence of 'He is a photographer' as meaning that *someone* is a photographer (even though this would be an implication of such an utterance); or that we can read an occurrence of 'The bus stops here' as meaning that the bus stops *somewhere* (even though the utterance would of course imply that). A similar effect can be observed with regard to expressions that are commonly recognised as relational, that is, associated with some extra argument-place in their semantic and/or syntactic structure, for instance 'home' or 'left'. An occurrence of 'Sam is home' cannot be read as meaning that Sam is just *at someone's* home; it seems the covert argument-place for the home resident should be somehow filled, either by Sam himself or by the speaker (*plus* her audience, perhaps). The same goes for 'left': an utterance of 'The restaurant is on the left' cannot be read as meaning that the restaurant is on the left *relative to some perspective or other* (or at least it is very difficult to create a scenario that would fit such a reading, and sure it would be something very far-fetched); a particular perspective has to be provided.

This asymmetry on indefinite readings tells us at least that the kind of indexicality involved in expressions like 'to rain', 'being ready' and so on differs from standard indexicality in a way that has to be accounted for. Some authors, such as Recanati, have taken this asymmetry to imply that no covert index is present in the syntax and even in the semantic structure of these terms (Recanati, 2010, Ch. 3). The fact that a location is usually provided for the sake of completing the content of 'It's raining' solely depends on the contingent fact that we are usually interested in rain events to the extent that they happen at some specific place; but from this nothing follows as to whether a locational index should be associated with the predicate 'to rain'. The same considerations could presumably be invoked with regard to 'being green' and 'being ready' as well: completions introducing particular respects in which something is green or particular purposes for which someone is ready depend on the contingent fact that we are usually interested in attributing greenness in particular respects and readiness with regard to particular purposes, but from this nothing follows as to whether any indexes are associated with the words 'ready' or 'green'.

I do not believe that we should go as far as Recanati goes in holding that completion of a sentence like 'It's raining' solely depends on pragmatic interests. As I will argue at length in Chapter 4, this kind of completion may be viewed as semantically guided, even though not in the same way as indexicality is semantically controlled. We could envisage the completion of semantically under-determined sentences as the result of frame effects, that is, effects created by the fact that we master certain concepts and their mutual relations (the concept of rain and the idea that it is a spatially located event, for instance). Thus, there are prospects for giving a semantic account of the resolution of semantic under-determinacy which is not modelled along the lines of indexicals.

(v) Rigidity effects

I believe a further asymmetry should be registered between real indexicals and expressions which have been associated with hidden indexes, namely that the former expressions, when embedded in intensional contexts, refer rigidly, that is they maintain their reference fixed with respect to the context of utterance even when they are evaluated in an arbitrary circumstance (cf. Kaplan, 1989, p. 500). Consider the sentence

(1) It is possible that I wear a bikini right now.

62 Semantic Under-Determinacy and Communication

Here the modal operator 'it is possible that' shifts the possible world in which the embedded sentence 'I wear a bikini right now' is evaluated, but it does not shift the reference of either 'I' or 'now', which remains fixed according to the context of utterance. So if the modal sentence is uttered by Amanda at 12 p.m., it will be true iff there is at least one world where Amanda is wearing a bikini at 12 p.m. – where all sorts of other factors could vary, for instance her whereabouts.

Rigidity effects seem not to obtain with expressions like 'to rain', 'being ready', 'being green', this meaning at least that the alleged indexicality of these expressions importantly departs from the indexicality of Kaplanian indexicals. Suppose the following sentences are uttered:

(2) It is possible that the leaves are green.
(3) It is possible that it's raining.

Again, in sentence (2) the modal operator shifts the possible world in which the embedded sentence 'the leaves are green' is evaluated, though the specific interpretation of the predicate 'green' need not be held fixed in accordance with the context of utterance. Suppose that, in the context in which the modal sentence is uttered, 'green' is used to mean 'dyed green'. The fact that 'green' is used with this particular content seems to have no bearing on the truth-conditions of the modal sentence – which could be true even if, in a world w_j, the leaves at issue were painted with a red dye but green underneath the paint.

To see this more clearly, we need to elaborate on the example. Let us suppose that the speaker utters 'The leaves are not green' meaning that they are not *naturally* green. This interpretation of 'green' is therefore particularly salient in context. Nevertheless, the interpretation would not seem to affect the truth-conditions of a modal sentence in which the predicate 'green' occurs. For instance, suppose that, right after having uttered 'The leaves are not green', the speaker utters: 'But the leaves *could* be green'. Here it seems that the interpretation of 'green' in the modal sentence need not be affected by the interpretation that is most salient in the context of utterance. This is revealed by the fact that a perfectly appropriate way to continue the discourse would be to say: 'For instance, they could be so painted'. This signals that, when a sentence like 'The leaves are (not) green' is embedded in a modal context, the fact that the predicate 'green' bears a certain content in the context of utterance need not fix the content of the predicate for all circumstances of evaluation.

The same applies to sentence (3): the fact that, in the context of utterance, Paris is very salient, need not constrain the truth-conditions of the modal sentence. The modal sentence could be true even in a world where it is raining in London or in Mexico City.

An elaboration of the example again may bolster the case. Suppose the speaker utters 'It's not raining' while meaning that it is not raining in Paris. As a consequence, the interpretation most salient in context is that it is not raining in Paris. Right after that, she utters 'But it *could* be raining'; here the fact that rain occurring in Paris is salient need not affect the truth-conditions of the modal sentence, which could be true even if there is a world where it is raining in London. Indeed, the speaker could go on and add: 'For instance, we could be in London'. That this way of continuing the discourse is legitimate signals that the content contextually assigned to the alleged hidden indexical in 'It's (not) raining' need not remain fixed for all circumstances of evaluation.

Contrast this with how an indexical like 'here' would behave. The speaker utters 'It's not raining here' meaning that it is not raining in Paris (the place of utterance). Right after that, she utters 'But it could be raining here'. In this case, it is clear that the reference of 'here' cannot be shifted. Indeed, it would be infelicitous to continue the discourse by saying: 'For instance, we could be in London'. There is no way to read the second occurrence of 'here' as referring to London rather than Paris. The contextual interpretation of that utterance of 'here' clearly rigidifies reference to the place of utterance.

Together with the previously noted discrepancies, this asymmetry between the semantic behaviour of real indexicals and that of alleged hidden indexicals should make us suspicious that the context-sensitivity of semantically under-determined expressions, such as 'to rain', 'being ready', 'being green' and so on, is to be rendered in terms of indexicality, albeit covert or hidden.

2.1.4 Semantic under-determinacy is not syntactic ellipsis

Ellipsis is primarily a syntactic phenomenon, consisting in the deletion of some linguistic material, where the missing components can be retrieved from a linguistic *antecedent*, either in the same or in a separate sentence (for an overview, see van Craenenbroeck and Merchant, 2013). Typical cases are:

(4) A: 'Who baked the cake?'; B: 'Bill'.
(5) Bill cooked the lunch, and Jill the dinner.

In (4), the verb phrase 'baked the cake' goes missing in B's response, yet it can be recovered from the sentence antecedently uttered by A. In (5), the verb 'cooked' is deleted in the second clause of the conjunction and can be retrieved from the first conjunct.

Now the question to be answered here is whether the semantic under-determinacy of such sentences as 'It's raining', 'Jill is ready', 'The leaves are green' and so on may be recast as syntactic ellipsis.

A first consideration suggesting that a syntactic ellipsis account may be out of order has to do with the different *degrees of infelicity* of bare utterances of 'The leaves are green' as opposed to bare utterances of elliptical forms like 'Bill' and 'Jill the dinner'. By 'bare utterance' I mean an utterance which takes place in a conversation which features no previously established linguistic or presuppositional background – that is, where the speaker and the hearer did not utter anything before and do not share any presuppositions.[4] In order to avoid any default interpretations associated with 'The leaves are green', let us focus on a bare utterance of 'It's too late' (supposedly under-determined) as opposed to a bare utterance of 'Bill' (supposedly elliptical). It seems to me that the *degree* to which these utterances would be judged infelicitous differs significantly: the former may be judged infelicitous because it omits some information, but nevertheless we may safely maintain that we have received hints as to the proposition that the speaker means based on what she says (that it is too late *for something*). The latter may be judged infelicitous because it omits information and, moreover, we fail to gain even the slightest insight into the proposition that the speaker means based on what she says (that Bill ... *what?*). It seems to me that a failure to provide enough resources for retrieval of the proposition meant by the speaker is a common trait of bare elliptical utterances – like 'Jill the dinner', 'Seven is', 'Grace has',[5] 'Me as well', 'Over there', 'Bread'. Yet, it is not a common trait of semantically under-determined ones – like 'Jill is ready', 'The leaves are green', 'Jamal is tall' and so on. This generalised discrepancy strongly suggests that semantically under-determined sentences and elliptical sentences are not manifestations of the same phenomenon.

A second problem for the idea that semantically under-determined sentences are just elliptical is what Stanley and Szabó (2000, pp. 87–8) call *under-determination*. Supposing that 'The leaves are green' is syntactically elliptical, there may be more than one way in which the ellipsis could be resolved by providing the missing words, and there is no principled reason for choosing one set of words rather than another. For example, suppose that 'The leaves are green' is completed as 'The leaves are painted green'; why not use the word 'dyed' instead of 'painted'? Or, why not complete the sentence so that it results as 'The leaves are covered by a green layer of dye', or 'The leaves are covered by a green layer of paint'? There is no reason to choose one completion rather than another: since 'any completion goes', as it were, there seems to be no easily available, principled account of how the completion should be effected. We are left in the dark as to a general and principled account about what, in a context, should and should not be taken into account in order to perform the linguistic completion.

Another problem for the view would be, I surmise, the *trivialisation* of syntactic ellipsis. If the proposal were right, sentences might count as elliptical even if they were not preceded by any articulated sentence or sentence component. But, then, all sentences could be syntactically elliptical, in the sense that all of them might be missing some component if compared to longer, more articulated sentences. Yet, certainly this trivialises the notion of syntactic ellipsis, which by no means coincides with the mere idea of 'missing some component in comparison to longer sentences'.

Thus, in light of considerations of lesser infelicity of utterance for semantically under-determined sentences, of under-determination and of trivialisation, there seem to be strong reasons for rejecting the view that semantic under-determinacy is just syntactic ellipsis.

2.2 The under-articulation view

One might still think that semantically under-determined sentences are in some sense elliptical, but perhaps in a less syntactically laden sense. Perhaps the ellipticality at play here is something broader than the syntactic notion considered so far. Sentences like 'The leaves are green', 'Jill is ready' and so on may exhibit a 'semantic ellipsis', that is an ellipsis of content rather than of syntactic structure. This option has been already explored with regard to incomplete definite descriptions ('the table', 'the horse', 'the house') and indeed has had some distinguished proponents.

Quine, for instance, states that our everyday use of descriptions is often *elliptical*, that is it leaves understood some parts of the condition to be satisfied by the denotatum of the description; as an example he cites 'the yellow house', which shortens the more complete description 'the yellow house in the third block of Lee Street, Tulsa' (Quine, 1940, p. 146). The same proposal is adopted by Sellars, who has it that utterances of sentences like 'The table is large' are often elliptical and are intended to state what would be non-elliptically stated by some more complete sentence, such as 'The table over there is large' (Sellars, 1954, p. 200).

Both Quine and Sellars are careful in their phrasings: they both talk of elliptical *uses* or *utterances*. This may signal that what they have in mind is something different from strict syntactic ellipsis; perhaps something more similar to abbreviation, or shorthand. Drawing from these terminological hints, Neale (2004, pp. 98–105) traces a distinction between syntactic ellipsis, a genuinely linguistic phenomenon, and what he calls 'utterance ellipsis', conceived as a mere way of using language. Syntactic ellipsis, on the one hand, is the deletion of one or more sentential components, which can be easily recovered in the material antecedently articulated, thus allowing the reconstruction of the non-elliptical sentence via a 'copy–paste' process. Uttering a syntactically elliptical sentence implies engaging in an elliptical use. However, the reverse does not necessarily hold. This is because one can have mere ellipsis *of use*: for example, one might use elliptically the sentence 'The table is large', in order to say that the table over there is large, a content that might have been encoded by the longer sentence 'The table over there is large'. Thus 'The table is large' is elliptical with respect to 'The table over there is large', that is a longer and more specific sentence that could have been used instead of it.

In order to avoid confusion between semantic and syntactic ellipsis, I suggest dropping talk of a sentence being 'elliptical' in the semantic sense and adopting the more neutral notion of 'under-articulation'. I shall say that semantic ellipsis obtains whenever a certain sentence S, whose meaning is q and is used to mean the richer content that p, is 'under-articulated' with respect to a longer sentence $S´$ which could have been used and that literally expresses the same content that p. When a sentence S is under-articulated with respect to another sentence $S´$, it contains less linguistic material than $S´$ although it is used to mean the same content that $S´$ literally expresses. One may thus be tempted to think that sentences like 'The leaves are green', 'Jill is ready', 'It's raining' are under-articulated: for instance, 'The leaves are green' may be under-articulated with respect to 'The leaves are painted green'; 'Jill is ready' with respect to 'Jill is ready to ski'; 'It's raining' with respect to 'It's raining in Paris' and so on.

One first difficulty with the notion of under-articulation may be the following: as Stanley remarks concerning semantic ellipsis (2005a, p. 191) it looks utterly non-explanatory. If the explanandum is that some sentences under-determine the content of their utterances, it is no explanation to say that these sentences are under-articulated with respect to longer sentences that literally express a more complete content. Appeal to under-articulation adds nothing to the facts that stand in need of an explanation – it is merely a redescription of them.

Besides the problem mentioned by Stanley, the under-articulation approach incurs the same troubles as the syntactic ellipsis approach illustrated above, namely under-determination and trivialisation. It incurs under-determination because, supposing that a sentence like 'The leaves are green' is under-articulated because its semantic content fails to be identical with the proposition intended by Pia, namely *that the leaves are painted green*, there is a range of longer sentences that could have been uttered in its place and that would express the same content (or at least have the same truth-conditions) as the intended one: for instance 'The leaves are *dyed* green'; 'The leaves are *coloured with green paint*'; 'The leaves are *covered by a layer of green paint*' and so on. There is no principled way of choosing one rather than another sentence, so once again, we are left at a loss as to which contextual features should be deemed responsible for selecting the correct, non-under-articulated sentence.

Trivialisation too besets the view, for it is easy to see that every sentence could be regarded as under-articulated. For every sentence S, a longer sentence S´ could have been uttered which has the same content as S, or is at least true in the same conditions as those in which S is taken to be true or false by its speaker. This condition could be satisfied *trivially*: suppose that the speaker uttered 'The leaves are green on the outer surface' meaning nothing more and nothing less than what the sentence means. The sentence could be deemed semantically elliptical with respect to longer sentences like 'The leaves are green on the outer surface *and* the leaves are green on the outer surface', '*Oh my God*, the leaves are green on the outer surface', '*Frankly*, the leaves are green on the outer surface' and so on, which all have the same truth-conditions as those intended by the speaker while uttering the sentence (even though they may be different in aspects that pertain to tone, colour, performative features and so on). Clearly, that under-articulation is so easy to obtain renders the notion trivial and does not help discriminate between those utterances that are 'seriously' under-articulated and those that are not so – since all of them could be affected by this kind of defectiveness.

Ultimately, then, under-articulation is not a fix for the defects of the syntactic ellipsis view, in that it points to a non-explanatory notion and, moreover, it runs into the same troubles, namely under-determination and trivialisation.

2.2.1 Under-articulation and Effability

In this section, I will consider a further important motivation not to see semantic under-determinacy as a form of under-articulation. Accepting that semantic under-determinacy is just under-articulation seems to imply that, were more material to be articulated, the semantic under-determinacy could be solved and a perfectly determinate content and truth-condition could be attained.

This view echoes those authors who hold that, for instance, indexical sentences or sentences containing incomplete definite descriptions could be substituted by 'eternal' sentences that achieve reference in a non-context-dependent way and thus express fully evaluable propositions. Thus, when faced with a sentence like 'Tom believes the door is open', Quine states that if we want to identify the reference of 'Tom' without the help of the circumstances of utterance, we should provide surname, address and other material that could identify him uniquely. The same holds for 'the door': if we want to achieve unique reference for the definite description, we have to specify where the door is and at what time (Quine, 1960, p. 193). Analogously, Katz claims that we may substitute indexical expressions like 'I', 'here' and so on with expressions that have the same reference but whose reference stays fixed across contexts and variations of speaker, time, place and so on (Katz, 1972, p. 126). This suggests that these theorists believed that linguistically articulating more information could make the proposition expressed by utterances of indexical sentences or sentences containing definite descriptions fully expressible, or *effable*, in eternal terms. Let us call this the Effability View.

Extending this view to semantically under-determined sentences, one might suppose that, by adding further material to the sentence, the under-determinacy could be dispelled. But it is easy to ascertain that, often, quite the opposite happens: adding more words means *reiterating the semantic under-determinacy*. So for instance, suppose 'Jill is ready' is under-articulated with respect to 'Jill is ready for the Spanish exam'. The latter sentence may express what a speaker means with an utterance of the former sentence, however it is far from being semantically determined, in that it fails to specify a number of details: is Jill ready in the sense of having studied enough, or is she psychologically and emotionally ready? Is the exam an exam about the Spanish language, or is it held in Spanish, or both? As one can see, adding more details has the effect of multiplying the possible under-determinacies rather than reducing them. (Indeed I have conceded something similar to this point in section 1.1.2, when arguing that every sentence (no matter how long and articulated) could be regarded as incomplete, while maintaining that, when the incompleteness is reasonably contained, speakers may be entitled to ignore it.)

One route for the proponent of the under-articulation idea would be to endeavour to establish just how much articulation would resolve the under-determinacy. This may be feasible in a principled way in some cases: for instance, supposing that the semantic under-determinacy of 'Jill is ready' is due to an argumental incompleteness, one could establish that articulating the missing argument would be enough, articulation-wise, to resolve the under-determinacy. Unfortunately though, in cases where the incompleteness is not attributable to an unfilled argument or parameter, this is much less easy to accomplish in a principled manner. Moreover, whether principled or not, the move would offer a merely practically useful remedy that would spare us undue prolixity, though it would not erase the possibility that semantic under-determinacy be reiterated. Thus, it would seem inevitable for the theorist inclined towards an under-articulation account of semantic under-determinacy to accept that articulation cannot solve semantic under-determinacy; in fact, the more a sentence is articulated, the more under-determinacy it seems to give rise to.

In conclusion, it seems that one should resist the idea of under-articulation also because it would seem very easy to associate it with the thesis of Effability. On the one hand, Effability is just wrong: it is just false that providing more linguistic material could generally resolve the problem of under-determinacy. On the other hand, the under-articulation account disjoint from the Effability idea is not particularly helpful: as noted in the previous section, it does not explain under-determinacy but only redescribes it (or at best it registers a co-occurrence between semantic under-determinacy and under-articulation without explaining it), *plus* it is subject to under-determination and trivialisation. All this strongly speaks against considering semantic under-determinacy as under-articulation.

2.2.2 Ineffability and the 'gappy picture'

The considerations run in the previous section seem to suggest the opposite of what Effabilists say, namely that no matter how much one articulates sentences, their content will not determine a truth-condition for their utterances. This is tantamount to embracing a thesis of Ineffability, whereby sentences in natural language generally fail to express truth-evaluable, propositional contents. The idea that, generally, sentences fail to express propositions or thoughts (understood as complete, eternally true entities) has been forcefully advocated by Robyn Carston (see 2002a, p. 29). Let us dub this the *Ineffability Thesis*. Carston argues for it by enumerating various cases in which language allegedly fails to determine a complete and evaluable content.

The first case is offered by so-called *private contents* – for instance, the way one is presented to oneself in the first person (see Frege, 1918/56); but also the way one is presented with objects other than oneself, with which one is acquainted perceptually and that give rise to phenomenologically unique and radically private experiences (for instance, the way I am presented with my mother as opposed to the way my brother is presented with her).

Then there are those contents of our attitudes that have 'perspectival aspects' and can be expressed only with the help of indexical terms, such as 'I', 'here' or 'now'. According to Perry (1979), these are *essentially indexical* sentences, because their content is not expressible in terms of 'eternal' or 'a-perspectival' sentences (see also Wettstein, 1979). For instance, it seems that the content expressible by the sentence 'I am being attacked by a bear' is not expressible by means of the non-indexical sentence 'The speaker is being attacked by a bear'. Though the latter sentence would express the same Russellian proposition, it would lack that genuinely perspectival component that allows the subject to reason and act accordingly with the fact that the person attacked by a bear is *herself* and not someone else.

The third example of Ineffability is offered by incomplete definite descriptions, such as 'the house' or 'the table'. For any use of these descriptions, it has been argued that there is no reason to pick one complete description rather than another ('the house over there', 'the house on the third block of Murray St, Tulsa, Oklahoma', 'the house of John Smith' and so on), since speakers are often not themselves clear about which complete description the incomplete definite description they use stands for. It follows that the content of incomplete descriptions is ineffable (cf. Carston, 2002a, pp. 37–9; Wettstein, 1981).

Complete definite descriptions also give rise to Ineffability, inasmuch as their reference could vary according to the conversational assumptions mutually shared by the speaker and her audience: for instance, one could use 'the current president of the US' to refer to Barack Obama, if it was mutually assumed that Barack Obama is the president of the United States. Yet, if the speaker knew that the audience believes that the president of the US is Frank Zappa, she could use the same definite description to refer to Frank Zappa. Since even the reference of definite descriptions could vary depending on shared assumptions, it is in turn ineffable. Similar considerations hold for proper names, too (cf. Carston, 2002a, p. 38; Recanati, 1994).

The next case is quantification: Ineffability here arises to the extent that a quantifier's contribution to the truth-conditions of an utterance can vary from context to context, depending on which domain of quantification is relevant. So for instance, the quantified phrase 'every bottle' could indicate every bottle in Charles' fridge, or every bottle of beer in Italy's supermarket shelves. Since quantifiers do not give a fixed contribution to truth-conditions, but a variable one depending on the context of utterance, their content also is ineffable (cf. Carston, 2002a, p. 39; Recanati, 1994).

Finally, predication too gives rise to Ineffability, in virtue of the under-determined contribution predicates generally give to the truth-conditions of utterances. For instance, the truth-conditional contribution of 'is green' is under-determined insofar as it could vary depending on the contextual background, ranging from 'appears green on the outer surface' (in a conversation where what matters is external appearance) to 'is green by its natural, genetically coded colour' (in a conversation where what matters is the generically determined features of a plant). Thus, insofar as predicates could pick out different properties depending on context, their content within an utterance counts as ineffable (cf. Travis, 1975, 1985, 1996, 1997 and Lahav, 1989).

Reviewing such a variety of cases supplies Carston with reasonable grounds for the thesis that language in general fails to determine fully evaluable propositions. Yet this conclusion has a worrisome consequence. This bad consequence springs from the fact that *mental contents may be conceived as propositional*. Thus Carston, who endorses a Fodor-style conception of thoughts as Mentalese sentences (Fodor, 1998, 2001), suggests that we should endorse a principle of semantic compositionality for Mentalese, whereby the semantic value of a Mentalese sentence is fully determined by the semantic value of its constituents and their syntactic arrangement. She is very explicit in her claim to the effect that Mentalese sentences do not under-determine their truth-conditions, do not display context-sensitivity, generality of sense, vagueness, polysemy and other kinds of semantic defectiveness. Their contents consist of context-invariant, eternal propositions (Carston, 2002a, p. 75). Wettstein (1979) too claims that, although the sentences that we use may contain some defective descriptions that do not guarantee any unique referent, speakers always manage to attain reference at the level of what they mean with their assertions (and hence, I take it, at the level of thought), and this makes the propositions/thoughts we entertain invariably determined. Both Carston and Wettstein seem squarely to espouse a conception of thought as fully propositional. If this is so, however, and insofar as propositions are inexpressible, our thoughts are themselves inexpressible.

Thus, Ineffability plus the conception of thought as propositional implies that language cannot express our mental contents. But this is hard to swallow. It would imply that understanding the sentences that speakers use would fail to give hearers a reliable insight into the mental contents of speakers; that those who interpret these sentences end up with non-propositional objects which could not be the contents of their beliefs, desires, hopes and so on. Hearers of utterances of these sentences could not appropriately end up with beliefs that they could evaluate as true or false, or on the basis of which they could make decisions and undertake actions. A gap would open itself between the mental life of language users, which would consist in the entertaining of full-blown propositions, and their linguistic life, which would consist in the production and interpretation of sentences that fail to express propositions.

The proponent of Ineffability could try and argue that Ineffability does not really have a detrimental impact on these tasks, given the capacity of hearers to contextually complete or flesh out the defective contents of the uttered sentences in order to work out a full-fledged proposition.

This answer has the merit of providing an account of how the gap between mental and linguistic content is filled; however, one might complain, it makes no steps toward a non-gappy picture of the relationship between the contents of our thoughts and the contents of the sentences that we utter. Moreover, the view presupposes that the contents of our mental states should be conceived as propositions. Yet this view looks like an unnecessary idealisation: why should our mental states coincide with propositional, eternally true or false contents? No doubt, some contents might possess these features, but certainly not all such contents need to. It seems that sometimes we may have non-propositional thoughts and that these could, in appropriate circumstances, be useful as far as running or mental life is concerned – including acquiring beliefs that we can recognise as true or false, undertaking actions and so on.

2.2.3 Effable mental contents

In this section, I will argue that our thoughts can be non-fully-propositional (henceforth, I will simply say non-propositional) and yet be determined enough for a thinker's purposes – as far as acquiring beliefs, evaluating their content and acting upon them is concerned. If this is so, then sentences that fail to express propositions can express the contents of non-propositional thoughts. This reinstates *a non-gappy picture* of the relation between mental and linguistic content. I will consider the pros and cons of the view and conclude that, on a cost–benefit analysis, this view fares better than the Ineffabilism propounded by Wettstein and by philosophers of Fodorian persuasions in general, like Carston.

First of all, the thoughts we entertain can arguably be non-propositional. Let us illustrate this with an example concerning mental predication. Suppose Charles looks at a kettle set in front of him and forms the belief that the kettle is black. Suppose also that the kettle's original colour is black; moreover, it is black because it is covered in soot. Charles is not privy to these facts or he simply does not care whether the kettle is black in one way or the other. It seems that the content that he entertains (*that the kettle is black*) has no clear truth-conditions, in that one might ask: is it true just in case the kettle is painted black? Or is it true just in case the kettle is black because it is covered in soot? If this is so, then the thought is semantically under-determined, that is, it fails to determine a truth-condition. Note that both the narrow, internalistically identified content is indeterminate, because the speaker has no intention to describe the kettle as black in one way or the other; but, importantly, the wide, externalistically individuated content is indeterminate, because it is not clear which individual–environment relation determines it (the kettle's being painted black or the kettle's being black because it is covered in soot?).

Another example – this time involving mental reference – is the following: suppose Charles sees a statue of David Hume in front of him and forms the belief that *that* is huge. Suppose he is not particularly interested in what exactly is huge, whether the statue representing Hume (suppose he does not even know the guy portrayed is Hume) or the lump of marble sculpted so as to look like David Hume. It remains under-determined whether the thought that he is entertaining is true iff the statue is huge or iff the lump of marble is huge. Whether what is huge is the statue or the marble lump could make a difference for Charles, because his opinion as to the size of the object could vary depending on whether he identifies it as statue or marble lump. Having seen larger marble lumps, he may not think that *that* marble lump is huge; but having seen much smaller statues, he may think that *that* statue is huge. Be that as it may, since he does not care or is ignorant about that distinction, the simple thought he entertains (that *that is huge*) is under-determinate, that is it expresses no truth-condition or proposition. Note once again that both narrow content is indeterminate, since the speaker does not clearly intend to refer to the lump rather than the statue; and wide content is indeterminate, since no externalistically individuated relation between the individual and the environment can determine that.

So far, it seems that our thoughts can consist of non-propositional contents. Far from being useless or ineffective, these contents could play a role in our linguistic, mental and practical life. The first thing to note is that these contents could be evaluable as true or false, given appropriate aims, interests and available information of the speaker. For instance, suppose that Charles' aim is to ascertain, by simply looking at the kettle, whether it appears black rather than red or yellow. In such a context, where what is at stake is simply what colour impression the kettle triggers when looked at, it does not matter much whether it is black because it is covered in soot or because it is painted black. So, as far as Charles' interests are concerned, it is true that the kettle is (or appears) black (rather than yellow or red). Together with evaluation, action upon the belief that the kettle is black is perfectly possible – for instance, Charles might fetch the kettle or continue to look for the kettle he wishes.

The same considerations hold for Charles' thought that *that is huge*. Suppose Charles is scared of huge objects and constantly tries to avoid them. Looking at the statue, he forms the belief that it is huge (in the particular way that scares him). This thought does not need to carve the world out in any finer-grained manner, as far as Charles' interests are concerned – namely, avoiding huge things. So, his thought that *that is huge* is true in that particular scenario. Action upon belief ensues: in consideration of the truth (relative to his interests and aims) that that is huge, Charles might go on and avoid it, for instance by changing his route or crossing the street.

All this shows that non-propositional thoughts may count as *semantically determined enough* given our purposes: whether or not a thought is evaluable might be a context-sensitive matter, where the aims, interests and available information of the speaker play a pivotal role. What is relative to aims, interest and available information is the *evaluability* of the thought, and consequently, its truth-value. So, for instance, the thought to the effect that that is huge is evaluable relative to the aims of its thinker (avoiding huge things), while it might not be evaluable for the aims of another thinker. For every thought, then, one will have to consider the aims, interests and available information of the thinker in order to judge whether it is evaluable (and usable for belief, reasoning and action purposes), and also in order to assign a truth-value to it.

In this scenario, it is clear that what we have started regarding as non-propositional thoughts can be expressed by sentences that fail to express propositions. In this way, we rescue the non-gappy picture according to which the sentences that a speaker utters express the thoughts that he or she entertains. The content a hearer grasps while interpreting an utterance gives her an insight into the mental contents of the speaker and puts her in a position to acquire a legitimate belief that, in appropriate circumstances, could be evaluated as true or false and be employed in reasoning and decision making or provide a ground for action. In other words, in this picture the gap between language and thought opened by Ineffabilism accompanied by a conception of thought as propositional is eventually closed. The contents of thoughts are conceived as expressible by means of semantically under-determined sentences, because thoughts might be non-propositional in the same way as the contents expressed by these sentences are non-propositional.

The view has some benefits and some costs. On the side of benefits, we have already emphasised that the present proposal allows us to rescue the effability of our mental contents, thus reinstating a *non-gappy view* of the relationship between the contents of our utterances and our thoughts, a result I consider valuable.

A cost of the view is that it tears thoughts and propositions apart. Some might protest that this forces us to abandon a convenient picture of the semantics of thoughts – where, for instance, thoughts are conceived as propositions and respond to the principle of compositionality. However, it is not clear that the picture needs to be abandoned. This picture is, first of all, still good for anyone who is interested in thought in the non-psychological sense (see Frege, 1918/56) and thus is interested in the laws that regulate our thought as rational thinkers at an idealised level, so to speak. Moreover, from the fact that thoughts qua mental contents tokened in our heads may be semantically under-determined it does not follow that we do not in some ideal sense 'aim' at entertaining thoughts that are fully propositional. So, ultimately, it seems that a propositional conception of thought can be retained by anyone interested in a non-psychological account of thought with no contrast with the project I am presently engaged in.

An account along the lines I have proposed is in general useful if one cares about psychological plausibility, that is, accounting for thoughts as they are actually entertained by thinkers. Admission of non-propositional contents would mean acknowledging that thought in the psychological sense is often, like thinkers themselves are, sloppy, gappy, skimpy or imprecise. This might be due, as some have already remarked, to the fact that subjects often think by relying on available spatio-temporal or subjective coordinates in their environment – the self, the temporal location of the thought, the spatial location of the thinking (see Perry, 1986; Lewis, 1979; Burge, 1977; Recanati, 1993, 2007). But thinkers are also sloppy in the sense that they think unspecific, not fully precise thoughts, by employing concepts they do not fully master or they are not interested in employing in a detailed manner. Or, they perform acts of mental reference which are not fully determinate in the sense that they do not pick a unique object, either because the thinker is careless in focusing attention, or because she is not interested in achieving full uniqueness of reference, or because she is ignorant of some facts. Also, the content of people's thoughts might end up being semantically under-determined because the world does not cooperate: it provides no reference, or too much reference and thus ambiguities that are not resolvable with a mere inspection of the circumstances of the thinking. Ultimately, the need for such a psychological plausibility might be a strong motivation for moving away at least partly from accounts of thought which conceive of its content as fully propositional.

To sum up, in this section I have defended the idea that thoughts can be effable as against the thesis that thoughts are in general ineffable, where this thesis follows from the joint acceptance of the ineffability of propositions and the propositionality of thoughts. In order to defend this insight, I have explicitly challenged the thesis of the propositionality of thoughts, arguing that our thoughts can be non-propositional and, therefore, expressible by means of sentences that express no proposition. This move is sustained by the motivation of restoring a less idealised and more psychologically plausible view of how our mental life is conducted, which need not picture thinkers as invariably entertaining propositions, but admits for incomplete, imprecise or gappy thoughts.

Conclusion

In this chapter, I have taken up the issue of the peculiarity of semantic under-determinacy, arguing that it is not a case of either ambiguity, vagueness, indexicality or ellipsis.

- A number of considerations suggest that semantic under-determinacy is not ambiguity; first of all, ambiguous words arguably have definitely many meanings (for reasons of learnability and memory), while semantically under-determined words can mean indefinitely many things; secondly, from various tests and inter-linguistic considerations it emerges that known ambiguous words and semantically under-determined words work differently;
- Semantic under-determinacy is not vagueness either, because supposing that vagueness generates unclarity in the application of predicates

and in the evaluation of sentences, semantic under-determinacy has to be resolved prior to establishing that vagueness obtains;
- Semantic under-determinacy should not be conflated with indexicality either. More than one theorist has tried to go down this path and reduce semantic under-determinacy to a form of indexicality – such as co-occurrence with an empty variable in logical form, extra argument-places in the logical form of a predicate or simply indexing relative to a context. Although semantically under-determined expressions might seem to align with indexical ones as far as some aspects of the former are concerned – for instance, the variability of their content relative to a context of utterance – it is not clear that they can live up to the comparison with other prima facie fundamental features of indexicals. Firstly, as Neale has noted, alleged hidden indexicals lack perspectivality; secondly, they do not seem to enter into anaphoric relations, nor they seem to give rise to a priori knowable truths, as Cappelen and Lepore have pointed out; thirdly, indefinite readings seem available for hidden indexicals, while they are not for genuine indexicals, as Recanati and Hall highlight; finally, I have stressed how genuine indexical expressions give rise to rigidity effects (for example, if embedded under modal operators), while alleged hidden indexicals do not;
- It can be argued that semantic under-determinacy is not ellipsis either: first of all, it is implausible that it is a case of syntactic ellipsis, in that syntactically elliptical sentences could not provide the hearer with a sufficient (albeit partial) insight into the proposition meant by the speaker, while semantically under-determined sentences could afford such an insight. Moreover, the syntactic ellipsis account suffers from under-determination and trivialisation;
- One might suspect that semantic under-determinacy is rather a case of 'semantic ellipsis', where this obtains when a sentence S is 'under-articulated' with respect to a longer sentence $S´$, that is, although it means that q, it is used to express a richer content content p that $S´$ literally expresses. Unfortunately, though, semantic ellipsis or under-articulation is not an explanation but merely a redescription of semantic under-determinacy; moreover, it is still exposed to the threats of under-determination and trivialisation;
- A further problem for the under-articulation account comes from the fact that the idea of under-articulation or semantic ellipsis is often accompanied by the view that further articulation could aid in overcoming semantic under-determinacy and thus achieving a propositional content (*Effability*). Unfortunately, quite the opposite

seems to be true: the more we articulate a sentence, the more the under-determinacy increases. This suggests what I have called an *Ineffability* thesis, to the effect that no sentence, no matter how much articulated, could express a fully evaluable proposition;
- The Ineffability View combined with a conception of thought as propositional has as its consequence that language users cannot express their thoughts by using sentences, or that hearers cannot grasp something believable when interpreting the sentence uttered by the speaker. I have argued that our thoughts can be (and indeed I think they often are) non-propositional but nonetheless they can have a role in our linguistic practices, mental and practical life. If this is so, semantically under-determined sentences can express our thoughts after all, and the gap between our linguistic and mental contents can be closed.

Part II
Semantic Under-Determinacy and Communication

3
Semantic Under-Determinacy and the Debate on Context-Sensitivity

The idea of semantic under-determinacy is typically accompanied by the thesis that the expressions that suffer from it are also somehow context-sensitive. A large debate has flourished in recent decades concerning the nature, extent and localisation of context-sensitivity in language. In the present chapter, I will present and critically assess the main positions that have emerged in the literature. These could be partitioned into two macro-positions: on the one hand, *Contextualism* has it that context-sensitivity plays a pivotal role in language, affecting the semantic content of utterances in ways that depart (either in quantity or in quality) from standardly recognised phenomena like indexicality. Three varieties of Contextualism – Extreme, Radical and Indexical – will be covered in the present chapter. On the other hand *Minimalism*, in a more conservative fashion, argues that context-sensitivity can affect sentence content only if it is triggered by already familiar and recognised semantic factors; all effects that are not attributable to traditional forms of context-sensitivity are to be traced to a different level of the semantics of utterances. Three positions which all subscribe to this thesis – Minimalism, Ultra-Minimalism and Non-Indexical Contextualism – will be illustrated and discussed.

3.1 Extreme Contextualism

Extreme Contextualism questions the idea itself that there is anything like meaning conceived as an abstract entity which linguistic expressions permanently and invariantly 'have'. This idea traces back to Wittgenstein's *Philosophical Investigations* (1953) and Austin (1950, 1962) and it is resumed and developed in detail by authors such as Charles Travis and John Searle.

There seem to be two ways of interpreting the Extreme Contextualist tenet. The first reading is to the effect that there is no such thing as the meaning of words, whether conceived as an abstract or a mental entity. Words do not 'have' a meaning independently of their being employed, but they acquire one when they are used in concrete situations: Wittgenstein's §432 of the *Philosophical Investigations* is very suggestive of this, as he remarks that a sign by itself seems dead and suggests that 'life is given to it' through use. So, in order to discover what the meaning of a certain expression is, we have to look at the ways in which this expression is used (§§37, 43).

This entails that no proper 'theory of meaning' can be developed, in that there is no sensible way in which one can generalise on the 'meaning' of a particular expression – all one can do is survey the different uses that can be made of it, with no aspiration to pursue any theoretical generalisation. This is explicitly maintained by Travis, who has it that all that can be acknowledged is the semantics an item has at the present moment, or anyway on some *particular occasion* – no prediction about the future semantics of that item can be made (Travis, 2002, pp. 29–30; see also Waismann, 1951 and Searle, 1978).

This claim is at odds with the fact that the import of words in language use seems to exhibit some *constancies*, which allow speakers to use the same words to talk about the same things across different contexts and comprehend the words that their fellow speakers use even when they are not familiar with the details of their situation of use. It is very tempting to consider the (truth-conditional, communicative) import that a word has across different contexts as its meaning, yet the Extreme Contextualist should refrain from doing so. However, there would seem to be no good reason for this – in fact it seems that the overwhelming evidence provided by such constancies or regularities should prompt the Extreme Contextualist to either abandon or at least mitigate her claim.

This brings us to the second way of interpreting the 'meaning is use' slogan, according to which there is something like meaning, for which the theorist should give a definition or at least an explication in terms of use (or conditions thereof). This position seems exemplified by Horwich's Use Theory of Meaning (see Horwich, 1998). Note that, in this second interpretation, Extreme Contextualism does not prevent 'regular uses' from building up what a certain word means: it just recommends that meaning is not thought of as an abstract or mental entity, but as something tightly linked with *use* (in that it is either defined or explicated in terms of it). Meanings thus conceived could be viewed as perhaps posing only loose constraints on use, as well as remaining open to a great deal of variations and interpretations. Still, if this second rendition of the view has any plausibility, it is less extreme than one might think and indeed it makes it possible to build a proper 'theory of meaning'.

Be that as it may, absent any clear and final interpretation, Extreme Contextualism is unstable between these two poles: if it is identified with the second interpretation, namely the thesis that meaning is cashed out in terms of use, it is not that extreme after all because it admits some sort of stable 'meaning'; if it is equated with the first interpretation, it is untenable in the face of semantic regularities and their lending themselves to forming what one would call a word's 'meaning'. Owing to this instability, I suggest that we cast Extreme Contextualism aside and move to other positions which are apparently less ambivalent and more tractable.

3.2 Radical Contextualism

Radical Contextualism is the view that the semantic content of a sentence is generally not the proposition that a speaker means by uttering it. Oftentimes, the semantic content of a sentence, despite disambiguation and the saturation of indexical elements, still fails to express a full-blown proposition. This happens with sentences like 'It's raining', 'Steel isn't strong enough', 'Jill is ready', 'Peter's book is grey' and so on, which exhibit a certain degree of incompleteness (see Introduction and Chapter 1) and thus fail to determine what a speaker may mean by uttering them *to the extent that they fail to express a proposition* in the first place. Furthermore, in a great deal of other cases, the semantic content of a sentence may express an evaluable proposition which, however, is generally not what speakers mean by uttering it. This happens with sentences like 'I've had breakfast', 'Everybody is going to the beach', 'John has three children', 'Jack and Jill are married', 'You are not going to die', 'It will take some time to get there' and so on, which all have a truth-condition that is however less specific than what a speaker might normally mean by uttering each of these sentences (see Introduction).

In order for the semantic content of a sentence to express a full-blown proposition, or in any case the proposition meant by the utterer, it has to undergo a number of processes of enrichment, expansion, specification or modulation. These processes, are, according to Radical Contextualists, substantially different from processes of indexicality resolution. The latter are semantically controlled or, as Recanati has it, 'bottom up', in that they are typically driven by a word's meaning or – in Kaplan's terms – character. If a sentence contains an indexical expression like 'I', the meaning itself of the indexical ('the speaker in context') prescribes that a referent is assigned to it according to who is doing the speaking in the context of utterance. By contrast, the processes of enrichment envisaged by Radical Contextualists escape the model of indexicality in that they are semantically unconstrained and thus 'free'. Recanati dubs these processes 'top down' in that they are not mandated by semantic features, but are triggered by purely pragmatic demands, such as a need for relevancy, informativeness, perspicuity, clarity and so on (see Recanati, 2004, p. 18; Carston, 2004, p. 818; Sperber and Wilson, 1986, pp. 188–9).

Processes of free pragmatic enrichment affect semantic content in many ways. One way in which they can supplement it is by adding material in the form of so-called *unarticulated constituents*. An unarticulated constituent is a propositional component which is not the content of any linguistic element articulated either in the superficial or deep syntax of a sentence (see section 1.1). One example is provided by the sentence 'It's raining', which could be uttered concerning (*à propos de*) Palo Alto, without either explicitly or implicitly articulating the locational information in its syntax. In this case, a Radical Contextualist would say that the addition of Palo Alto in the proposition is the result of a pragmatic process by means of which one seeks to make the content of a sentence more informative. The hearer would exploit such a pragmatic process to obtain the proposition that it is raining *in Palo Alto*, which thus contains Palo Alto as an unarticulated constituent.

Another way in which free pragmatic processes could act on sentence content is by adjusting meaning, thus making it 'ad hoc'. Suppose Charles asks Geena whether she would like to go to the movies and she replies 'I am tired'. In order for the answer to count as pertinent, the sense of the word 'tired' may have to be adjusted and made more precise, so as to indicate the property of being tired to an extent that prevents one from going to the movies (see Sperber and Wilson, 1998, pp. 194–6; Carston, 2002a, pp. 143–52). Or, suppose Charles utters 'Geena likes to wear rabbit': in this case, a pragmatic process is said to cause the sense of the words 'rabbit' to be adjusted or modulated so as to indicate rabbit *fur* – rather than rabbit meat, say (see Recanati, 2004, p. 24; 2010, pp. 84–5, 169).

The result of such pragmatic processes is an expansion, enrichment or refinement of the content of a sentence which corresponds to a full-blown proposition or, in any case, to what the speaker really means. It differs from sentence content in that it includes elements that are not articulated in the syntax of the sentence; at the same time, though, it could not be identified with a conversational implicature, in that it is too closely related to the content expressed by the sentence – being a mere 'fleshing-out' of it and not a separate and truth-conditionally independent proposition. It is in effect a 'third level' of content, to be kept apart from both sentence content and conversational implicature. Recanati dubs it 'what is said' (see Recanati, 1989, 2001, 2004, 2010), whereas Carston and Sperber and Wilson coin the term 'explicature' (Carston, 1988, 2002a, 2004; Sperber and Wilson, 1986) in order to indicate it (both notions correspond to what, in the Introduction, was defined as 'utterance content').

Radical Contextualism has enjoyed a huge success in the last three decades, giving rise to a heated debate that has come to touch a range of diverse aspects, from its cognitive underpinnings to its relationship with syntactic theory. Providing a detailed assessment of the position would be beyond the scope of this section. In what follows I will focus on some difficulties that relate to the substantiality of the Radical Contextualist view and its sustainability in the face of rival theories.

One weakness of Radical Contextualism seems to be its being exposed to what I will call the 'divide and conquer strategy'. Radical Contextualism holds that a variety of effects are pragmatic in nature (that is, they are triggered for pragmatic purposes) and, moreover, that they affect the content of a sentence, thus 'fleshing it out' or enriching it in various ways. In this sense, Radical Contextualists emphasise how pragmatics intrudes into semantics, so that the distinction between the two becomes blurred. However, an opponent of such a view, inclined towards a sharper separation between semantics and pragmatics, could adopt a 'divide and conquer' strategy and argue, for each single case presented in support of Radical Contextualism, that it is either really a case of semantic process or that it falls in the domain of conversational implicature, or anyway of pragmatically conveyed content. The Radical Contextualist could implement some strategies aimed at defending her view to the effect that there exists a 'grey area' which hosts a mixture of semantic and pragmatic phenomena (Recanati's 'what is said' and Relevance Theorists' 'explicature'). As we shall see, though, these strategies prove rather unsatisfactory.

First of all, let us illustrate what a 'divide and conquer' strategy consists of. Consider for instance an utterance of 'I've had breakfast': in opposition to the Radical Contextualist's contention that this utterance gives rise to free enrichment, it could be argued that the tensed verb 'have had' occurs with an implicit temporal variable, which gets assigned the appropriate time or time interval in accord with what is salient in the conversation (see King and Stanley, 2005), thus delivering the correct content to the effect that the speaker has had breakfast *on that very morning*. Similarly, consider an utterance of 'Geena likes to wear rabbit': it could be argued that the word 'rabbit' is polysemous between 'rabbit fur', 'rabbit meat' or 'rabbit stuff', and that comprehending this utterance implies selecting the right sense of 'rabbit' according to what the linguistic and extra-linguistic context looks like. Or, consider an utterance of 'John has three children': Radical Contextualists hold that 'three children' gets enriched so as to express the same as '*exactly* three children'. By contrast, one could argue that an utterance of this sentence may trigger the following reasoning leading to a scalar implicature: since the speaker did not say that John has more or less than three children, and since she would have said it had she known that, she must imply that John has exactly three children (see Levinson, 2000). Finally, consider the sentence 'Susan got married and had a kid': here instead of a process of free enrichment that takes 'and' and returns 'and *then*', one might suppose that the following (perhaps default) inference might lead to deriving an implicature: supposing that the speaker is abiding by the Gricean sub-maxim of Manner, 'Be orderly', she must imply that the two events happened in the order in which she presented them; hence, that Susan got married *and then* had a kid.

In general, the 'divide and conquer' strategy may be viewed as a reaction to a tendency of the Radical Contextualist to lump together a great number of cases as instances of free enrichment, without considering whether a more traditionalist solution is available first, either in terms of semantically driven processes or in terms of Gricean implicature. But what does lead the Radical Contextualist to such a seemingly undiscriminating treatment of context-sensitivity? The answer, as far as I understand, lies in the Radical Contextualist's methodology, which makes ample use of *intuitions* as to 'what is said' in order to decide whether a certain aspect of content belongs to the content of an utterance or to a different, entirely pragmatic level.

In general, the Radical Contextualist will say that the mark of the effect of a free pragmatic process is that we have the intuition that it forms part of 'what is said', or the utterance's content. Typically, language users are not aware of the processes' effects and immediately judge their product as part of 'what is said'. For instance, in interpreting an utterance of 'Julia took the key and opened the door' normal speakers would be immediately aware of the enriched content to the effect that Julia took the key and *then* opened the door *with the key*, and not also of the content literally expressed by the sentence *plus* the effect of the pragmatic process on it (for experimental results that confirm this hypothesis, see Gibbs and Moise, 1997). By contrast, with conversational implicature, it is held that one would have to be aware of the sentence's content, of the implicated content and the inferential connection between the two (Recanati, 2010, p. 144): for instance, if we imagine that by uttering 'I am French' one implies that one is a good cook, the typical language user will have to rely on the assumption that the speaker has just said that she is French in order to derive the desired implicature. So, the normal language user will be aware of 'what is said', what is implied and of the connection between the two. Since this does not occur with examples of free pragmatic enrichment, it is concluded that the result of these processes is not anything akin to an implicature.

Yet, for one thing it is not obvious that the derivation of a conversational implicature is such that the hearer is (even potentially) aware of the sentence's content, of the implicated content and the connection between the two – and, by the way, it is notable that Grice himself (1967/1989, p. 31) conceded that conversational implicatures might be 'intuitively grasped'.

Moreover, one ought not to downplay the possibility that what-is-said intuitions are due to semantics proper. This means not only that, unbeknownst to us, some effects might be generated by covert indexicality, value-assignments to hidden variables (as with 'I've had breakfast') or unrecognised polysemy (as in the case of 'rabbit'): these are open possibilities that need to be brought to the fore by apt semantic arguments. What I have in mind is that there is always the possibility that already familiar semantic effects shape our intuitions as to what is said – that is, that our intuitions as to what is said track the semantic (pragmatically untouched) features of the sentences that we utter. If this were so, then what-is-said intuitions would not help to establish the range of free-enrichment effects, because they would capture semantically and pragmatically determined contents indiscriminately. Actually, empirical tests have shown that literal, purely semantic content *is* available to our intuitions. Noveck (2004) has devised experiments aimed at showing whether scalar implicatures are intuitively judged part of what is said. Subjects had to listen to an utterance of 'Some turtles are in the box', look at a number of pictures and judge whether the sentence were true or false. In one picture, some turtles were in the box and some were outside; in the other, crucial one, they were *all* in the box. In the latter case, approximately half of the subjects judged the sentence false, while approximately another half judged it true. This has been taken to show that the sentence's literal content (that *some* turtles are in the box – as opposed to *not all*) is available after all, and so that what-is-said intuitions do not reliably capture the product of free pragmatic processes (see Carston and Hall, 2011 for discussion).

In sum, intuitions as to what is said do not conclusively establish that something is subject to free pragmatic processes: on the one hand, it could be part of a conversational implicature, for even intuitions about conversational implicatures could be as direct as those about enriched utterance content; on the other hand, intuitions as to what is said may include the result of semantic processes, both unrecognised and familiar.

It could be argued that pragmatic effects operate on 'what is said' because their products pass a number of tests that conversational implicatures typically fail. Recanati (1989; 2010, p. 145; see also Cohen, 1971) stresses that the pragmatically enriched 'what is said' falls within the scope of logical operators like negation and the conditional, while implicatures generally do not: for instance in the sentence

(1) If Mary took the key and opened the door, then she is sober; but if Mary opened the door and took the key, then she is not sober

it seems that the enrichments pertaining to Mary's opening with the key and the temporal order are retained; by contrast, in

(2) If I am French, then I am European

it is not clear that the implicature that one is a good cook could still arise. Recanati explains this asymmetry with the idea that free pragmatic enrichment occurs locally, for example in the antecedent of each of the conjuncts in (1), while the implicature would have to occur globally, as a result of uttering the whole sentence (2). The Radical Contextualist may thus argue that the products of pragmatic enrichments pass these embedding tests, so they do not belong to the level of implicature. Yet, passing such embedding tests may count as evidence that these contents are not *particularised* conversational implicatures, however this is still not conclusive evidence that these contents could not be identified as generalised conversational implicatures (see Grice, 1967/1989; Levinson, 2000)[1] or other 'standardised' but still pragmatically derived contents.[2] Not to mention the possibility that the processes in action may in some cases be semantic in kind.

Carston (1988, 2002a) puts forth a different criterion for distinguishing between enriched sentence content (which she calls *explicature*) and implicatures: the guiding principle is one of 'Functional Independence', to the effect that implicatures *should not* entail what is said (they should not be logically stronger than it), otherwise the latter would be cognitively redundant, that is, it would play the same cognitive role in inferences. For instance, we could suppose that 'Susan got married and had a kid' gives rise to the implicature to the effect Susan got married *and then* had a kid, through the sub-maxim of Manner 'Be orderly'. If this were so, Carston argues, the implicature would imply what is said – which would in turn play the same inferential, cognitive role as the implicature. Carston then concludes that there is no implicature and the enriched content is in fact an explicature. The principle of Functional Independence has been judged wrong by more than one author, in that it is clearly contravened by some bone fide implicatures, which *do* entail what is said. Think of an utterance of 'Claire danced with a man' used to implicate that Claire danced with a man different from her husband, brother and so on; this is arguably an implicature which logically entails what has been said (see Garcia-Carpintero, 2001, p. 113; Recanati, 1989 for other examples). Moreover, as Saul (2002, pp. 360–1) notes, entailed contents *can* play different cognitive roles than those played by the propositions that entail them – for instance, logical and mathematical propositions in proofs. So that of Functional Independence does not appear to be an effective criterion for the sake of determining whether something is part of an utterance's content rather than an implicature.

Finally, Carston and Hall (2011) argue that what sets the difference between explicature and implicature is that explicature is *local*, or sub-propositional, while implicature is *global*, or propositional. As they explain, with implicature one processes the sentence first, establishes what has been said and then works out the implicated proposition through (more or less implicit) reasoning. With explicature, things are different: one does not process the sentence and then move to working out the explicature; pragmatic mechanisms already kick in during reconstruction of what the speaker is saying. But this is a good distinction to be made *once we have discovered* which are the implicatures and which the explicatures. Before this, the criterion cannot help us to discriminate between implicature and explicature, because each example could be reconstructed equally well at the cognitive level as a case of implicature and as a case of explicature. For example, it seems that we can account for the way in which 'Every bottle is in the fridge' is interpreted by reconstructing the process either way: (i) for the implicature account, it is enough to suppose that one apprehends the semantic content to the effect that every bottle *tout court* is in the fridge and, through some more or less compressed or implicit reasoning, concludes that the speaker must have meant that every bottle *in the house* is in the fridge; (ii) for the explicature account, one could suppose that, in light of certain assumptions concerning the conversation, the speaker immediately considers the words 'every bottle' as meaning 'every bottle in the house' and then proceeds by composing the other elements of the proposition expressed. As one can see, both accounts are prima facie plausible. It might be objected that cases like 'Every bottle is in the fridge' strongly suggest that the enriched content is an explicature because the enrichment seems to concern only sub-propositional elements (the phrase 'every bottle'). But this still tells nothing about the underlying cognitive mechanisms for the enrichment – whether the whole sentence is processed first and the phrase is subsequently enriched; or whether the enriched version is straightforwardly introduced in the proposition the hearer interprets as what is said, during the interpretive process. That a certain feature is highly suggestive of a certain cognitive mechanism certainly does not prove whether that mechanism actually takes place.

To sum up, in this section I have raised some problems concerning the tenability of Radical Contextualism: I have argued that Radical Contextualism has no easy way of defending itself against the opponent who is adverse to a 'third level of meaning', that is, an amalgam of semantics and pragmatics. The opponent might adopt a 'divide and conquer' strategy in order to undermine the account. The problem seems to spring from the methodology adopted by the Radical Contextualist, in which intuitions as to what is said have central importance. I have pointed out how recourse to intuitions does not conclusively make a case for free pragmatic processes, and neither do other methods for setting the difference between explicature or implicature, such as embedding tests, functional independence tests and the local vs global contrast.

3.3 Indexical Contextualism

The main tenet of Indexical Contextualism is that all context-sensitivity is traceable to indexicality broadly construed, where this is importantly seen as having a *syntactic* articulation. In this way, the context-sensitivity of these expressions becomes controlled by their syntax and, consequently, by their semantics, rather than being affected by free pragmatic processes.

In sentences like 'It's raining', the predicate 'to rain' comes with an argument-slot for times, which is filled by the time of utterance, and *also* introduces a location-slot which is occupied by a free variable; the variable can be saturated with contextually provided places, thus yielding a richer proposition which however is the result of a semantically controlled process of variable assignment, rather than one of free enrichment. A host of other expressions, such as gradable and comparative adjectives like 'tall', 'small', 'rich' (see Stanley, 2000, 2002b), nouns like 'bottle', 'student', 'question', mass terms like 'water' (Stanley and Szabó, 2000; Stanley, 2002b) and colour adjectives like 'green', 'blue' and so on (Szabó, 2001; Rothschild and Segal, 2009) have been given an Indexical Contextualist semantics in order to account for the apparent context-sensitivity of their use. An Indexicalist treatment has also been offered of tense, which is to be represented as a covert variable in the logical form of sentences which could either undergo binding by temporal quantifiers ('in the past', 'in the future', 'now') or be assigned a specific value in context (cf. King, 2003; King and Stanley, 2005; Partee, 1973).

The term 'Indexical Contextualism' has also been adopted to indicate other approaches that do not particularly stress the syntactic source of context-sensitivity. These accounts are not so much concerned with nailing the context-sensitivity of these terms down to their syntax; they limit themselves to emphasising how the context-sensitivity of these words is to be traced to some specific *parameter* in their semantics, in such a way that their content changes as the values of the parameter change. The context-sensitivity thus becomes apparent only when the truth-conditions of sentences are spelled out, in such a way that one could locate it at the *metalinguistic* level. Thus, the semantics of a term like 'know' has been modelled so as to incorporate a parameter for epistemic standards in order to explain sceptical paradoxes (see Cohen, 2000; DeRose, 1995; Lewis, 1996). Moral terms like 'good', 'ought' (see Harman, 1978; Unger, 1995; Dreier, 1990) as well as predicates of personal taste like 'delicious' or 'disgusting' (see Glanzberg, 2007; Cappelen and Hawthorne, 2009; Lopez De Sa, 2008; Sundell, 2011) have been treated as featuring a parameter on moral codes or standards of taste, in order to account for the fact that the truth of moral or taste judgements depends on the inclinations of the speaker (or of a group which is salient to the speaker).

In this section, I will focus attention on Indexicalism understood as a *syntactic* proposal concerning context-sensitivity; my main aim will be that of stressing the problems of the syntactic thesis and of gesturing at a purely semantic alternative.

The main argument in favour of Indexical Contextualism has been offered by Stanley (2000, 2002a, b, 2005a) who, drawing partly on

92 *Semantic Under-Determinacy and Communication*

Partee (1989), appeals to the phenomenon of binding of implicit variables in quantified contexts in order to show that some expressions feature a hidden index or argument-position which is articulated in their syntax. Firstly, he shows that sentences like

(3) Every time John lights a cigarette, it rains
(4) Most species have members that are small
(5) Every student answered every question

can have bound readings, that is, readings where an implicit variable in the embedded clause is bound (its assignment of values is controlled) by a binding operator like a quantifier ('every time', 'most', 'every student'). This implies that (3) is read as meaning that every time John lights a cigarette, it rains in the location *where he lights a cigarette*; (4) is read as meaning that most species have members that are small *for those species*; (5) is read as meaning that every student answered every question *that was posed to her*.

Stanley also endorses what he calls the *Binding Assumption* (2000, p. 412), according to which a semantic binding invariably co-occurs with a syntactic binding. Binding operators do not have effects on unarticulated variables, so if an implicit variable is bound by such an operator, this variable must be syntactically articulated. Stanley's argument concludes that this must mean that predicates like 'to rain', 'being small', or nouns like 'question' occur with a hidden index in logical form. These additional indexes or argument-places are phonologically null but nonetheless articulated in syntax and they serve to account for these expressions' context-sensitivity.

Stanley's argument has been the target of a number of criticisms: among these are charges of overgeneration[3] and methodological[4] qualms, about which a vast literature already exists. In this section I will concentrate on two difficulties with Stanley's insistence on syntax as the *locus* of context-sensitivity, which will allow me to hint at an alternative view which appeals to semantics solely.

First of all, it is not clear why, even admitting that an articulated variable occurs in the embedded clauses '... it rains', '... that are small', or in the quantified noun phrase 'every question', the argument-slot occupied by that variable should belong to the logical form of the very predicates 'to rain', 'being small' or to the noun 'question' even when these are *not* controlled by quantifiers. Stanley's ideas on these matters do not seem entirely clear: he talks of 'to rain' as co-occurring with either an event variable or with a temporal and a locational node

(2000, p. 416); he then maintains that nouns like 'question', and 'bottle' cohabit a terminal node in the sentence's tree structure with a domain index (Stanley and Szabó, 2000, p. 101; Stanley, 2002b, p. 113). All these phrasings are actually ambiguous between the idea that the covert positions belong to the lexical structure of 'to rain', 'question' or 'bottle' rather than simply to the sentence's syntax. Eventually, in a footnote of his (2005, fn. 15) and in a postscript of his (2007, pp. 248–9), Stanley rejects the idea that domain indices are part of the lexical structure of nouns and opts for the view that they occupy their own separate nodes in the sentence tree. Yet this is once again ambiguous between the view that the noun co-occurs with a separate node occupied by a domain index in all sentences (as a matter of convention), or only in some constructions. If the second view were to hold, then Stanley's Binding Argument would prove something rather weak, namely that the context-sensitivity of 'to rain' or 'every question' *when these occur in certain linguistic constructions* (*like quantified sentences*) is to be traced to the sentences' syntax or logical form. Yet Stanley seems to be after a stronger claim, namely that the context-sensitivity of the predicate 'to rain' or the phrase 'every question' is to be traced to their syntax or logical form in all sentences in which they occur. This entails that he has to commit to the idea that these expressions are conventionally and invariably associated with hidden syntactic positions, whether they occur embedded or unembedded.

If this is the view he is bound to embrace, though, one could protest that the Binding Argument does not quite prove it: this is because the argument only gives us reasons to think that there is a position articulated in logical form when these expressions occur embedded, but not when they occur unembedded, or in any other linguistic construction (see Recanati, 2002a). So, there is a sense in which Stanley's Binding Argument is inconclusive if the desired conclusion is that language context-sensitivity is traceable to syntax or logical form *in the generality of cases*.

The point can be bolstered by observing that binding cases may be dealt with by saying that the structure itself of the sentences is such as to allow the 'creation' of a free slot articulated in logical form, where a variable is subsequently bound by the quantifier; if this were so, nothing could be concluded concerning the syntactic set-up of individual predicates or other sentences which do not involve quantification. Recanati (2002a) and Martí (2006) have proposed precisely this account of Stanley's bound readings. The view is that the syntax of 'to rain' leaves it completely optional whether or not a locational variable should be generated. What happens with quantified sentences like 'Every time John lights a cigarette, it rains' is that the quantifier 'Every time' creates the location-slot in the sentence's logical form, fills it with a variable and binds it (Martí, 2006, p. 161). According to this account then, binding proves the presence of a hidden position but only as a consequence of that particular linguistic construction, and nothing could be inferred concerning whether the predicate 'to rain' is associated with a locational variable in a fixed way in all sentential constructions.

A second difficulty with the Binding Argument is that it is not clear on what grounds the Binding Assumption should be accepted and why the binding exhibited by 'Every time John lights a cigarette, it rains' could not just be a matter of semantics, with no syntactic correlate.

Stanley seems to assume that, if the phenomenon is not syntactically grounded, it will inevitably be a product of strong pragmatic processes which provide so-called *unarticulated constituents* to the utterance's content, that is, constituents that are not the semantic value of any sentential component. Unarticulated constituents pose a problem to the extent that they undermine the compositionality of the content of utterances: Stanley assumes that utterance content is (only) determined by assigning a content (relative to context) to each component of the uttered sentence and by assembling the resulting contents according to compositionality rules (see King and Stanley, 2005; Stanley, 2000). However, if some constituent which is not the denotation of a sentential component can intrude into utterance content, compositionality is questioned, in that utterance content becomes the result of assembling the contents of sentential components *plus* unarticulated constituents. Moreover, if pragmatic processes are unconstrained by the meaning of sentential components and obey independent criteria, it becomes impossible to account in a systematic way for how certain linguistic forms will contribute to the utterance's truth-conditions. What gets lost, together with compositionality, is the systematicity of a theory of meaning which allows the theorist to maintain that the same word or linguistic construction will give the same contribution to utterance truth-conditions regardless of the context in which it is used.

Stanley's postulation of hidden syntactic positions seems to be a way of rescuing these features of a semantic theory. However, postulating hidden syntax is not the only way to preserve the compositionality and systematicity of an utterance's content: as an alternative to it, one could suppose that variable-like elements are straightforwardly introduced in the proposition as a response to semantic/conceptual requirements. For instance, suppose that 'to rain' were associated, at the lexical or conceptual level, with a slot for locations; or that 'small' contained as part of its lexical meaning or its conceptual structure, a slot for comparison classes. These lexically or conceptually articulated slots would call for completion in a context of utterance; so the lexical or conceptual semantics would guide the contextual provision of a propositional element. It is also under the guidance of such semantic/conceptual constraints that a hearer could introduce a bindable element and thus obtain a bound reading *directly in the proposition understood*, where this were interpretively appropriate. This entails that the bound reading to the effect that *for every place x where John goes, it rains in x*, obtains only at the interpretive level, as a result of 'to rain' being associated with a location-slot as a matter of its lexical meaning. Also a reading of 'It's raining' which completes its content as being that it is raining *in Paris* is such that Paris is introduced in the proposition as an effect of filling in a slot that is merely present at the level of the predicate's lexical structure. The added propositional constituent respects the compositionality and systematicity of the utterance's content, in that its introduction is after all controlled by semantic/conceptual aspects of the expressions at issue, and not by any other strongly pragmatic criterion such as relevancy, salience and so on. At the same time, one has to posit no hidden positions in the sentence's syntax, but only an element straightforwardly expressed in the proposition.

This way, the constituents introduced would be unarticulated after all (in that they would not be the semantic values of any articulated element in the sentence's syntax), but they would nonetheless comply with compositionality and systematicity at the level of utterance content – thus sufficiently soothing, I take it, Stanley's concerns. This option really remains unexplored in Stanley's essays, but it is by all means open and, to my mind, definitely worth investigating.

The upshot of these considerations is twofold. On the one hand, Stanley's argument is not conclusive in that, even conceding that complex sentences like 'Every time John lights a cigarette, it rains' contain a hidden articulated position, it is not clear why the same position should be articulated in the logical form of 'to rain' and other predicates when these occur unembedded. On the other hand, binding could as well be a solely semantic phenomenon (that is, one that occurs at the level of the proposition expressed) and still, if we follow a proposal in terms of lexical/conceptual slots, respect compositionality and systematicity at the level of utterance content. Therefore, the syntactic solution is not strictly necessary to preserve these features of a semantic theory, contrary to what Stanley seems to assume.

This completes the presentation and critical discussion of the three main varieties of Contextualism. In the remainder of the chapter, we will turn to a discussion of those views I have grouped under the family of Minimalism. Adherents of Minimalism usually think of themselves as defenders of a 'traditional' approach to the semantics of natural languages – which they trace back to authors such as Davidson, Montague, Kaplan and Lewis – according to which the role of context in the determination of an utterance's truth-conditions is rather limited, being confined to the resolution of familiar indexicals, perhaps demonstrative expressions and a handful of other relational terms. The first two varieties of Minimalism that I am going to present – plain Minimalism and Ultra-Minimalism – tend to view enrichments as pertaining to some further level of content distinct from what the sentence expresses in context. The third variety of Minimalism – also known as Non-Indexical Contextualism – helps itself to an enriched version of what is called 'circumstances of evaluation'.

3.4 Minimalism

The main tenet of Semantic Minimalism is that all sentences express a complete, invariant, evaluable proposition, which is the proposition they 'semantically' express (cf. Cappelen and Lepore, 2005; Borg, 2004, 2012a). For Cappelen and Lepore, the proposition semantically expressed by 'It's raining' is *that it's raining*, full stop; or the proposition semantically expressed by 'The leaves are green' is *that the leaves are green*, full stop. For Borg, it is the proposition *that it's raining somewhere* or *that the leaves are green in some way*.

The second tenet of Minimalism is that context-sensitivity is only triggered semantically: this has the consequence that the only kind of context-sensitivity admitted is indexicality (broadly understood). Cappelen and Lepore state that context-sensitivity thus conceived is confined to a small set of known indexicals and demonstratives, like 'I', 'you', 'he', 'she', 'it', 'that' and 'this', 'here', 'there', 'now', 'today', 'yesterday', 'tomorrow', 'ago', but also 'actual' and 'present' – all words that in some way introduce a function from some parameter of the context (the speaker, the addressee, salient objects, the moment of the speaking, and so on) to content. Borg is more liberal as to the extent of context-sensitivity in language and, in the last chapter of her book (2012a), she seems open to the idea that some lexical aspects determine constraints on syntax, where this may require the saturation of some covert free positions. This is not incompatible with the second tenet of

Minimalism that all context-sensitivity must be semantically governed – it just diverges from the view held by Cappelen and Lepore that this context-sensitivity must be kept to a minimum and that there be no 'unexpected' indexicals in language.

If all sentences express a truth-evaluable proposition and context-sensitivity is only triggered semantically, why is it that utterances of the same sentences, in which no clearly context-sensitive expression occurs, are evaluated differently across different contexts? Cappelen and Lepore explain these 'context-shifting' phenomena with the idea that our intuitions concern the propositions expressed by the *speech acts* performed in each of these situations, and not the propositions semantically expressed by the sentence-tokens. Minimalism on semantic content is therefore accompanied by *Speech Act Pluralism*, the view that every utterance of a sentence expresses a variety of propositions. These propositions need not be determined by features of the speaker's context, and neither by the speaker's intentions. The view is therefore extremely liberal as to what counts as 'the proposition expressed' by a certain speech act: it may vary depending on whether one takes into account the beliefs of the speaker or of the interpreter, facts about the world, facts about the speaker's or interpreter's background assumptions, logical relations and so on (see Cappelen and Lepore, 1997, p. 290; 2005, p. 193; Cappelen, 2008).

Minimalism has been regarded by more than one theorist as doomed from the start, mainly on the account that the theory's notion of proposition semantically expressed, or 'minimal proposition' (especially that propounded by Cappelen and Lepore) is hardly tenable. As MacFarlane (2007, p. 246) observes, minimal propositions seem to provide no truth-condition in that, if we think of propositions as selecting certain possible worlds and excluding others, they do not seem able to 'rule out' any precise set of possible worlds. With regard to the minimal proposition *that Chiara is tall*, *tout court*, it may be asked at what possible worlds exactly is this proposition true – those where she is tall for a seven-year-old, for a basketball player, for a dwarf person? The alleged minimal proposition does not specify that.

The main reply to MacFarlane's objection, which can be found in Cappelen and Lepore (2005, pp. 157–75) and Borg (2012b, p. 524), goes as follows: the critic's point is that minimal propositions do not describe a state of affairs such that it could make them true in a possible world. However, Minimalists note, this is a problem which obtains with all propositions, even those we would not deem as minimal. Even the (non-minimal) proposition *that Chiara is tall for a seven-year-old* may fail to determine a truth-condition relative to a possible world. After all, one may wonder: is Chiara tall for a seven-year-old if we measure her height in the evening (when she is 1 centimetre less tall than in the morning); if she is an undernourished child and we compare her with a bunch of well-fed children; if she is a well-nourished child and we compare her with undernourished children, and so on? No proposition – no matter how many details it includes – fully specifies what has to be the case in the world for it to be true. So it is claimed that the objection has no bite against Minimalism, for it points to a difficulty that afflicts all contents in general. The reply seems to play with the idea that no (or almost no) sentence can express a proposition which is *maximally* specific, so as to specify to the closest detail what should be the case for an utterance of that sentence to be true. This is certainly true, but unfortunately from this it does not follow that minimal propositions are not problematic. Granted that no sentence expresses a maximally specific proposition, it might still be the case that some propositions have contents that help answer MacFarlane's challenge ('In which worlds is this true or false?') better than others. Importantly, minimal propositions may not be among these.

However, Borg (2009, pp. 48–9; 2012a, pp. 108–9) insists that even minimal propositions are such that they determine a set of possible worlds where they are true. For instance, the proposition *that Chiara is tall* is true in all those worlds where Chiara is tall with respect to some comparison class.[5] To the extent that this content is capable of sorting worlds into those where it is true and those where it is false, it does count as a proposition. It is another issue, she continues, whether or not this sorting of worlds enables the subject to determine whether the proposition is true or false in some specific possible world: this is an epistemic difficulty, as a result of which it may take some extra effort for subjects to establish whether a minimal proposition is true in a possible world. However, it is not the task of semantics to facilitate language users in such a way. So, as long as a content succeeds in partitioning worlds in the way just described, it may legitimately count as a proposition. Borg's line, then, is to maintain that arguments that play on the truth-conditional incompleteness of minimal propositions suffer from an epistemic bias – that is they consider as a proper truth-condition something that allows a subject to ascertain, for a given possible world, whether a proposition is true or false at that world. Yet, as she complains, this is to conflate conditions of truth with *conditions of verification* and to demand too much from a semantic system (2004, p. 230; 2009, p. 48).

First of all, it seems to me that this conception of a proposition leads to an extremely implausible implication: since the proposition is, by Borg's admission, true in all those worlds where Chiara is tall relative to some comparison class, then it is true in all those worlds where Chiara is tall in any of the following ways: as a seven-year-old, as a basketball player, as a ballerina, as a dwarf, and so on. If this is true, then the proposition expressed by the sentence 'Chiara is tall' is not something that a speaker may reasonably or at least typically mean. Typically, when we ascribe the property of being tall to someone, we do it in order to indicate that he or she is tall *in some unique* way, and not to indicate that he or she is tall in a variety of ways depending on the possible worlds we consider. So, these minimal propositions would be hardly what a speaker would typically express.

Secondly, even if I agree with Borg that it would be too much to ask of a semantic theory that it provide us with conditions of verification, I do not think this is what critics of minimal propositions have in mind. As I have tried to show in section 1.1.1, the dissatisfaction with sentences like 'It's raining', 'The leaves are green', 'Chiara is tall' and so on, is that these express *generic* contents, that is contents that do not describe a particular state of affairs understood as a configuration of particular objects and properties: for instance, Chiara's being tall for a seven-year-old, for a basketball player, for a dwarf person. Specification of a particular state of affairs might help one select the world, or set of worlds, where the utterance should be evaluated and thus might help to respond to MacFarlane's 'at-which-worlds' challenge.

Yet, I have highlighted that having a non-generic truth-condition is not yet to have a *maximally* specific truth-condition. So it might be the case that even propositions that determine particular truth-conditions (like *that Chiara is tall for a seven-year-old*) might fail to enable the subject to settle in which possible worlds these truth-conditions hold, because the truth-conditions they specify are far from being maximal. So the 'at-which-worlds' challenge is to be taken with a pinch of salt, as a request to specify a particular rather than generic truth-condition, but certainly not a maximally specific truth-condition.

Ultimately, as already observed, it seems that whether a truth-condition counts as exhaustive enough may be a matter of threshold: above a certain threshold, the sentence counts as semantically well determined and the absence of certain details is not even noticed; below a certain threshold, the conversants may feel like the sentence encodes too little information to be evaluable. It seems that particular truth-conditions, depicting particular states of affairs (that is, configurations of particular objects and properties) are specific enough to meet the 'at-which-worlds' challenge, while of course being by no means maximally specific. By contrast, if a sentence expresses a generic content (like *that Chiara is tall tout court*), it is definitely exposed to such a challenge. Yet, the challenge is not, as Borg alleges, a challenge on conditions of verification – it is a genuine challenge concerning the granularity of the content expressed by minimal propositions.

Be that as it may, suppose we granted that minimal propositions are propositions in some loose, but still legitimate sense – in virtue of their capability to sort worlds in some way. It seems that, even so, the proposition *that Chiara is tall* is rather rarely what speakers mean with an utterance of 'Chiara is tall', for usually they mean to convey a richer content. The question then arises of what minimal propositions are for: what is their function at the semantic level? Do they have a role to play in our cognitive life and in our linguistic practices? Proponents of Minimalism strive to show that minimal propositions do play a role because, for instance, they are the content shared by various utterances of the same sentence and they are what inter-contextual speech reports hinge on (Cappelen and Lepore, 2005, 2006). Moreover, they illuminate our linguistic competence and explain language productivity and systematicity (Borg, 2012a).

Yet, it seems that these roles could also be played by things that are not propositions. Indeed, nothing dictates that the 'shared contents' of our speech acts should be truth-evaluable, nor that the sentences by means of which we manifest our linguistic competence should express full-blown propositions. In other words, there seems to be no requirement that the contents that play the roles Cappelen and Lepore and Borg assign to them also be the minimal propositions they propound (see Bach, 2006). So, the Minimalist would find herself in a rather embarrassing situation: she would be advocating the existence of entities like minimal propositions, ascribing to them various roles that could be fulfilled even by entities that are not propositional. This would imply that minimal propositions would be utterly superfluous from a theoretical point of view, because their function could be performed even by entities that are not propositional. Theoretical parsimony would dictate we should discount these entities and prefer an account in which the same roles could be accounted for with no need to posit any extra propositional object.

To sum up, the core notion of Minimalism, namely that of minimal proposition, seems to fail to qualify as properly propositional in that (if we try fully to spell out MacFarlane's objection) it fails to determine a particular truth-condition, something which would help answer the 'at-which-worlds' challenge. What is more, even if one granted to minimal propositions the status of propositions, that would not take Minimalism very far: given that the roles assigned to minimal propositions would be equally well played by non-propositional contents, minimal propositions would turn out as superfluous and, on the basis of parsimony considerations, dispensable.

3.5 Ultra-Minimalism

Unlike plain Minimalism, Ultra-Minimalism marries the view that the meaning of a sentence in context (even provided disambiguation and indexicality resolution) is *not* generally a proposition, but rather what Bach (1994a) calls a 'propositional radical'.[6] This is to be understood along Russellian lines, as a structured *n*-tuple of properties and objects. For instance, the proposition expressed by 'Jill is ready' is to be understood as consisting of the pair <*b*, being ready> consisting of the individual *b* to which the name 'Jill' refers and the property of being ready. Such a structured entity does not amount to a proposition to the extent that, in the case at hand, it fails to specify for what Jill is ready – that is to say, it leaves a gap or slot in the sentence's semantic content (even relative to a context).

A further claim endorsed by the proponent of Ultra-Minimalism is again a radicalisation of the Minimalist contention that context-sensitivity is only triggered semantically. According to Bach (2005, pp. 39–40), not only is context-sensitivity semantically controlled, but has to be kept to a minimum: in particular, only indexicality in a narrow sense is allowed to have effects on a sentence's meaning. This means that the only effects of context on sentence meaning are those mandated by the meaning of a small set of indexicals, notably *pure* indexicals such as 'I', 'today', 'tomorrow', whose referent is fixed in an 'automatic' way (provided they are not used in any non-literal way). Demonstratives are excluded from this highly restricted circle in that their referent is fixed not (or only to a minor degree) with the help of their meaning (or character), but with the help of clues as to the intentions of the speaker.

Finally, Ultra-Minimalism has it that processes of pragmatic enrichment do not operate on sentence content thus conceived, but on a pragmatically characterised level of content. This means that intuitions as to contextual shifts in truth-value do not concern semantic content proper, but rather a further, pragmatic level, which Bach (1994a) calls 'impliciture'.

In Bach's view, an *impliciture* is a middle ground between what is explicitly said (in context) by a sentence and a Gricean implicature. What is explicitly said corresponds to the sentence's meaning-in-context and might coincide with a propositional radical; it is identified according to a syntactic criterion which Bach draws from Grice (1969/1989, p. 87), whereby the content expressed by a sentence (in context) must track the constituents of the sentence in the order in which they are presented and with the syntactic features they display. That is, the content explicitly expressed (in context) by 'Jill is ready' is nothing but the result of combining the meanings of 'Jill', 'is' and 'ready' in accordance with the way they are arranged in the sentence and the syntactic categories to which they belong ('Jill' is a noun forming a noun phrase, while 'is ready' forms a verb phrase). An impliciture is a way of communicating something implicitly that is closely related with what one is explicitly saying, while an implicature strongly departs from what one explicitly says. Thus, one may utter 'Jill is ready' in order to suggest or implicate to someone else that it is late and that he or she should move on; however, besides the implicature, one would plausibly communicate that Jill is ready for something specific as well – going to the movies, for instance – thus conveying a content that is closer to the sentence's conventional meaning. Importantly, according to Bach, in both cases what allows us to arrive at either the impli*ca*ture or the impli*ci*ture are Gricean processes relying on conversational maxims and speaker's intentions.

Bach uses the term 'impliciture' in apparently the same way in which Radical Contextualists like Carston and Sperber and Wilson use the term 'explicature' and Recanati uses 'what is said': in all these cases, it is the level of content which is obtained whenever one 'enriches', 'develops', 'completes' or 'expands' a content which is somehow semantically under-determined. However, as Bach explains, the term 'explicature' is misleading in that it suggests that there is something explicitly communicated, while exactly the opposite is true: the supplementary aspects are only *implicitly* communicated (Bach, 1994b, 1998, 2010).

Ultra-Minimalism and Radical Contextualism nevertheless agree on at least these two factors: (a) the idea that semantic content (even provided ambiguity and indexical resolution) is under-determined, in that it fails to result in a complete proposition, and (b) the idea of there being a 'third level' in between strict semantic content (in context) and Gricean implicature. What they disagree on is where to locate this intermediate level of content. While Radical Contextualists locate 'explicature' or 'what is said' on the side of semantics, thus subscribing to a view in which semantic content is irremediably contaminated by pragmatic processes, Ultra-Minimalists locate 'impliciture' on the side of pragmatics, in that they see implicitures as responding to Gricean maxims just like implicatures. This leaves semantic content uncontaminated by the effects of conversational mechanisms.

The difference between the two approaches is admittedly subtle and it may raise the suspicion that the controversy is merely verbal (see Chalmers, 2011): it all comes down, one might protest, to what one wants to call 'semantic' as opposed to 'pragmatic'. Radical Contextualists call 'semantic' everything that has to do with conventional meaning *plus* some pragmatic effects, while Ultra-Minimalists work with a more austere notion of semantics and locate under the heading of 'pragmatics' every slight augmentation of sentence content which goes beyond 'automatic' reference assignment to indexicals. The latter authors belong in the tradition of Formal Semantics initiated by Montague and Davidson, so they are inclined to view sentence meaning in a context as either totally invariant or depending on a limited amount of contextual effects, all of them governed by semantic rules with (almost) no room for speaker's intentions; at the same time, they follow Grice's idea that everything that goes beyond semantically governed context-sensitivity lies in the domain of pragmatics – that is, of what is communicated 'on top' of what is said. The former authors instead draw largely from the work of the later Wittgenstein and Austin, in particular from the idea that use greatly affects linguistic meaning; as a result they see no sharp distinction between sentence meaning and speaker meaning and they allow non-semantically (pragmatically) driven contextual processes to affect sentence content. By way of dispelling the complaint that these theorists are merely talking past each other, a charitable way of regarding the debate is to see it as a meta-theoretical clash between two *conceptions* of semantics, its role, its methodology and its relationship with pragmatics.

Ultra-Minimalism as presented and defended by Bach is, therefore, a view closer to the tradition than that propounded by Recanati, Sperber and Wilson and Carston. Yet, in virtue of its positing a third level of content in between sentence content-in-context and Gricean implicature – namely Bach's impliciture – it suffers from difficulties analogous to those of Radical Contextualism. Ultra-Minimalism depicts impliciture as the result of Gricean pragmatic inference on semantic content, however it does not offer any conclusive arguments in order to rule out that the involved processes are really either semantically controlled (on the model of indexicality) or give rise to proper Gricean implicatures. It seems that anyone who is a friend of a more cut-and-dried separation between semantic content and speaker's content could launch a 'divide and conquer' campaign against the Ultra-Minimalist, analysing each single case as either the upshot of semantics or of Gricean pragmatic mechanisms leading to proper conversational implicature.

Bach (1994a, b) distinguishes, at the level of impliciture, between cases of expansion and completion: expansion occurs whenever a sentence does express a proposition, however this is trivially either true or false, and thus needs to be qualified. Cases in point are: 'You are not going to die', uttered by a mother to her child who is crying about a minor cut in his finger, and 'I haven't eaten', uttered by someone who clearly has recently eaten. By contrast, completion concerns cases of semantic under-determination or incompleteness, where a sentence's content fails to amount to a proposition owing to a failure to specify an argumental or complemental element. Cases is point are: 'Jill is ready [*for what?*]', 'Jamal is tall [*for what?*]', 'Steel isn't strong enough [*for what?*]'.

A divide and conquer strategy could then try to track cases of expansion and completion down to different processes than those of impliciture creation. With 'You are not going to die', one might suppose that the verb 'to die' occurs with an implicit temporal variable which gets filled in with a contextually provided time, so as to return the content to the effect that the child is not going to die *at time t*. This could raise the particularised implicature that the cut is not serious. With 'Jill is ready', one might suppose that the search for a contextually provided purpose for which Jill can rightly said to be ready is triggered by aspects of the semantics of the word 'ready' – for instance, that it contains a slot in its argument structure, concerning purposes or activities.

In sum, Ultra-Minimalism counters Minimalism with a refusal of the idea that semantic content is propositional; at the same time, it opposes Radical Contextualism in its picturing free enrichment as operating on pragmatically conveyed content rather than on semantic content. As has been noted, the difference between Ultra-Minimalism and Radical Contextualism is subtle and almost terminological, such that it is most charitably seen as a divergence between two distinct conceptions of semantics. Finally, Ultra-Minimalism shares with Radical Contextualism its being exposed to a divide-and-conquer move on the part of the proponent of a sharper division between semantics and pragmatics.

3.6 Non-Indexical Contextualism

Non-Indexical Contextualism is the view that the *truth-value* of utterances depends on one or more contextual features. It thus diverges from

Indexical (or even Radical) Contextualism in that it sees content as invariant and thus context-insensitive, while it is truth-value that varies depending on contextual aspects. The formal machinery behind Non-Indexical Contextualism is the picture of semantics adopted by theorists since the work of Kaplan (1989), Lewis (1980) and Stalnaker (1970). These authors outline a *two-tiered* semantic machinery which distinguishes between a context of utterance and a circumstance of evaluation. The role of a *context of utterance* is that of assigning a denotation to those expressions which do not have a fixed content across utterances – indexicals and demonstratives, whose referent varies as a specific *parameter* of the context varies (the speaker, the time of utterance, the contextually salient objects). A *circumstance of evaluation* corresponds to a further set of parameters, with respect to which evaluation is effected. Usually, the circumstances of evaluation consist of a possible-worlds parameter, however, in general, whether a parameter is part of the circumstances of evaluation depends on whether one is ready to admit an intensional operator which can affect it – for instance, temporal operators ('in the past', 'now').

The 'basic move' of Non-Indexical Contextualism consists in positing *extra parameters* in the circumstances of evaluation of the sentence at interest, in addition to the possible-world parameter w, with respect to which truth-value is made to vary.

An example of *ante litteram* Non-Indexical Contextualist approach is *Temporalism* (see Prior, 1968; Kaplan, 1989): the truth-value of a sentence like 'Carl is showering' is relative not only to a possible world w, but also to a time t. This implies that the proposition *that Carl is showering* is invariant in content across times, though it can be true or false depending on the value of the time parameter in the circumstances of evaluation. For example, it may be true at time t_1 iff Carl is showering at $<w, t_1>$ and false at t_2 iff Carl is not showering at $<w, t_2>$.

The model exemplified by Temporalism has been replicated in giving the semantics of other expressions in various areas of discourse. Thus, for example, Lasersohn (2005) argues that the truth of utterances of sentences containing predicates of personal taste like 'tasty' and 'delicious' is to be relativised to a world–time–individual triple $<w, t, i>$ rather than to a world–time couple $<w, t>$.

An extra-parameter approach has been adopted to deal with epistemic modals, too. Egan et al. (2005) argue for the postulation of truth relative to *centred worlds*, cashed out as triples $<w, t, i>$ of a world, a time and an individual, in order to account for the semantics of epistemic 'might' and 'must' (see also Egan, 2007, 2011; von Fintel and Gillies, 2008).

106 *Semantic Under-Determinacy and Communication*

Gradable adjectives like 'rich', 'tall', 'fat' and 'fast' have received a treatment in terms of Non-Indexical Contextualism by Richard (2004, 2008), who claims that the truth-value of an utterance of a sentence like 'Naomi is rich' is relative not only to a comparison class, but also to a parameter on standards which sets the cut-off point for the application or non-application of the predicate adopted by the speaker.

Kompa (2002) gestures at a Non-Indexical Contextualist account of the semantics of epistemic verbs like 'know', while Brogaard (2008) develops this conception formally. Brogaard has it that the truth-value of knowledge attributions like 'A knows that P' depends on the values of a judge parameter *j* in the circumstances of evaluation, where the context of utterance fixes the value of *j*.[7]

The extra-parameters move has been adopted in order to cope with semantically under-determined expressions as well, such as 'green' or 'ready'. At the root of the strategy lies a general idea about the relation between semantically under-determined expressions and context (defended, for example, by Predelli 2005a, b), a very straightforward development of which is certainly the postulation of extra parameters. On the one hand, traditional semantic systems such as those designed by Kaplan and Stalnaker are concerned with assigning intensions (functions from 'points of evaluation' to truth-values) to pairs <*s, c*> consisting of a clause, or interpreted logical form *s* and an index of the context *c* corresponding to a list of parameters like agent, time and location. Provided absence of indexicality, different utterances of the same sentence certainly have the same intension. Nevertheless, variability of truth-value despite sameness of intension seems possible. According to Predelli, the conversants' interests and standards determine different 'applications' of the intension, that is to say, they determine different sets of circumstances in which the utterance might be true/false (see 2005a, p. 366). This implies that, taking Travis' green leaves as an example, Pia's utterance of 'The leaves are green' is true in the photographer scenario because the photography-related interests that are operative in the conversation determine circumstances which are such as to make the sentence 'The leaves are green' true. Pia's utterance is however false in the botanist scenario because, given the botanist's interests and standards, the circumstances determined by such interests are such as to make the sentence 'The leaves are green' false. Predelli's idea is that of maintaining the traditionally accepted Kaplan-style semantics while allowing that the same proposition be evaluated in different circumstances, the configuration and composition of which are shaped by the conversants' interests and standards. As one may realise, the idea that the conversationalists' interests, goals and presuppositions determine different circumstances is altogether neutral with respect to the structure one may want give to the index of the circumstances of evaluation at the formal level. Predelli remains uncommittal in this sense: he is happy to still regard these circumstances as 'possible worlds', if by 'possible world' one merely means a 'point of evaluation'. Instead of using possible worlds, one may as well use world–time pairs, or even *situations* in the sense of Barwise and Perry (1983): for example, authors such as Corazza and Dokic (2007, 2010), Barba (2007) and, to a certain extent, Gauker (2012) take this latter option.

Yet, the path is short from Predelli's solution to an account in terms of extra parameters in the circumstances of evaluation. MacFarlane (2007, 2009) suggests such a strategy by introducing a 'counts-as' parameter in the circumstances of evaluation, beyond that of possible worlds, whose role is that of fixing how things have to be like in order for an object to fall in the extension of predicates such as 'green', 'tall', 'ready' and so on, thus affecting the overall assessment of the sentence (MacFarlane, 2007, p. 246).

Non-Indexical Contextualism seems compatible with a twofold position about the semantic content of sentences like 'It's raining'. On the one hand, they are semantically defective in the sense that their truth-value depends on some aspects that have to be settled in the circumstances of evaluation of the context. On the other hand, they are not semantically defective in that their content need not be supplemented by context in any way. Non-Indexical Contextualism thus may seem in agreement with Minimalism because of this second contention. However, on closer inspection, this is not really the case: the propositions countenanced by Non-Indexical Contextualism may not exhibit any unexpected form of context-sensitivity at the level of content, but, unlike minimal propositions, they are nevertheless unevaluable unless a value is provided for a relevant parameter. So, equating Non-Indexical Contextualism with Minimalism on the basis of an alleged agreement on the status of propositions (as context-*in*sensitive) would be quite inaccurate. What is more, Minimalism and Non-Indexical Contextualism differ fundamentally in how they conceive of the *truth* of propositions: Minimalists stick to an *absolutist* conception of truth, whereby a proposition is true or false *tout court* in a possible world w; by contrast, Non-Indexical Contextualists advocate a *relative* notion of truth for propositions, whereby a proposition is true or false in a world w depending on some parameter x (time, place, individual, standards of precision, epistemic standards and so on).

Doubts have been raised over whether the 'basic move' of adding extra parameters in the circumstances of evaluation is justified in all cases. As we know from the work of Lewis (1980, p. 27) and Kaplan (1989, p. 502), the justification for adding a coordinate in the circumstances of evaluation, such as a world coordinate, is provided by the presence of what is called *intensional operators*, like 'possibly' and 'necessarily', that are capable of 'shifting' its values. It seems that the presence of operators is an important motivation for positing a certain parameter, to such an extent that, were a theory to fail to display such operators, that would be a reason to look at it with suspicion. This has led Stanley (2005b) to criticise Non-Indexical Contextualism on 'know' on the account that, if we wish to countenance an epistemic standards parameter in the circumstances of evaluation, there must be an operator in our language that is purported to shifting it; but in the case of knowledge predicates, there seems to be no such operator,[8] so this would seem to deprive the Non-Indexical Contextualist's 'extra parameters' move of its legitimacy. The same argument could clearly be replicated for other forms of Non-Indexical Contextualism – on 'might', 'tasty', 'good' and so on. I will not discuss this argument here, mainly because I think that, even supposing it was legitimate on the part of the Non-Indexical Contextualist to take the 'extra parameters' step, greater reservations would loom large concerning whether the account really makes a difference with respect to other forms of Contextualism already present in the arena. I will devote the remainder of this section to such reservations.

In the Non-Indexical Contextualist's view, sentences do not by themselves express context-sensitive contents, but propositions are unevaluable anyway outside of a context. Thus, in a sentence like 'Julia knows that penguins eat fish' the word 'know' does not behave like an indexical, and so content is strictly speaking context-*in*sensitive. Yet the sentence is not evaluable unless a value is provided for a specific parameter (the epistemic standards *e* for 'know'), given that the content is 'neutral' with respect to a certain feature of the circumstances of evaluation. The combination of the 'neutral' content, call it σ, with the relevant value of the parameter in the circumstances of evaluation, call it *e*, gives rise to a content $<\sigma, e>$ which is complete and non-neutral, usually called an 'Austinian proposition'.[9] So one might think that, by filling in the relevant parameters, one is actually completing *some* level of content, namely the Austinian proposition: by specifying the parameter in the circumstances of evaluation, one specifies a component of an Austinian proposition. Seen from this angle, there appears to be little difference between Indexical and Non-Indexical Contextualism: in both cases the content and evaluation of an utterance depend on retrieving the value of a contextual parameter; it is just that in the former account, the parameter serves for fixing the denotation of a predicate (knowledge-at-standard-*e*); while, in the latter account, the parameter serves for fixing a feature of the circumstances of evaluation and a component of the Austinian proposition. Under this light, it is tempting to see Non-Indexical Contextualism as a mere notational variant of Indexical Contextualism (see Stojanovic, 2007).

In addition, if we consider the 'counts-as' parameter envisaged by MacFarlane and the conversationally determined 'points of evaluation' set forth by Predelli for resolving cases of semantic under-determinacy, we may wonder how exactly one should go about settling these features of the circumstances of evaluation. There is no systematic way of reconstructing the process – indeed, it depends on what is salient in the context of utterance, the speaker's intentions, the conversational background and so on: in other words, on factors that escape the control of semantics and are presumably purely pragmatic. If we reconstruct these processes as specifying components of the Austinian proposition, then since providing the value of these parameters is a process regulated by purely pragmatic demands, it appears as a re-edition of free enrichment. So, this version of Non-Indexical Contextualism would seem to offer a mere notational variant of Radical Contextualism, whereby free pragmatic processes provide a value for the 'counts-as' parameter or narrow down the relevant 'point of evaluation' while also filling gaps in the Austinian proposition, rather than enriching the sentence's content. Yet it is not clear whether this is a valuable or even interesting difference.

It may be objected that Non-Indexical Contextualism is superior to both Indexical and Radical Contextualism, in that it looks simpler, more systematic and elegant once compared with accounts which increase complexity by positing hidden indexicality (Indexical Contextualism) or undermine systematicity by introducing processes not controlled by the semantics (Radical Contextualism). In contrast with these accounts, Non-Indexical Contextualism manages to preserve some fundamental features of formal semantic systems, such as systematicity and a certain parsimony in adding any extra context-sensitivity. Yet, as I will contend, allegiance to the tradition comes with some costs, which do not exactly seem to outweigh the benefits.

The first cost has to do with how the Non-Indexical Contextualist explains intuitions of semantic under-determinacy. Typically, these intuitions tell us that there is an incompleteness or lack of determinacy in the content of a sentence like 'Jill is ready'. The 'felt' defectiveness thus concerns *content* in the first place. But this is not what the Non-Indexical Contextualist accepts, for in her view the content expressed by a sentence like 'Jill is ready' is complete (it has no gaps other than those created by regular indexicality). So, how should one understand intuitions of incompleteness? Perhaps the Non-Indexical Contextualist should say that ordinary language users mistake the 'neutrality' of contents for incompleteness; they realise that these contents could not be evaluated unless a parameter is specified, but they wrongly believe that this parameter is part of the sentence's content, and not of the circumstances of evaluation. This is because they adhere to a 'folk' semantics which is not sophisticated enough to distinguish between incompleteness of content and mere neutrality with respect to a feature of the circumstances of evaluation. One first cost for the Non-Indexical Contextualist is thus a divorce between ordinary speakers' intuitions and semantic theory. This cost is clearly not paid by either Indexical or Radical Contextualism, where semantic under-determinacy is an under-determinacy of content, something which is in sync with intuitions as to semantic incompleteness of sentential content.

A second cost of Non-Indexical Contextualism is that it has to relinquish an intuitively plausible explanation of how utterance comprehension works cognitively. The process whereby a hearer interprets an utterance of a semantically under-determined sentence like 'Jill is ready' might be thus reconstructed by the Non-Indexical Contextualist: first, the hearer apprehends the content *that Jill is ready*; subsequently, one searches for the right 'background' (the circumstance or situation) against which the content could be evaluated as true or false. By doing this, though, one would be throwing out a much more intuitive, compelling conception of comprehension according to which the hearer of a certain incomplete content interprets it by 'fleshing it out'. This conception regards utterance comprehension as a matter of (re)construction and supplementation of *content*. Subscribing to Non-Indexical Contextualism again implies departing from this model of utterance comprehension, while no such departure is required for either Indexical or Radical Contextualism, which both regard utterance comprehension as a process of content completion, through saturation or enrichment.

Finally, a third cost of Non-Indexical Contextualism lies in its pledging loyalty to a semantic orthodoxy while marrying a semantic unorthodoxy on another level. Even though the Non-Indexical Contextualist might be happy with ditching the context-sensitivity of content, what she accomplishes is really a trade-off whereby she gives away some unwanted context-sensitivity, but only to embrace truth-relativity. So, she restores orthodoxy on the side of content but has to go unorthodox on the side of truth. Ultimately, it is not clear how this allows the theorist to remain in line with the precepts of Formal Semantics.

Overall, it seems that choosing Non-Indexical Contextualism could be motivated by the desire to stick with a traditional account of semantics. Yet, as I have argued, the theoretical virtues afforded by this choice do not seem to outweigh the costs it imposes, so I doubt that Non-Indexical Contextualism represents a viable alternative to the other forms of Contextualism covered so far. For the purposes of this book, then, Non-Indexical Contextualism will not count as an interesting option over and above those already surveyed in this chapter.

Conclusion

In this chapter, we have gone through the main current theories concerning context-sensitivity in language. From the critical discussion of each of these positions, some points have emerged, which I shall summarise by way of conclusion:

- Concerning both Radical Contextualism and Ultra-Minimalism, I have noted that positing a third layer of content in between sentence content and implicature – whether it is called 'impliciture' or 'explicature' or 'what is said' – exposes one to the threat of a *divide-and-conquer strategy* aimed at tracing each aspect to either a purely semantic or purely pragmatic process. This strategy may be launched by someone who wishes to maintain a traditional, sharp separation between semantics and pragmatics.
- While presenting Radical Contextualism, I have questioned its methodology of using intuitions of untutored, competent speakers in semantic theorising. This, I have urged, is not a successful strategy: intuitions of untutored speakers are not reliable enough to establish whether an aspect of content is part of what is said or of what is implicated. On the one hand, even implicatures could be intuitively grasped (as even Grice conceded): this may distort the results of the theory, which would classify as 'what is said' things that are really implicatures. On the other hand, semantically driven processes could shape the content of our intuitions: so our intuitions would not especially reveal the effects of free pragmatic processes.
- While presenting Indexical Contextualism as the thesis that context-sensitivity could be traced to syntax or logical form, I have urged that

a purely semantic solution is available. This has been argued with respect to binding phenomena. Stanley takes binding cases to show that context-sensitivity has syntactic roots, something which would allow the theorist to preserve compositionality and systematicity in a semantic theory. Yet I have suggested that we can see binding as a purely semantic phenomenon (occurring at the propositional level) guided by lexical or conceptual constraints. This non-syntactic solution would still ensure compositionality and systematicity and it would at the same time be more economical in terms of the amount of postulated syntax. It is hence preferable to Stanley's proposal.
- While discussing Minimalism, I have argued that minimal propositions do not qualify as propositions because they fail to specify particular states of affairs, even though they encode enough semantic information to partition possible worlds in some (rather coarse-grained) way. Yet, even if they did qualify, they would seem rather superfluous because their alleged theoretical role – acting as the shared contents of speech acts, shedding light on semantic competence – could be played even by non-propositional entities.
- Finally, I have explained why I think that Non-Indexical Contextualism is not an interesting option at least for the purposes of this book: first of all, it appears to be a mere notational variant of Indexical and Radical Contextualism; secondly, even though it may prove superior in its remaining faithful to the semantic tradition, I have argued that fidelity comes with a cost. Non-Indexical Contextualism divorces intuitions of semantic under-determinacy from what semantic under-determinacy really is (according to the theory); it is bound to relinquish a plausible and cognitively compelling view of utterance comprehension; it disposes of unwanted context-sensitivity thus restoring orthodoxy, but has to go unorthodox on the side of truth.

4
Semantic Under-Determinacy and Conceptual Constraints

In this chapter, I will articulate and defend an account concerning the context-sensitivity of semantically under-determined sentences. The central thesis I will defend is that the context-sensitivity of semantically under-determined sentences such as 'It's raining', 'Jill is ready', 'The leaves are green', 'Steel isn't strong enough', 'Bill cut the grass' is to be accounted for in terms of *conceptual constraints*, that is constraints that govern concept use – and derivatively, language use.

Before presenting the account in greater detail, some argument needs to be offered to justify the position. Firstly, I will need to defend the claim that a characterisation of the context-sensitivity of semantically under-determined sentences should be *primarily semantic* rather than pragmatic, thus opposing Radical Contextualism (section 4.1). Secondly, I will stress that the conceptual constraints proposal strives to defend the idea that the context-sensitivity of semantically under-determined sentences has no *syntactic articulation*, thus going against Indexical Contextualism as it has been understood by its main proponents (section 4.2). Formulation and defence of the conceptual constraints view will be the subject of section 4.3, while in section 4.4 I will take up some issues concerning the relationship between the conceptual and lexical semantics I am presently defending and the question of meaning Molecularism as opposed to Atomism and Holism.

4.1 A preference for a semantic (rather than pragmatic) account

In this section, I will defend the insight that an account of the context-sensitivity of semantically under-determined sentences should be primarily in semantic terms (if such an account is available), rather than in pragmatic terms.

That the context-sensitivity should be accounted for in semantic terms means that the contribution made by the context is guided or controlled by some standing, context-invariant semantic features of the expressions occurring in the sentence. This conception is modelled along the lines of indexicals and demonstratives, where a standing, context-invariant semantic trait of these expressions provides an instruction for reference assignment in context. For instance, it is the standing, context-invariant meaning of 'I', which could be spelled out as 'the speaker in context', that provides an instruction as to how context should contribute with reference.[1] Also relational predicates offer a good model: consider a sentence like 'Sam is an enemy'. The term 'enemy' seems to apply only to those individuals that are hostile *to someone* (certainly not to individuals that are hostile to *no one*). So it is part of the meaning itself of 'enemy' that whoever is indicated as such, is to be considered so relative to someone else. This relational aspect built into the term's semantics will plausibly instruct the interpreter to search for some contextual information, so as to make the sentence fully evaluable.

After having laid down what I mean by 'a semantic account' of the context-sensitivity of a certain expression, what I wish to argue in this section is that, *other things being equal, we should privilege an account of the context-sensitivity of semantically under-determined sentences in semantic rather than pragmatic terms, when this is available*. Why so?

One major motivation is that the incompleteness of semantically under-determined sentences often concerns conceptual aspects which are clearly identifiable independently of pragmatic considerations. This strongly suggests that the semantic defectiveness of these sentences could be resolved by appealing to semantic resources *plus* some contextual information, rather than by appealing to pragmatic principles and maxims. For instance, the incompleteness exhibited by 'Jill is ready' typically depends on a failure to specify *for what* Jill is ready, a failure which seems to be due to disregarding some aspects linked to the way we think about being ready – being ready for *this*, for *that* and so on. We only need to be somehow cognisant that the predicate or concept BEING READY mandates retrieval of such an element in context, *plus* some contextual information, in order to provide the desired completion; what we do *not* need to do is go through pragmatic reasoning in order to figure out the implicit purpose or activity for which Jill is ready. Employing the resources supplied by the semantics of 'ready' or the conceptual structure of BEING READY seems to be a convenient enough heuristics for us. So, what one does when one fails to articulate *for what* Jill is ready is primarily fail to live up to the structure of the predicate 'ready' or the concept BEING READY, not so much fail to observe maxims of relevance, informativeness, perspicuousness – even though the former failure often de facto coincides with the latter failure. That this is a semantic failure rather than a pragmatic one becomes even more apparent once one considers that the incompleteness exhibited by a sentence like 'Jill is ready' is a context-invariant one: there is never a context in which it is OK to leave the content incomplete, and even when it seems there is, it will probably be because it is understood that Jill must be ready for something, since she cannot be ready *tout court*. That is, the purpose or activity for which Jill is ready is not specified but it is (implicitly) existentially quantified over, since the purpose or activity slot cannot just remain vacant. Similarly, there is no context in which it is OK to utter a sentence like 'It's raining' and leave the content incomplete; and even in those cases where it seems OK to do it – as in Recanati's weatherman example surveyed in section 2.1.3 – it will probably be because it is understood that it must be raining somewhere, that is, the rain location is (implicitly) existentially quantified over and the location slot does not just remain vacant.[2]

The case of 'Jill is ready' should be contrasted with an example like 'You are not going to die' said by the mother to the son who has suffered a minor finger cut. Here we may feel that there is some incompleteness too, but arguably this is primarily a pragmatic flaw: firstly, there is no obvious conceptual truncation nor a failure to specify any *relatum* of a polyadic predicate; secondly, there actually are some contexts in which it is OK to express the bare sentence's literal content, to the effect that the speaker is not going to die, *tout court* (think for example of a context in which one is speaking to a member of some alien community which does not technically die – because they are immortal, or they reincarnate). Here whether or not the sentence's content should be completed by specifying *from what* the addressee is going to die is something that depends on pragmatic considerations, which include considering what the speaker is talking about, what she could reasonably mean with that utterance, in what way she wishes her assertion to be relevant and so on. It seems that the *pragmatic route* is the most convenient way a hearer could use to figure out what the speaker means here – and that no appeal to standing, context-invariant semantic features of the sentence could help.

Let us now compare the two examples: it seems that in the second case a pragmatic account of both the incompleteness and its resolution is appropriate enough. In the first case, however, a semantic account is available and my claim is that, *other things being equal, an available semantic account is to be preferred to a pragmatic one*.

The first reason for this lies in the *stability* afforded by such an approach: a semantic account would exploit standing, context-invariant semantic features of the expressions at issue. This entails that it is one's stable, context-invariant competence on the very concept of BEING READY (which allows one to derive, for instance, that being ready implies being ready for something), that triggers search for contextual information as to the activity or purpose for which the person referred to is ready and, if no such purpose or activity is spotted in the context of utterance, simply allows one to drop the task and perhaps conclude that the person is just ready for *some* activity or purpose. A purely pragmatic account of how an utterance of 'Jill is ready' would be understood would have to invoke only context-dependent aspects such as the speaker's beliefs, intentions, the goal of the conversation, and would have to invoke, *as a matter of ordinary practice*, the mobilisation at least of the hearer's ability to make inferences about what the speaker is thinking about or meaning, or a capacity to handle conversational maxims, where these abilities seem more appropriate for *extraordinary* circumstances, where communication breaks and the parties need to make adjustments in their respective assumptions concerning what is going on in the conversation. A semantic account, with its stress on features that are stable and context-invariant, is more apt to account for how utterance interpretation goes on in *ordinary* cases, where no special attention is to be credited to the specific intentions of the speaker or the conversation's goal, and where the hearer proceeds simply by exploiting her well-acquired semantic (or conceptual) competence *plus* a minimal ability to inquire into the salient aspects of utterance context.

An account which exploits stable semantic (conceptual) competences as a matter of ordinary procedure is to be contrasted with two, independent approaches in the literature. On the one hand, an account in which one's mind-reading and inferential abilities have centre stage in ordinary cases in figuring out an utterance's truth-conditions (see Sperber and Wilson, 1986, 2002; Sperber, 2000). On the other hand, an account in which information different than the semantic one intervenes in the working out of the content of an utterance – as for instance when world knowledge affects the interpretation of utterances. The latter approach is useful in explaining how an utterance of, for example, 'The ham sandwich is getting restless' is interpreted as meaning that the ham sandwich *orderer* is getting restless: here chunks of genuine world knowledge (which I assume is at least intuitively different from semantic or conceptual knowledge) do seem to enrich utterance content (Nunberg, 1978; Fauconnier, 1985).

Secondly, a semantic account ensures a *continuity* between the interpretation of (i) context-insensitive sentences, like 'Barack Obama is the president of the United States of America in 2014'; (ii) context-sensitive sentences, typically containing indexicals and demonstratives, like 'I am tired' or 'This is beautiful'; (iii) and semantically under-determined sentences, like 'It's raining' or 'Jill is ready'. This continuity seems to be welcome in virtue of the fact that the interpretation of utterances of all these sentences arguably need only be a matter of *convention* and *compositionality*. In particular, determining the content of these utterances need only require that what enters into meaning composition is properties of the sentence's components that are nothing but (or are derived from) their standing, linguistic meaning. For instance, in sentences of type (i), utterance interpretation requires reference assignment to the proper name 'Barack Obama' according to extant conventions; in sentences of group (ii), it requires assigning a reference to 'I' or 'this' according to their conventional linguistic meaning; and, arguably, in sentences of group (iii), it requires completing the truth-conditions of 'It's raining' by observing the semantic requirements with which the meaning of the verb 'to rain' is conventionally associated (that there be a place, for instance). *If* sentences (i)–(iii) all have this common trait, ensuring a continuity between their accounts seems to be a desideratum.

An account that ensures such a continuity would diverge from accounts that see a cut-off between, on the one hand, context-insensitive and context-sensitive (indexical or demonstrative) sentences and, on the other, everything else – ranging from semantically under-determined sentences, to non-literal talk, to implicatures. This idea cross-cuts a variety of views, including Radical Contextualism, which assigns a special role to 'free' pragmatic enrichment as opposed to 'linguistically controlled' pragmatic processes; Ultra-Minimalism, that even rules out reference assignment to demonstratives as semantic and recognises a pragmatic level of impliciture; and Minimalism, that only admits a semantically 'safe' context-sensitivity (indexicals and demonstratives) and allocates any other kind of context-sensitivity to speech-act theory (see Chapter 3 for further details).

These considerations having been made, it is important to keep in mind that pragmatics could *still* have a role in all this: in particular, pragmatics could help the hearer to identify what is salient in context (what the speaker is talking about, what she is referring to, and so on);

moreover, pragmatics could help the hearer to decide whether or not the enterprise of resorting to context is worth embarking on or not, depending on various factors. For instance, suppose the speaker utters 'Jill is ready', but the hearer has the reasonable suspicion that the speaker is not cooperating: in that case a pragmatic reasoning could make the hearer refrain from trying to figure out what the speaker is talking about, therefore saving the effort of understanding an utterance whose contribution is unimportant.

What about those cases in which a semantic account is not available and only a pragmatic account is? In these cases, we should definitely go for an account in terms of pragmatics. Moreover, once we have embraced a pragmatic account, my inclination would be to remain open to various 'shades of pragmatics', that is to a variety of pragmatic mechanisms determining different pragmatically conveyed contents, ranging from free enrichment and ad hoc meaning construction to generalised implicature, to proper conversational implicature. My attitude towards views that posit an interplay between semantics and pragmatics, like Radical Contextualism or Ultra-Minimalism, is therefore one of hospitality. Pragmatically conveyed meaning may come in a plurality of 'shades', depending on how close it stands with respect to sentential content – whether it is a mere enrichment, strengthening or loosening of it, whether it is more indirectly derived from it and so on. The point of the present section was to defend the claim that *if* a semantic strategy is available, other things being equal, this should have a priority with respect to a pragmatic strategy. Thus, should it turn out that a semantic account is available after all even for cases in which only a pragmatic account was thought to be available, we should embrace the semantic option, for the reasons delineated in this section.

4.2 The plausibility of a semantic, non-syntactic account

The idea that the context-sensitivity of semantically under-determined sentences should be accounted for in semantic terms is not news. Other theorists have defended it before, yet their angle was somewhat different from what I am trying to advocate in this chapter: in their view, the context-sensitivity of semantically under-determined sentences is a matter of semantics because it has a *syntactic* representation in the first place (Stanley 2000, 2002a, 2005a; Stanley and Szabó, 2000). This means, for instance, that resolving the context-sensitivity of a semantically under-determined sentence like 'It's raining' is a matter of semantics because it comes down to complying with the syntactic structure of the sentence, which allegedly contains an empty position that calls for filling-in. In contrast with this, I will argue for the claim that, *although the context-sensitivity of semantically under-determined sentences should follow a semantic track, it need not have a syntactic articulation.*

4.2.1 Semantic structure can be more complex than syntactic structure

Arguing for a semantic, non-syntactic account of the context-sensitivity of under-determined expressions involves admitting that the resolution of the semantic under-determinacy of these expressions obeys semantic instructions that need not correspond to syntactically articulated positions. In order to show that this is plausible, we should be able to identify at least one case where these semantic constraints are operative without there being any syntactically articulated form. Applying the example to a predicate like 'to rain', this implies arguing that, *at the semantic or conceptual level*, it expresses at least a dyadic relation RAIN(X, Y), whose argument-places call for completion, but that *at the syntactic level* it could behave like a monadic predicate or, in any case, fail to occur with articulated positions in syntax.

Here it is important to distinguish two levels of representation: on the one hand, the *semantic representation* of the predicate's logical form, or of the logical form of the sentence which contains it. This is a level of analysis that has been introduced by logicians and philosophers in order fully to spell out the semantic structure of these typologies of expressions – and it usually employs the notation of first-order predicate logic. On the other hand, we have *syntactic representations*, like Chomskyan Logical Form (LF). Although LF specifies aspects that serve for semantic interpretation, it still counts as a genuine level of syntactic representation (Haegeman, 1994; Hornstein et al., 2005). My point here will be to argue that semantic representation could be more complex than syntactic representation, and hence that this could justify the view that there are semantic/conceptual constraints which could operate and trigger processes of context-sensitivity resolution, independently of syntactic forms.

In order to make this point, I will show that there are sentences in which predicates like 'to rain', 'being green', 'being ready' could correctly be used as monadic, although obviously the employed predicates display a certain degree of complexity at the semantic level. In these sentences, the use of the predicate as monadic is correct from a *syntactic* point of view, in the sense that it generates no intuitions of ill-formation or unintelligibility and there are no independent syntactic reasons to postulate any extra syntactic complexity. Clearly, though, the concept (and meaning) associated with the predicate has a more complex (though perhaps implicit) structure which it would be a mistake to disregard. These cases will serve mainly as 'intuition pumps' and, as I will show in what follows, they have important implications for a strategy which invests much in syntactic complexity, such as Stanley's position.

I will introduce the notion of *zero-reading*, that is, of a reading in which the predicate is correctly used with a less than dyadic syntactic structure, in order to refer to this phenomenon. The sentence

(1) Whenever there is a place where water falls from the sky, it rains

is such that the predicate 'to rain' that occurs in it can get a zero-reading, that is, a reading where 'to rain' is used as a monadic predicate (of times, in this case). This may be seen clearly by spelling out the most plausible interpretation of (1), which could be read as stating that, whenever there is a place where water falls from the sky, *an event of rain occurs*, where the stress is not much on the whereabouts of the raining episode as much as it is on the happening of the phenomenon (at a certain time) (see also Recanati, 2002a, 2004, 2010 and Cappelen and Hawthorne, 2007). At the syntactic level, the sentence could be regarded as roughly displaying the following structure:

(1´) Whenever (t) there is a place (s) and water falls from the sky at (s), it rains (t).

Here I contend that there is no need to represent, at the syntactic level, any locational variable (s) in the embedded clause '... it rains'. Note that a locational variable is introduced and bound by a quantifier operator in the main clause ('there is a place (s) and water falls at (s)'), but this *by itself* mandates no postulation of the same variable in the embedded clause.

Moreover, an independent syntactic reason for postulating the time variable (t) is absent in the case of the locational variable (s). The time variable (t) could be supposed to be introduced in the embedded sentence independently, as a consequence of the verb's being tensed; on the other hand, there seems to be no parallel, independent syntactic reason to posit a locational variable in the embedded sentence.

One could argue that postulation of the location variable (s) is mandated by the fact that a bound reading is possible, whereby whenever there is a place where water falls from the sky, it rains *at that place*. It is undeniable that such a bound reading is possible, but the question here is whether this mandates postulation of such a variable. In order to conclude, from the possibility of a bound reading, that a variable is present in syntax, one needs an assumption to the effect that, for every semantic binding, there corresponds a syntactic binding: this is in effect the move made by Stanley with his Binding Assumption. But this assumption need not be avowed, for more than one reason.

The main motivation is that semantic and syntactic binding need not coincide. As a number of theorists have pointed out, (a) 'semantic' binding, where the interpretation of a covert pronominal or variable is controlled by some operator, need not coincide with (b) properly 'syntactic' binding, where there is a well-identified syntactic connection between two items – such as c-command. Consider, for instance:

(2) John bought exactly one donkey and fed it.

Here, Neale (2007) notes that we have a semantic binding between the quantifier expression 'exactly one donkey' and the pronoun 'it', but no possible syntactic relation occurs, because the binding is *cross-sentential*, that is, the binding operator and the bound element are in two distinct sentences. Similarly, Pupa and Troseth (2011) observe that in the sentence

(3) Some manager didn't succeed to persuade every shareholder in the company

there seems to be a binding between the restricted quantifier expression 'every shareholder in the company' and 'some manager', where the latter is read with the restriction 'some manager *in the company*'; however, no syntactic relation holds, because the bound expression is located in a higher hierarchical position than the binding expression, and therefore cannot be controlled by it.

Even more radically, Collins (2007) doubts whether semantic binding could possibly be accompanied by a syntactic binding. Consider a sentence like

(4) Every student answered every question

where 'every student' seems to affect through binding the interpretation of 'every question' – delivering the interpretation to the effect that (for instance) every student x answered every question y that was posed to x. A first potential syntactic relation between the two elements could be *c-command*:[3] However, Collins argues, c-command already obtains anyway between 'every student' and 'every question', and it in no way reveals whether any bound variable is there to be c-commanded as well. A second potential syntactic relation could be *adjunction*.[4] The relation would have to obtain between the quantified phrase 'every question' and a domain variable x, where the domain variable would be supposed to play the role of adjunct, the result being 'every question x'. Yet, adjuncts are generally phrases, and it is difficult to see variables qua logical/mathematical objects as equivalent to phrases. Moreover, adjuncts are essentially optional – their specification is not demanded at the level of theta-structure – so their nature is deeply different from the nature of the alleged hidden variables, which occupy positions that are to be filled in a mandatory way.

For these reasons, it is not obvious that, just because a semantic binding is available as an interpretation of (1), then we have to postulate a syntactic element which is subject to syntactic binding at the level of LF.

The second motivation for refraining from positing elements at the level of LF is that it is perfectly possible to make sense of the bound reading without making any commitment as to syntax. In fact, proponents of a Davidson-style event analysis could accomplish this, as Cappelen and Hawthorne (2007) show: it is sufficient to suppose that the predicate 'to rain' is monadic and applies to events, which are identified in terms of their spatio-temporal coordinates; these coordinates can be represented in the semantic interpretation of the sentence (when appropriate) by variables ranging over times or locations and be bound accordingly by quantifying operators. In this way, one does not buy into the syntactic complexity of either the predicate 'to rain' or sentence (1), and manages to capture a bound reading of (1) anyway.

A further, alternative and purely semantic solution is adopted by Pagin (2005), who proposes to render bound readings such as that of 'Whenever John lights a cigarette, it rains' as involving quantifications over contexts. The reading would be cashed (semi-formally) as follows: 'The sentence "Every time John lights a cigarette, it rains" is true in the context of utterance c iff, for every context $c´$ different from c as to time t and location l, if John lights a cigarette at $t(c´)$ at $l(c´)$, then it rains at $t(c´)$ at $l(c´)$'. In this way, the bound interpretation remains a purely semantic phenomenon, with no commitment at the level of syntax; indeed, the semantic binding becomes apparent only at the level of *meta-language*.

Other examples of zero-readings are:

(5) Whenever she is prepared for an activity, Jill is ready.
(6) Whenever something or some salient part of it looks like this, it is green.

(5) and (6) contain predicates for which a zero-reading is appropriate, that is, in which 'being ready' and 'being green' are consistently used as monadic predicates (I will ignore the quantification over times for convenience). The structure of (5) and (6) could be the following:

(5´) Whenever there is an activity (*a*) and she is prepared for (*a*), Jill is ready.
(6´) Whenever there is something (*o*) or some part (*p*) of (*o*) and (*o*) or (*p*) looks like this, it is green.

It is easy to read (5) as stating that whenever there is an activity for which she is prepared, Jill is in a state of readiness, full stop. And it is easy to read (6) as stating that whenever something or some salient part of it looks like some demonstrated shade, it has the property of being green, full stop. The same considerations that have been invoked for (1) could be replicated for (5) and (6): firstly, there is no independently syntactic reason for postulating an activity variable in the embedded clause '... Jill is ready' and for postulating a part variable in the embedded clause '... it is green'. Secondly, invoking the possibility of a bound reading of (5) and (6) does not by itself mandate the postulation of a bound variable; endorsing the Binding Assumption could enable one to infer the presence of the articulated variable, however there is no need to avow this assumption, for the reasons listed previously. Even in these cases, then, there appears to be no need to postulate any syntactic complexity.

Absence of syntactic complexity does not entail absence of semantic complexity. Of course, that these predicates can be correctly used with a monadic syntactic structure does not imply that the concepts (meanings) we associate with them do not have a more complicated structure. Clearly, the lexical concept TO RAIN does not apply just to times, it also concerns places. This implies that a zero-reading of (1) would not make sense at the semantic level: that rain has a locational component *must* be part of the sentence's truth-conditions, even though it is a background aspect that is bracketed and seems of little importance in the occasions in which (1) would be usually uttered. This aspect must be contemplated at the semantic level on pain of the sentence's interpretation resulting in nonsense: think of how unacceptable it would be to interpret (1) as saying that whenever there is a place where water falls from the sky, it rains, *punkt*, as if raining could somehow not be a spatially located event. The upshot of these considerations is that the zero-reading that seems correct at the syntactic level is not correct at the semantic level. This could be explained by saying that, although the predicate 'to rain' could be used as monadic, that is as having – say – just one slot for times at the level of logical form, the lexical concept TO RAIN is not monadic, in that it has at least one slot for times and one for places, which must be taken into account in interpreting any occurrence of the predicate, even when this seems to be correctly used as monadic at the syntactic level. This seems to offer a case in favour of the claim with which I have opened this subsection, namely that *the semantic structure of a predicate (or sentence) could be more complex than the syntactic structure (LF) of that same predicate (or sentence)*. Similar considerations hold for examples (5) and (6).

Zero-readings have served so far as 'intuition pumps': the peculiar semantic interpretation that they generate makes it easy to appreciate that the syntactic structure of their sentences, which encourages a reading of the predicates as monadic, could be less complex than their semantic structure, which however must take account of some fundamental semantic/conceptual constraints. Yet the considerations advanced so far about zero-readings could be extended to sentences which greatly encourage bound readings, such as

(7) Wherever I go, it rains
(8) Whenever John lights a cigarette, it rains

in which it is easy to hear a bound reading for (7) to the effect that wherever the speaker goes, it rains *there*; or a bound reading for (8) to the effect that whenever John lights a cigarette, it rains in the place where he lights a cigarette. In this case as well, it is not evident from the structure of (7) or (8) that there is any need to posit a variable in the embedded sentence '... it rains'. The ease with which we obtain the bound interpretation is probably the strongest rationale for positing any such syntactic complexity, but in order to construct an argument for this one needs something like the Binding Assumption. Yet there is no need to avow such an assumption, as argued before. It follows that, since in this case as well we could have a bound reading at the semantic level without a binding at the syntactic level, semantic structure could be more complex than syntactic structure (or LF).

In conclusion, these considerations lead to a claim as to a gap between 'logical form' in the sense of semantic analysis and 'logical form' (LF) in the sense of the representation of the syntactic relations that govern specific linguistic items (such as quantifiers and indexed variables). On the view that I am proposing, there can be a certain degree of complexity at the level of semantic analysis which, however, does not correspond to any syntactic complexity.

As a result of this, my claim is also that the context-sensitivity of these expressions is primarily implemented at the purely semantic/conceptual level and I advance no thesis at the level of syntax. In this, I distance myself from Stanley, who champions the view that a good deal of syntactic complexity should be posited along with semantic complexity, in order to account for context-sensitivity.

In his view, a purely semantic account would correspond to a 'revisionary move' in the spirit of the fathers of analytic philosophy, whereby logical form is used to give a more perspicuous representation of the semantic structure of natural language sentences. By contrast, there exists a 'descriptive' and empirical task, whereby isolating a sentence's logical form means discovering its 'real structure', which might be found to be different from its superficial grammatical form. Here the theorist may have to attribute some hidden complexity to natural language sentences, and this would be the upshot of an empirical investigation. Stanley is quite clear that his proposal falls on the descriptive side:

> It is in this [the descriptive] sense that I intend the thesis that all context-dependence is traceable to logical form. What I shall defend is the claim that all truth-conditional context-dependence results from fixing the values of contextually sensitive elements in the *real structure* of natural language sentences. (Stanley, 2000, 391–2, my italics)

While I do not question that, in some cases, context-sensitivity could imply fixing the values of syntactically articulated elements, I question that this happens *in all cases*, as Stanley boldly declares in this passage. If my arguments are correct, and hence if semantic structure could be more complex than syntactic structure, then we may have to complete a sentence on the basis of semantic/conceptual constraints which, however, are by no means represented by positions in the syntax of the sentence. For instance, we would have to complete at the semantic level a sentence like (1), (7) or (8) on the basis of mastery of the (at least dyadic) concept TO RAIN(x,y), even if the predicate 'to rain' could be correctly used as monadic at the level of syntax. This clearly goes counter to the contention that *all* such completions come down to the fixation of the value of elements in a sentence's real syntactic structure. This is therefore a semantic, non-syntactic (or at least not primarily syntactic) account of the context-sensitivity of semantically under-determined expressions.

It could be objected that, in this picture, harmony between syntax and semantics is lost, which might constitute an inconvenience. The proponent of the syntacticist strategy might retort that his view preserves such a harmony. Yet, harmony between syntax and semantics is a virtue of the theory only if it is justified. As we have seen, there seems to be no justification for postulating syntactic positions in the binding cases, although their postulation would establish a harmony with the semantically posited slots. Absent this justification, it seems that harmony will have to be forgone and that, in these circumstances, it need not be a regrettable loss. Note also that, as a compensation for the lack of harmony that would seem to afflict the present proposal, the drawback for the syntactictist would be a charge of overgeneration, that is, the charge of generating *excessive and implausible syntactic positions* just because their presence could explain bound readings. This risk would, however, not upset the proponent of a conceptual constraints account in the least.

One might nevertheless insist that the semanticist view mandates compliance with an excessive number of semantic/conceptual 'slots', so that the proposal is still subject to the overgeneration or proliferation charge. As I will argue in section 4.3.3, this worry is far less problematic than it would seem at first glance.

Finally, one may find that the idea that there are 'slots' in semantic structure is just trivial; that it is accurate, but also rather uninteresting to make context-sensitivity explicit *only* at the semantic level (see Stanley, 2000). This is because, I presume, the fact that these semantic slots exist is already something that more or less anyone would be ready to recognise; using a formal language to represent them only serves to make them more explicit, but it adds nothing to what almost everyone would be ready to acknowledge on the basis of a simple exercise of semantic/conceptual analysis. I agree that confining oneself to making these semantic aspects explicit would be rather unexciting, yet I believe I have not contented myself with such a humdrum and innocuous task. The point I have tried to make is quite different: by arguing that semantic structure could be more complex than syntactic structure, I have argued that at least in some relevant cases there need be nothing more to the context-sensitivity of some expressions than what can be revealed by semantic/conceptual analysis, and that the prospects for a syntactic account are dim. *This* claim is not trivial, if only because it contrasts the line pursued in recent literature by those syntacticists that claim that all context-sensitivity can be traced to syntax.

4.3 The Conceptual Constraints View

The previous sections were aimed at preparing the ground for an account of the context-sensitivity of semantically under-determined sentences which is (i) genuinely semantic rather than pragmatic and (ii) regards these sentences' context-sensitivity as implemented at the semantic, and not necessarily at the syntactic, level. The central proposal of the chapter will be stated and developed in the following subsections.

4.3.1 Stating the view

In this section, I will articulate a positive proposal according to which the context-sensitivity of semantically under-determined sentences could be traced to a number of *conceptual constraints*. I take conceptual constraints to be primarily *ways of structuring and organising thought about certain matters*. We structure thought about meteorological matters in terms of phenomena such as rainfall, snowfall and so on happening at times and locations, possibly with varying intensities; we structure thought about being ready in terms of individuals and objects being prepared for a number of different purposes or activities; we structure thought about being green in terms of objects that are green in some respect, or part, or against some comparison class.

To characterise the phenomenon in terms familiar to cognitive psychologists or cognitive semanticists, we may view conceptual constraints as being part of very general and fundamental *schemata* (Minsky, 1975; Rumelhart and Ortony, 1977; Rumelhart, 1980; Cohen and Murphy, 1984), or *frames* (Fillmore, 1982, 1985, 2003; Fillmore and Baker, 2010). These are typically structured configurations which feature various interrelated items, where each item occupies a particular 'slot' or 'dimension'. A good illustration of a schema or frame is that associated with trading and commercial relationships, which contains the concepts *buy, sell, pay, spend, cost,* all of which are connected semantically and evoke one another. For example, the selling and buying relationships come as interrelated insofar as, depending on which relatum one decides to focus on, the same agents and items that could enter into the relation of x *selling* y *to* z could enter in the relationship z *buying* y *from* x, by changing their roles and thus occupying different 'slots'. Similarly, the frame associated with family relationships features different interrelated nodes such as *mother, father, child, son, daughter, husband, wife* and so on, all connected through semantic links and evoking one another in such a way that, again, depending on what relatum one decides to focus on, the same elements that enter the relation x *is the father of y* could enter in the relation *y is the child of x*, and so on (Petruck, 1996).

Utterance comprehension has been regarded as greatly affected by frames (Fillmore, 2003). Appeal to frames allows one to reconstruct a background against which one may determine what the speaker is talking about. Frames could be *invoked*, that is 'searched for', in order to gain full comprehension of certain utterances. A famous example involves a sentence like 'We usually wait to open our presents until it's midnight', in which a specific frame, namely the Christmas frame, must be invoked in order to gain full comprehension of what the speaker is talking about (Fillmore, 1985). Alternatively, frames could be *evoked*, that is suggested, by some words or phrases in the sentence itself, which could equally help clarify what the speaker is talking about. A well-known example in the literature is provided by the following sentence: 'The men were happy to spend some time on land today' (Fillmore, 1982, 1985). Here the locution 'on land' evokes a sailing frame, whereby being 'on land' is opposed to being 'at sea', and immediately suggests that the speaker is talking about sailors (as opposed to an aircraft crew, say).

Drawing inspiration from these examples, something similar is bound to happen, I venture, with semantically under-determined sentences like 'It's raining', 'Jill is ready', 'The leaves are green' and so on. Reading or listening to one of these sentences evokes a *very general and fundamental schema or frame*, to which the interpreter might appeal in trying to understand an utterance of that sentence in a specific context. The schema or frame will include some 'dimensions' or 'slots' to be filled with information possibly drawn from context; to complete these slots is to abide by the specific *conceptual constraints* that arise from the schema or frame.

The to-rain schema, for instance, may include a slot for times, one for locations, possibly a slot for different ways and intensities of raining, and so on. The being-ready schema may include a slot for the subject or object which is ready and a slot for the purpose or activity for which it is ready, together with slots for times and locations, presumably. The being-green schema may include a slot for the object to which the colour is attributed and a slot for the part or respect in which the colour is manifested, *plus* probably a slot for the comparison class against which the shade is ascribed, and again time and location. Gaining comprehension of utterances of these sentences means correctly responding to the conceptual constraints posed by the relevant schema evoked.

An objection that might be easily raised at this point has to do with *proliferation*: one might not be attracted by a picture in which a concept has such an articulated structure as to include slots for nearly everything – from times and places, to manners and so on. This worry is legitimate, but I do not think it poses too serious a problem in the framework I am proposing here: see section 4.3.3 for a more detailed response to this worry.

4.3.2 Conceptual constraints and the argument/adjunct distinction

Conceptual constraints as part of these schemata pose some restrictions thought and language use must comply with, on pain of massive incoherence, nonsense or absurdity: for instance, the conceptual constraint to the effect that rain occurs at a location is one to which thought and language use *must* comply with, on pain of nonsense or absurdity; the conceptual constraint that a father is a parent is equally a conceptual constraint that has to be observed, in order to avoid serious incoherence. Conceptual constraints might be regarded as giving rise to *conceptual truths* or, perhaps in a less epistemologically laden and more innocuous sense, '*conceptual truisms*'[5] that, as such, are all on a par as to their import in our cognitive and linguistic life.

Yet, failure to abide by some of these constraints in language use is bound to result in intuitions of outright ill-formation and unintelligibility; while a failure to observe other constraints may simply result in intuitions of 'conceptual truncation' and truth-conditional incompleteness. I will argue that this difference is best captured by presuming that some conceptual constraints correspond to an expression's *argument*, which it is typically mandatory to saturate; while some other conceptual constraints correspond to simple *adjuncts*, whose specification is merely optional.

As a first example, consider the concept TO COMPLETE: the schema associated with this concept will surely include at least two slots, for the completer and the completed object. A sentence like

(9) Mary completed

strikes one as ill-formed and unintelligible to the extent that it fails to specify the 'completee' slot. From this intuition, we may gather that the conceptual constraint dedicated to the completee also acts as a *syntactic* constraint, because disregarding it in language use gives rise to a judgement of ill-formation and unintelligibility. By contrast, consider other (more or less familiar) examples:

(10) It's raining.
(11) Peter is singing.

(12) Claudia is dancing.
(13) Clark is eating.

Here these sentences fail to specify some aspect that seems required by conceptual constraints – namely *where* the rain is falling, *what* Peter is singing, *where* Claudia is dancing, *what* Clark is eating and so on. Yet this in no way results in an intuition of unintelligibility or ill-formation: the sentences are perfectly well formed and intelligible even if none of the above-mentioned aspects is articulated at the surface level. This phenomenon goes under the label of Null Instantiation, in which conceptually core arguments are omitted at the syntactic level (Fillmore, 1986).[6] These conceptual constraints therefore do not correspond to syntactic constraints. At most, a failure to specify these aspects could trigger the intuition that (10)–(13) are semantically incomplete, that is, that the contents they express lack some features that could help to spell out the truth-conditions of utterances of these sentences. This may happen more often with a sentence like (10), and less often with a sentence like (12), but this is arguably due to contingent facts about how these sentences are used. Semantic incompleteness is bound to be sensed more often in the case of 'It's raining', for usually utterances of this sentence are performed while implicitly referring to a specific location; but nothing prevents using (10) as it is, leaving it to the hearer to suppose, as a default move, that it is simply raining somewhere – as in my interpretation of Recanati's weatherman case and in the zero-reading cases I have proposed (see section 4.2.1). Fewer intuitions of semantic incompleteness are bound to be had with 'Peter is singing', 'Claudia is dancing' and 'Clark is eating', for often little attention is paid to *what* is sung, *where* one dances or *what* is eaten when these linguistic forms are used, though nothing prevents a scenario obtaining in which even (11)–(13) sound semantically incomplete. Suppose, for instance, that Claudia is a famous dancer and is on tour. A fan of hers reads of her upcoming performance in a newspaper and utters 'Claudia is dancing'. It seems that in this case the speaker has failed to provide a piece of information that might be useful to the audience, namely the place – the city, part of city or venue – where the performance will be held. Or, suppose that depending on what Clark eats, his friends could predict what his mood will be. A friend sees Clark in the distance and utters 'He's eating': here the sentence might sound incomplete for it fails to specify what he is eating, which by assumption is the focus of the friend's interest. Be that as it may, even though any of (10)–(13) could be regarded as semantically incomplete in its own way, again this incompleteness by no means amounts to an instance of syntactic ill-formation.

These considerations seem to license a distinction between conceptual constraints that coincide with restrictions on the syntax of a certain expression and those conceptual constraints that instead coincide with merely semantic requirements, which could generate an intuition of semantic incompleteness but also be presumed as satisfied in a default way. Here the distinction between an *argument* and an *adjunct* may come in handy.

On the one hand, the arguments of a predicate correspond to the participants minimally involved in the state or activity described by it (Haegeman, 1994). The number of arguments of a predicate determine its adicity: for instance, two argument-places determine a dyadic predicate. Specifying a value for one such argument-place reduces the 'adicity' of the predicate (Heim and Kratzer, 1998). In virtue of the arguments' specifying the minimal number of admissible role-fillers for a certain predicate, saturating these argument-places is something mandatory in order for the expression to contribute to a well-formed and intelligible sentence.

An *adjunct*, in contrast, does not correspond to a minimally required element in a state or event. Specifying an adjunct does not decrease a predicate's adicity. It merely acts as a modifier of the expression (see Heim and Kratzer, 1998). Specifying an adjunct is not a mandatory step for the building up of a well-formed expression; adjuncts are typically *optional*.

The resulting picture is the following: cognitively mature subjects possess a wide number of conceptual frames, which pose a number of conceptual constraints that could turn out useful in interpreting linguistic utterances. These constraints are all *on a par* as to their conceptual import (they all express conceptual truths or at least 'truisms'), though in language use they give rise to more stringent or more relaxed requirements. Some conceptual constraints give rise to *syntactic* requirements which, if disregarded, could result in intuitions of ill-formation and unintelligibility: these conceptual constraints could be seen as corresponding to *arguments*. By contrast, other conceptual constraints pose no syntactic requirements but could at most give rise to intuitions of semantic incompleteness (unless they are presumed to be satisfied by default): these constraints could be argued to correspond to *adjuncts*.

Going back to our favourite examples, then, from these considerations it follows that a predicate like 'to rain', at the syntactic level, has only one argument-place (perhaps filled by the dummy subject 'it' in 'It rains'), and that any specifications as to time and location would not be ways of saturating argument-places, but rather ways of specifying adjuncts. This, however, does not mean that the concept TO RAIN cannot be polyadic at the semantic level – in virtue of the conceptual constraints that apply to it. Similar points hold for 'being ready' and 'being green'. At the syntactic level, they are both monadic, while at the semantic level they apply to more than one relatum, again in virtue of conceptual constraints. BEING READY applies at least to both individuals (or objects) and activities (or purposes), but the purpose or activity plays the role of an adjunct. As to BEING GREEN, it applies at least to objects and parts of these objects (or respects), where the 'part' relatum corresponds to an adjunct.[7]

As a consequence of the fact that a failure to comply with conceptual constraints may generate intuitions of semantic defectiveness, those very conceptual constraints can act as a *guide* to retrieval of the information appropriate to finally achieve a complete and evaluable content. Thus, upon listening to an utterance of 'It's raining', a hearer might exploit the conceptual constraint to the effect that raining occurs at locations in order to provide a completion to the sentence's semantically under-determined content. The location-related conceptual constraint may trigger the search of a salient location in the utterance's context (Paris, London, Bogotá), or, when the location cannot be retrieved, prompt the hearer to opt for an existentially closed interpretation, to the effect that it is raining *somewhere*. Similarly, upon hearing an utterance of 'Jill is ready', the hearer might exploit the conceptual constraint to the effect that being ready is being ready for a purpose or activity and, on this basis, try to figure out in the context of utterance for which purpose Jill is said to be ready (to ski, for the Spanish exam, and so on), or otherwise, opt for an existentially closed interpretation to the effect that Jill is ready *for something*.

4.3.3 Conceptual constraints and their semantic effects

The view I am proposing conceives of both the peculiar context-sensitivity of semantically under-determined sentences and of the very resolution of this context-sensitivity as an entirely *semantic* matter. There is more than one reason to think so.

First of all, conceptual constraints can legitimately be considered as 'semantic constraints' in that they arguably contribute to the semantically correct use of words, where by 'semantically correct use' I mean a use that does not result in incoherence, absurdity, nonsense or category mistakes. Relatedly, following the conceptual constraints associated with the concept TO RAIN helps us build up thoughts like *it's raining now in Paris*, or *it rained last Christmas in Barcelona*, or *it will rain tomorrow in Courmayeur* (and the corresponding sentences). These are all thoughts or sentences that, irrespectively of their being true or false, are 'correct' from a semantic point of view, in that they comply with some basic semantic features of this kind of discourse. Semantically incorrect (or weird-sounding) constructions would be ones in which these constraints are somehow flouted, or constraints not pertinent to the currently attended discourse are applied.

Conceptual constraints also seem to guarantee the *systematicity* of our thought and discourse, which is once again a semantic feature. So, for instance, the fact that a weather concept like TO RAIN responds to constraints about locations and times seems to ensure that, if a subject can entertain the thought that it rains on 2 January in Paris, she can also entertain the thought that it is raining on 24 July in London. Or, if she masters the conceptual constraints on BEING READY, she will be able to entertain the thought that Jill is ready for the Spanish exam as well as the thought that Mark is ready to eat pizza and the thought that the pizza is ready to be eaten (this requisite is also known as the Generality Constraint from Evans, 1982).

Conceptual constraints arguably also help to respect the *compositionality* of our utterances, where compositionality squarely qualifies as a semantic feature. So, for instance, the conceptual constraints on TO RAIN operate so as to preserve the compositionality of the content of utterances of sentences like 'It's raining', that is, they preserve the idea *that the content of these utterances is determined by the content of their constituents and their syntactic arrangement*. Whenever 'It's raining' is uttered, conceptual constraints ensure that it is an aspect of the meaning (or concept) TO RAIN that triggers retrieval of the salient location – when this is available – so that the content of such an utterance results from semantic features of the predicate 'to rain' (established with the aid of contextual clues) *plus* syntax alone. All this rules out – as argued in section 4.1 – that what triggers selection of any salient location is pragmatic factors, such as the presumption that the speaker is cooperating, the search for a relevant, informative or perspicuous content, and so on.

Furthermore, conceptual constraints can legitimately be regarded as giving rise to semantic effects because they operate on *what is said* by an utterance, rather than on what is implied. This point requires particularly careful scrutiny. What we need to do at this point is rule out that the processes posited here in terms of conceptual constraints give rise to some sort of implicature, whether conventional or generalised.

From Grice (1967/1989),[8] we know that a conventional implicature is part of what a speaker suggests (without saying it) with her use of a certain expression, for the simple fact that she has used that expression.

This happens with 'therefore': using this word in the sentence 'He is an Englishman, he is therefore brave' raises the implicature that the man's being brave is a consequence of his being an Englishman; though this is not strictly speaking said by the sentence, use of the word 'therefore' is sufficient to suggest that a relation of consequence obtains.

Can we say that, with the conceptually constrained processes presently at issue, we are facing just another case of *conventional implicature*? One feature, it seems to me, sets the present case apart from cases of recognised conventional implicature. As Grice and others admit, the consequence relation suggested by use of 'therefore' is not part of the truth-conditions of the sentence 'He is an Englishman, he is therefore brave'; it is simply a suggested aspect. If the person referred to by 'he' were brave, but not as a consequence of being an Englishman, the speaker would still have said something true, although she would have *implied* something false. Now consider an utterance of 'It rains'; even though there may be 'zero-readings' of this sentence – where the predicate 'to rain' is correctly used as monadic from a syntactic point of view (see section 4.2.1) – any felicitous use of such a sentence nevertheless *evokes* a locational component. Suppose one were to utter the sentence 'Whenever drops are falling from the sky, it rains'. Even though this is true even if it is not actually raining in any particular place, still, that rain episodes are spatially located follows from the concept itself TO RAIN. Suppose this information was somehow conventionally implicated by an utterance of 'Whenever drops are falling from the sky, it rains'. Being a conventional implicature, it should not be easily cancellable. Indeed, one cannot consistently claim 'Whenever drops are falling from the sky, it rains, but not in any place'. Yet, it should be rather easily detachable, which is not. Whatever combination of words we may choose which results in a sentence with the same truth-conditions as 'It's raining', it will always be accompanied by a presumption that the phenomenon occurs in a location: try it with expressions like 'it's pouring', 'drops are falling from the sky', and so on.

Similar considerations hold for the idea that conceptually constrained processes give rise to *generalised conversational implicatures*. What is a generalised conversational implicature? Once again, we have to make reference to Grice (1967/1989, but see also Levinson, 2000): a generalised conversational implicature is a conversational (hence non-conventional) implicature, which has become customary, or habitual. For example, it has become customary, when uttering a sentence like 'I saw him with a woman, last night', to imply that the woman in question is neither the wife, nor the sister or mother of the man referred to with the pronoun 'he'. Another example is the use of 'Some' to imply 'Not all': when a speaker says 'Some of the protests were shut down' she usually implicates, and hearers normally take her as implicating, that not all protests were shut down. The implicature is elicited by default, but it is always cancellable. For example, the speaker could say 'I saw him with a woman, last night. In fact it was his sister' and 'Some of the protests were shut down; indeed, all of them were'.

Is content enrichment through conceptual constraints a case of generalised conversational implicature? It is hard to deny that every use of 'It's raining' or 'Jill is ready' or 'The leaves are green' carries with it some customary, or habitual aspect. As García-Carpintero observes,

> When a speaker utters a token *i* of 'is raining' (as in 'it is raining'), he takes for granted that more information is available in context about the place he is referring to than that it is salient when the token *i* is produced. But it is a conventional fact about the use of the present tense with verbs meaning located events such as 'to rain' that the place referred to is indicated in that way, as it were, by default, and speakers rely on their audiences sharing with them this knowledge. (García-Carpintero, 2001, p. 110)

What García-Carpintero is ultimately suggesting is that use of semantically incomplete sentences such as 'It's raining' or 'Jill is ready' triggers a generalised conversational implicature, that is an implicature that it has become habitual or customary to convey in those circumstances: namely *that some contextual information is salient*. This implicature concerns some facts about the conversational setting and it is indeed altogether distinct from the content semantically expressed by the sentence uttered. This idea is borne out by the cancellation test, which reveals that it is perfectly semantically consistent – albeit a bit pragmatically infelicitous – to erase the implicature by stating something like:

(14) It's raining, but there's no contextually salient place where it's happening.
(15) Jill is ready, but there's no contextually salient purpose for which she is.

García-Carpintero's suggestion is therefore acceptable, but it has nothing to do with the kind of content enrichment we are after, which does not lead one to derive a proposition about the status of the conversational setting, rather it brings one to expand utterance content with extra elements drawn from context. Here again, there is a fundamental difference between generalised conversational implicatures and these cases of enrichment, namely that the former are *cancellable*, while the latter are not. In normal circumstances, it would be greatly incoherent to say:

(16) It's raining, but there's no place where it's actually raining.
(17) Jill is ready, but there's no activity for which she is ready.
(18) The leaves are green, but there's no respect in which they are such.

These would not be just instances of implicature erasing; they would be plain contradictions. Note that the same holds even for *zero-readings* of 'It rains', since even these uses evoke a locational aspect which would be erroneous to cancel as if it was an implicature. As already noted, it would be a straightforward incoherence to utter:

(19) Whenever drops fall from the sky it rains, but not in any place.

To conclude, we have reasons to believe that conceptual constraints do not give rise to either conventional implicatures (because they are not easily detachable) or to generalised conversational implicatures (because they are not cancellable).

Finally, conceptual constraints do not ban recourse to context, and in this sense *they are compatible with a certain amount of pragmatics*; yet, as mentioned in section 4.1, the model of context-sensitivity they embody is one where conceptual/semantic aspects *control* pragmatic mechanisms. Conceptual constraints may be thought of as opening 'semantic slots', which on appropriate occasions may be filled in with contextual information. For instance, the rain-location constraint for 'to rain' may be regarded as opening a semantic slot to be filled with a location (Paris, London, San Francisco Bay, and so on). Saturation of these slots calls for retrieval of contextual information, perhaps by inquiring into the speaker's intentions, beliefs and so on, something which may take a certain amount of pragmatic work. Note, however, that this does not make the resulting process any more pragmatic than other processes of reference assignment to linguistic expressions (such as 'this', 'that'). Since the location-dedicated slot is opened up for semantic/conceptual reasons, the saturation of the slot is analogous to reference assignment to indexical or demonstrative terms or the saturation of any other free argument-place through contextual variable assignment.

The conceptual constraints view guarantees that the effects these constraints give rise to are genuinely semantic, however the idea that every time a hearer engages in the task of understanding an utterance, she faces multiple slots to be filled, may not sound tremendously appealing. This objection amounts to the proliferation complaint that was mentioned in sections 4.2.1 and 4.3.1. Although I do not wish to deny that for each concept, there will be a number of slots corresponding to a number of conceptual truths (or truisms) that *need* to be lived up to and hence *mandate* completion, I do not think this kind of issue is fatal for the view. In order to see this, we need to understand that the proliferation objection could play at two different levels.

The first is the cognitive level: the objector might be dissatisfied that, given the multiplicity of 'slots' that need to be filled by the hearer in order to make the sentence's content semantically complete, the task might turn out unbearably long and cognitively costly. But this need not be a consequence of the conceptual constraints account. True, for each concept there will be a number of 'slots' that are open in virtue of conceptual truths or 'truisms' that are associated with that concept: for instance, the conceptual truth (or 'truism') to the effect that when it rains, it rains at a location, will create a location slot; also the conceptual truth (or 'truism') that when it rains, it rains with a certain intensity will create a 'manner' slot. And these slots have, in an important sense, to be saturated somehow, in order to avoid nonsense, absurdity or incoherence. But this by no means implies that the hearer has *consciously to attend to* each single slot and saturate it explicitly. Some slots may come filled by default, if not by specific elements, at least through an existential quantification; and they may not be consciously attended to by the subject, but they may *remain in the background* as information that is taken for granted, or obvious. For instance, although by the lights of the theory every instance of 'It's raining' will have to respond to the conceptual truth (or 'truism') to the effect that when it rains, it rains with a certain intensity and thus will be associated with a 'manner' or 'intensity' slot, this slot may be filled by default with a standard value (such as 'average intensity'), or with an existential quantification ('some intensity'). Moreover, the 'intensity' slot need not be attended to consciously by the interpreter, but may remain in the background of her process of understanding, where the fact that it rains with an average intensity, or some intensity, is somehow taken for granted. In special contexts, the question of the intensity with which it rains might be brought into relief and prompt the interpreter to consider the specific slot and assign some other value to it, but other than that, the slot may generally be filled always in the same way; the matter may be treated as background information, and it might suffice that the hearer has a disposition to recognise its truth-conditional role.[9] Thus, the proliferation worry has little or no traction at the cognitive level, since there is no general requirement that all the putative slots be consciously attended to – it suffices that they remain in the background and the interpreter has a disposition to appreciate their truth-conditional role.

The second level at which the proliferation objection could play is the theoretical level: one may protest that the lexical semantics that results from the Conceptual Constraints View posits far too much complexity. But, provided that this complexity need not have damaging reverberations at the cognitive level, the complexity of the theory may just be something that we have to accept and live with. For lexical semantics *just might be complex* and it may be ill-advised to expect that it were not (more on lexical semantics will be said in section 4.4). The excessive complexity worry at the level of theory might thus be dispelled on the grounds that it poses unrealistic demands on the theory itself, demands which could be ignored for our purposes since, in addition, the alleged complexity here does not even bring bad implications at the cognitive level.

A further potential objection that deserves mention may be called the objection from 'smuggled metaphysics': at least some of those that I call conceptual constraints are really just metaphysical constraints: for example, constraints on time, location or manner. So the view conflates the metaphysical with the semantic. In response to this complaint, suffice it to say that it seems undeniable that, even if these were only metaphysical constraints, it would be *mandatory* to observe them on pain of describing impossible states of affairs (for instance, it raining in-no-place), something which would impact semantic evaluation after all. Whether it is necessary to consider these constraints consciously, when engaged in utterance comprehension, is another matter: I think it is not, as already argued.

The bottom line of these considerations is that there are good prospects for a view of the context-sensitivity of semantically underdetermined sentences as rooted in what I have called conceptual constraints, that is, ways of structuring and organising thought and discourse about certain topics. Conceptual constraints could be seen as part of *schemata or frames* that are evoked by some elements in the sentence (the word 'rain' in 'It's raining' evokes the rain frame and the conceptual constraints it carries with it). Some conceptual constraints are better seen, at the syntactic level, as *adjuncts* rather than arguments.

Finally, employing conceptual constraints to remedy to semantic under-determinacy ensures that the ensuing processes of enrichment or completion will be *semantic* rather than primarily pragmatic.

4.4 Concepts and words: towards Molecularism

In this section, I will argue for the idea that the picture of the conceptual (and somehow derivatively, lexical) realm so far adopted is best accompanied by a semantic Molecularism proposal. My argument in favour of this contention will be based on two, purely negative, considerations. The first negative consideration starts with the observation that the account of concepts (and lexical meaning) that I have been defending conceives them as both *internally structured*. As has been argued, the latter contention seems to be bound to lead to Holism about the semantic properties of concepts and of words, which is seen as a highly undesirable view (Fodor and Lepore, 1992). However, I will argue that two implicit premises of this argument can be rejected and the Holism threat can be thwarted. The second negative consideration relies on the point that the most radical alternative to Holism, namely Atomism, is not very promising either, in that it retains too restricted a notion of what counts as meaning-constitutive features – namely punctuate semantic properties based on causal and nomic relations between symbol and world. The conclusion of these negative arguments will be that Molecularism is the most reasonable account for the semantics of both concepts and lexical items, as it has been defended so far.

Admitting conceptual or lexical constraints immediately seems to imply subscribing to a view whereby concepts or the meaning of words are internally structured and complex. In the Generative Grammar tradition, the thought that the meaning of words is composite goes back to Katz and Fodor (1963), Katz (1972) and to more recent contributions like those of Bierwisch (1983), Jackendoff (1990), Pustejovsky (1995) and Pinker (2007). In philosophy, the position is represented by those authors who regard concepts or the meaning of terms as depending on their role in language – typically, an inferential role (cf. Brandom, 2000; Boghossian, 1994). Philosophers like Taylor (2001, 2003) and Neale (2007) also seem close to an idea of lexical complexity when they put forth the idea that the 'subsyntactic' structure of terms is complex.

Such a conception of concepts or lexical meaning is exposed to the following 'slippery slope' risk indicated by Fodor and Lepore (1992), whereby once it is recognised that the content of a concept or meaning of a word is composite and depends on the semantic properties of other concepts or words, it seems that there is no principled way of setting an upper limit to how many such concepts or words it depends on. One could seek help in the analytic/synthetic distinction, trying to say – for instance – that the meaning of a word only depends on the meaning of those words which are connected to the former through analytic inferences (and ditto for concepts, *mutatis mutandis*). Unfortunately, Fodor and Lepore observe, the analytic/synthetic distinction was convincingly criticised by Quine as being unprincipled, so little help is forthcoming from that in order to contrast the slippery slope effect. This leaves the way open to *Holism*, which they cash out as the idea that, if a word (or concept) has semantic properties, a lot of, and potentially every other word (or concept), must have them. Holism has been criticised as having all sorts of unpalatable consequences: for instance that, in order to know (learn) the meaning of a word *w*, one would have to know (learn) the entire language. Or, in order to understand what a certain word *w* means in someone's idiolect, one would have to understand all of it (cf. Dummett, 1973). Ultimately, as urged by Dummett (1991), Holism would render communication impossible. Other unpleasant consequences have to do with the possibility of maintaining scientific Realism and retaining a respectable theory of the contents of our intentional states (Fodor and Lepore, 1992).

The argument that goes from the supposition that concepts and words are internally structured (or *anatomic*, as Fodor and Lepore have it) to the conclusion that their semantic properties must (most probably) be holistic, relies on two implicit premises: firstly, that if the analytic/synthetic distinction will not work, nothing else will. Secondly, that what would be needed to interrupt the slippery slope is a distinction which is *principled*. The analytic/synthetic distinction being unprincipled, together with the assumption to the effect that if the former will not work, nothing else will, allegedly licenses the conclusion that meaning will most probably have to be conceived holistically. But this need not be so.

It may be that some distinction different from the analytic/synthetic distinction, which is moreover not principled, *could* do the job. It may be that the most appropriate distinction between the semantic properties that count and those that do not count for an item to be meaningful *cuts across* the analytic/synthetic divide, including not just truths that are analytic, but also empirical truths, both contingent and necessary and with varying degrees of revisability (see Marconi, 1997). Moreover, it may be the case that the distinction is to be individuated on a *case-by-case* basis, that is, not by employing general, all-purpose principles, but by investigating the features that compose the meaning of words in actual, day-to-day use by competent speakers (see again some considerations in Marconi, 1997). Moreover, the features that count for an item's having semantic properties need not be invariably the same for all speakers and for all situations; it may be that, among a set of features, at least *some* features should be shared by any two speakers who happen to employ the same concept or word during a certain exchange, but these features need not constitute a take-it-or-leave-it package: that some of them are shared is necessary, but not that all of them are *jointly* shared. This view is considered but somewhat dismissed by Fodor and Lepore (1992, pp. 27ff.), yet Perry (1994) manages to build a fairly plausible case for it.

All in all, what emerges is that the threat of Holism waved by Fodor and Lepore is not as looming and inevitable as they make it seem. A number of strategies are available in order to trace a distinction between what counts and what does not for an item's possession of semantic properties, which do not involve appealing to the analytic/synthetic or to any other principled distinction, but which nevertheless seem to provide a promising way of stopping the slippery slope to semantic Holism.

The most radical alternative to Holism is *Atomism*, according to which the meaning of a word is 'punctuate', that is, it does not depend on any other meaning of any other word. Fodor's (1998) famous version of conceptual Atomism has it that concepts (and derivatively, word meanings) are nothing but mental symbols in the language of thought, whose content is determined by symbol–world relations and not by structural aspects such as inferential role or their relationship to other concepts. The content of a concept is the object or property which is 'locked' to it through a causal–nomic link, and as such it bears no internal structure, nor requires that any other concept is in place. Adopting Fodor's Atomism for the conceptual and lexical realm certainly avoids falling prey to Holism, but at the same time is bound to leave one at a loss as to a number of aspects.

One of these aspects has to do with the fact that adopting an atomistic approach with respect to concepts or lexical meaning implies supposing that concepts or words give a semantically determinate contribution to sentences, that is, that in virtue of their causal–nomic link with their reference, these invariably have a semantically determined content. This presumption, however, contrasts with the widespread intuition to the effect that words may give incomplete or under-determined contributions to the truth-conditions of the utterances in which they occur. So, for instance, the atomist would say that, in a sentence like 'Jill is ready', the word 'ready' contributes the property BEING READY, which is internally unstructured and is simply linked to the word through causal-cum-nomological connections. Yet listening to an utterance of this sentence is likely to trigger requests of completion such as 'Ready for what?' If the atomist supposes that the sentence is semantically determined, such a question is not easily accounted for. (Note that similar considerations apply not just to sentences in the natural language, but also to sentences in the language of thought. The fact that the mental symbol READY is locked to the property of being ready still does not answer such a question as 'Ready for what?'.)

A possible way for the atomist to explain intuitions of incompleteness and requests for completion is that the word (concept) 'being ready', for instance, is associated with some constraints like 'being ready is being ready for something', which express semantic or conceptual truths, but nevertheless play no role in fixing the meaning of the lexical entry, that is, they are not meaning-constitutive.

These constraints may not be meaning-constitutive in the sense that they do not fix a word's reference in the way privileged by Fodor – through causal and nomic links. Yet, if these atomistically conceived semantic properties do not suffice to provide a determinate truth-conditional contribution *and* there are semantic/conceptual truths that provide guidelines as to how to obtain complete truth-conditions, then these would seem meaning-constitutive after all, at least in the following sense: they state truths that, if disregarded, can result in intuitions of semantic incompleteness or other kinds of defectiveness. For instance, disregarding the truth to the effect that rain falls in some location brings to intuitions of semantic incompleteness – an incapability to specify the sentence's truth-conditions; and the same happens if one disregards the truth to the effect that being ready is being ready for something. Moreover, as already mentioned in section 4.3.3, conjoining an affirmation of, for instance, 'It's raining' with a denial of one of these truths results in outright contradiction, as testified by a statement of 'It's raining, but not in any place'. So there is an important sense in which these truths *are* meaning-constitutive, for disregarding them may result in intuitions of semantic incompleteness and even contradiction – although they may not be meaning-constitutive in Fodor's sense, in that they are not needed to fix a word's or concept's reference.

Thus, the point here is that the notion itself of meaning-constitutiveness is ambivalent: in Fodor's treatment, that a certain aspect is meaning-constitutive means that it fixes the word's or concept's meaning through causal and nomic relations with the world: we may speak of it as an *external* meaning-constitutiveness. External meaning-constitutiveness is not incompatible with *another* notion of meaning-constitutiveness which focuses on the semantic relations and effects associated with a correct or incorrect application of the lexical item at issue: we may call this *applicative* meaning-constitutiveness. Since constraints like 'to rain is to rain in some location' or 'being ready is being ready for some purpose' clearly pose restrictions on correct and incorrect applications of attendant concepts and words like 'to rain' and 'being ready', and since these constraints are not – in principle – in contrast with a Fodorian construal of meaning-constitutiveness (because they relate to *a different notion* of it), it follows that there is no reason not to endorse the *applicative* understanding of meaning-constitutiveness perhaps along with an external, Fodor-style conception of meaning-constitutiveness. This, however, implies departing from Fodor's word and adopting *a dual account of meaning-constitutiveness*, which clearly goes counter to the Atomist theory which aspires to a single, external notion of meaning-constitutiveness.

A recent proposal made by Borg (2012a), which may be regarded as an attempt to block a combination of these two takes on meaning-constitutiveness, argues that, on the one hand, meaning is punctuate and constituted by relations that obtain between words and the world; on the other hand, lexical entries do contain some information which, however, matters only for our *syntactic competence* with the word and not for our semantic competence. Thus, according to her proposal, the meaning of the verb 'hit' is established through causal and nomic relations with the property of hitting; the lexical entry 'hit' may be associated with information such as 'hitting is a manner of motion' or 'hitting implies making contact with something' but this information would only matter for a speaker's competence on *which syntactic constructions* the word is allowed or not allowed to enter. As she remarks, it would be possible for a speaker to know the meaning of 'hit', that is to know that 'hit' refers to hitting, but to be ignorant as to the information that hitting is a manner of motion or that it implies making contact. On the assumption that this kind of semantic information affects the syntactic behaviour of the word, a person who were ignorant as to such information would be predicted to have mistaken ideas on the syntactic environments the verb 'hit' is admitted to. For example, she might think that 'Jack hit at Jill' is incorrect, while it is in fact correct (see Borg, 2012a, p. 195).

Borg's proposal is ultimately that, although 'hitting is a manner of motion' and 'hitting implies making contact with something' are pieces of semantic information, this information only impacts a speaker's syntactic competence, not her semantic competence. Yet it seems to me that being ignorant of this information jeopardises not only one's syntactic competence, but also one's *semantic* competence. To see this, let us grant that there is a sense in which one *is* semantically competent on 'hit' if one knows that 'hit' refers to hitting; here again the notion of competence may be tailored to one's semantics, so that one counts as competent insofar as one knows the facts that are meaning-constitutive in one's privileged sense. Meaning-constitutiveness here is understood along externalist lines, in such a way that a certain aspect is meaning-constitutive if it fixes meaning through causal and nomic relations. Consequently, the notion of competence will fit the externalist account too, in such a way that being competent amounts to being appropriately causally and nomically related with the world in such a way as knowing that 'hit' refers to hitting. The question here is whether there is *a pre-theoretical notion of semantic competence* according to which a person who does not know that, for instance, hitting is a manner of motion, but knows that 'hit' refers to hitting is competent. My inclination would be not to regard such a person as *fully* semantically competent: although she has a partial grasp of what the meaning of 'hit' is by being appropriately related with the property of hitting (whatever that may be), she lacks knowledge of those truths that would allow her to articulate, for herself and for others, the notion of hitting by 'unpacking it' so to speak, by decomposing it into simpler constituents. The account of semantic competence that does justice to this pre-theoretical insight is one in which an 'externalist', reference-based semantic competence combines with an 'internalist', structure-based one, thus sanctioning a *dual approach* to semantic competence. This approach would run parallel to a dual semantic approach to meaning-constitutiveness, according to which there is both an *external* meaning-constitutiveness, whereby what constitutes meaning flows from causal–nomic relations, and an *applicative* meaning-constitutiveness, whereby what constitutes meaning flows from truths that constrain semantic relations, inferences and intuitions.

The upshot of our critical assessment of Atomism is that *there must be some meaning-constitutive constraints built into lexical meaning.* This goes counter to Atomism as the theory that meaning is internally unstructured, even though it does not rule out that meaning-constitutiveness could be specified *also* in externalist, referential terms.

The conclusion to be drawn from these – purely negative – considerations is that: (i) if, on the one hand, there are resources available to counteract the Holism threat, and (ii) if, on the other hand,

Atomism should be superseded by a conception of meaning which regards concepts and words as *also* internally complex, then we have enough ingredients to support the position that concepts or word meanings are internally structured and that their semantic properties are dependent on the semantic properties of some, *but not all*, other concepts or words (see Dummett, 1993, p. 44). This is tantamount to opening the door to a *Molecularist* proposal concerning the semantic properties of concepts and words.

Conclusion

In this chapter, I have advanced and defended a positive proposal concerning the context-sensitivity of semantically under-determined expressions like 'It's raining', 'Jill is ready' and so on.

- The first step prior to elaborating on the proposal has been that of defending its legitimacy. Firstly, I have argued that, other things being equal, if a semantic account of the context-sensitivity of semantically under-determined expressions is available, it would be preferable to a pragmatic account. The main reasons for this are: first, a semantic account appeals to *stable features* of an expression and thus to one's well-acquired and consolidated competence, which are the resources that are mobilised in *ordinary* situations of communication; secondly, a semantic account ensures a *continuity* between the treatment of context-insensitive, context-sensitive (indexical or demonstrative) and semantically under-determined expressions: the semantics of all these expressions seems to be based on compositionality and convention, and it is an added value of a theory that it captures this continuity.
- I have claimed that it is plausible to envisage an account of the context-sensitivity of semantically under-determined sentences that traces this context-sensitivity to their semantics and not necessarily to their syntax. I have argued that it makes sense to pursue the idea that a sentence's semantic structure may be more complex than its syntactic structure. In order to show this, I have drawn attention to what I have dubbed 'zero-readings' – that is, sentences in which a predicate like 'to rain' is correctly used as monadic. The aim of my arguments was to license the idea that, at times, we may have to complete a sentence's content only with the aid of semantic/conceptual constraints, which correspond to no syntactic constraint.
- I have moved to the chapter's positive proposal, according to which the context-sensitivity of semantically under-determined sentences

and the resolution of this under-determinacy are to be traced to *conceptual constraints*. Conceptual constraints are ways of organising and structuring thought and language use with regard to a number of areas of discourse. For instance, a conceptual constraint associated with 'to rain' is that rain has to occur at some location; a conceptual constraint concerning 'ready' is that being ready is being so for some purpose, or activity. Conceptual constraints may be thought to be part of conceptual *schemata* or *frames*. Moreover, some conceptual constraints seem to be represented linguistically as *arguments*, others as *adjuncts*.

- The resolution of semantic under-determinacy is guided by conceptual constraints; that is, it is our competence with these constraints that provides us with directions as to how to complete the content of these sentences. The completion thus effected is an entirely semantic process, for different reasons. First of all, conceptual constraints help us to structure thought and discourse in a *semantically correct* way (where this is contrasted by nonsense, category mistakes and so on); they ensure *systematicity*; and they preserve the *compositionality* of the content of our utterances; they act at the level of *what is said* with an utterance, and not of what is implicated, as shown by detachability and cancellation tests; and they admit a certain amount of pragmatics, though the processes are still *controlled by semantics*.
- The picture of conceptual (and derivatively lexical) semantics I have promoted so far is most reasonably accompanied by a Molecularist account of their semantic properties. I defend this thesis with two purely negative arguments. Firstly, I resist the argument to the effect that, once it is admitted that concepts or lexemes are internally structured and that the analytic/synthetic distinction is not tenable, there is no way to avoid semantic Holism. Secondly, I criticise semantic Atomism on account of its too restricted notion of meaning-constitutiveness and semantic competence. I conclude that Molecularism, namely the thesis that the meaning (of a concept or word) is composite and that it depends on some but not all meanings (of other words or concepts), is the most reasonable compromise between the two extremes of Holism and Atomism.

5
Semantic Under-Determinacy, Comprehension and Meta-Representation

The problem I will be concerned with in the present chapter may be stated as follows: *how is utterance comprehension possible, given semantic under-determinacy?* The question concerns in particular the mechanisms through which a hearer comes to understand what the speaker means with the utterance of a semantically under-determined sentence. Utterance comprehension may be equated with knowledge of the truth-conditions of a certain utterance *u*; if semantically under-determined sentences fail to determine a truth-condition for their utterances (even provided ambiguity and indexicality resolution), how do hearers manage to understand utterances of them?

The chapter is structured thus. I will provide an overview of some of the main positions defended so far concerning utterance comprehension, *given* semantic under-determinacy: in section 5.1 I will present what I shall call the 'Inferentialist' view (mainly due to Grice, and refined by Carston and Sperber and Wilson), while in section 5.2 I will introduce what I shall call the 'anti-Inferentialist' view (in two versions, Millikan's and Recanati's). In section 5.3, I will argue against the anti-Inferentialist view, defending the claim that utterance comprehension is, after all, (also) a matter of inference. In section 5.4, I will argue, against the Inferentialist view, that the inferences we use in order to gain comprehension of utterances of semantically under-determined sentences need not result in *meta-representations,* meaning that their conclusion need not be about the intentions and beliefs of speakers. In section 5.5, I will outline a picture of comprehension as inferential and not distinctively meta-representational, compatible with the Conceptual Constraints View presented in the previous chapter. In section 5.6 I will illustrate the benefits of the view and face some major objections. In section 5.7 I will finally compare the model proposed in this chapter with an approach to utterance understanding in terms of 'egocentricity'.

5.1 Inferential approaches: from Grice to Relevance Theory

The idea that utterance comprehension is a matter of inference may find a precedent in Grice's views concerning the working out of implicatures. Grice famously articulated the difference between *sentence meaning* and *speaker's meaning*. Linguistic competence (plus knowledge of the context) is sufficient for a hearer in order to identify a sentence's meaning (in context), however it does not suffice in order to figure out the speaker's meaning, that is, that portion of what is communicated by an utterance that depends on the intentions of the utterer. In order to obtain the latter content, distinctively inferential competences are needed, together with other capacities that we may call 'meta-representational'.

Grice's model is specifically designed to account for all those cases in which, by uttering a certain sentence, the speaker *implies or suggests* something in addition. Here is a rather typical example. John asks Mary if she would like to go to the cinema and she answers 'I am tired'. Mary's utterance suggests that she does not want to go to the cinema, but in order to arrive at this, some reasoning needs to be done. Grice suggests that John starts from the premise to the effect that Mary said that she is tired and goes on with considerations like 'She wouldn't have said so if she didn't want to go to the cinema', 'She knows that I can suppose this [that she doesn't want to go to the cinema]', 'She hasn't done anything to stop me believing this', 'She intends me to believe this', 'Therefore, she means or implies that she doesn't want to go to the cinema'.

The first important feature of this 'working out' schema is that it is an instance of *inference to the best explanation*, where the explanandum is Mary's utterance of 'I am tired'. The hearer assumes that, despite the seeming irrelevance of what has been said, the speaker is nevertheless cooperating with the communicative enterprise; with this assumption in the background, the hearer follows the above train of reasoning that leads him to conclude that the speaker is implying that she does not want to go to the cinema.

The second important feature of this inference is that its premises and conclusion all feature an attribution of attitude to the speaker, for instance a belief attribution or an intention attribution. Attributing a belief, or intention, or desire to another subject is a way of representing what is going on in that subject's mind; it is a way of representing another subject's mental representation. Let us call any representation of another's mental representation a *meta-representation*. Thus, the inferential schema set forth by Grice contains, at each step, a meta-representation, such as 'Mary believes that φ', 'Mary means/implies that φ'.

Fully cognitively developed adults are naturally capable of forming and entertaining meta-representations, so Grice's model is plausible insofar as it is possible for any such individual to go through one of these inferences. Yet there is an interpretation of Grice's proposal that makes it *cognitively too demanding*, as some authors have remarked (see Sperber, 2000; Wilson, 2000; Sperber and Wilson, 2002).

First of all, it is implausible that even fully developed adults ordinarily interpret utterances by performing such complex inferences in an *overt and in a step-by-step fashion*. That is, it is implausible to suppose that listeners explicitly formulate the reasoning's premises in their mind, explicitly follow a linear train of reasoning and explicitly draw the conclusion.

The same considerations have been advanced with respect to *meta-representation*: it is implausible that fully developed adults consciously or explicitly formulate meta-representations (even second-order ones) like 'She intends me to believe this' or 'She knows I can suppose this' and so on. Quite to the contrary, it seems that if we entertain any meta-representations, we do that implicitly or 'by default'. Significant evidence on this point comes from developmental psychology. Experiments have shown that pre-verbal infants, who most certainly lack the capacity to explicitly form meta-representations, are nevertheless capable of inferential communication (Bretherton, 1991; Behne et al., 2011; Grassman et al., 2009; Tomasello, 2001). This suggests that meta-representations are taken care of by capacities that are implicit, covert and probably *much less sophisticated* than the ones that are involved at a conscious level.

These considerations have brought Relevance Theorists to propose a revision of the Gricean model. This revision is inscribed in the more general programme of Relevance Theory, in which implicature derivation and utterance comprehension are seen as responding to the same mechanisms. The operation of these common mechanisms is defended on the account of what seems a greater psychological plausibility.

The whole model is still inferential, albeit inference is here construed as implicit, subpersonal, fast and painless (Sperber, 1995; Carston, 2002b). Moreover, it is based on and driven by the notion of *relevance*, where a stimulus is defined as relevant when it has the most cognitive effects at the lowest computational cost. Thus, interpreting an utterance is a matter of deriving the content that is most cognitively useful by following a path of least effort (see Sperber and Wilson, 1986, p. 153). Most importantly though, the inferences employed in utterance understanding are performed by a *modular component* of our mind specifically dedicated to mind-reading or meta-representation.

With respect to meta-representation, then, the two models differ in the *level of sophistication*: a Gricean inference has both meta-representational premises and conclusion, and it could be easily interpreted as requiring the performer to have quite developed representational and reflective capacities.[1] By contrast, Relevance-Theoretic inference, being carried out by a modular component, only needs to give a meta-representational conclusion ('X means that φ'), while its premises need not be meta-representational and, in fact, they do not even need to be accessible to one's awareness. As Sperber explicitly claims,

> The conclusion of such an interpretation process is an attribution of a meaning to the speaker, hence a metarepresentation, but the premises in the inference process need not be metarepresentational. Therefore this procedure can be followed by a relatively unsophisticated metarepresenter. (Sperber, 2000, p. 133)

I will return to the Relevance-Theoretic view of utterance comprehension, and especially to Sperber's proposal in section 5.4, where I will criticise precisely the contention spelled out in this passage. As I will argue, we have reasons to think that the conclusion of an interpretation process *need not be* a meta-representation. This will suggest an alternative to the Gricean/Relevance-Theoretic account of utterance comprehension presented in this section. Prior to turning to this task, though, I will present and resist a view of utterance comprehension which is diametrically opposed to the Inferentialist approach just considered, in that it regards utterance comprehension as non-inferential.

5.2 Non-inferential approaches

A position which strongly contrasts with the account just presented has it that understanding tokens of sentences of a natural language is an altogether *non-inferential* activity. According to Ruth Millikan, for example, there is no inferential step between hearing an utterance and knowing what state of affairs it speaks about. Language understanding is as direct as perception. Of course, the reflective speaker could voluntarily focus on the items that serve as a vehicle – the phonemes or graphemes, the words, their meanings, the sentence's syntax – and from those infer

Semantic Under-Determinacy, Comprehension and Meta-Representation 151

the content of the uttered sentence. However, this is likely to happen only in a minority of cases, and it implies performing a less natural or spontaneous task (see Millikan, 2004, p. 121).

Even though language understanding does not require inference on the part of the hearer, this still does not mean that there are no processes whatsoever that allow the hearer to go from the auditory perception of a certain utterance to the perception of the state of affairs spoken about. These processes are not inferential, but rather merely *translational*: they involve moving from one representation to another. In particular, these processes are not inferential in the sense that: (i) they cannot be modelled in terms of premises and conclusion; (ii) they involve 'functionally insulated' signs, that is, symbols that are designed to serve only one purpose (or very few ones) and can interact only with items very limited in number and format.

The translational model returns a picture in which hearers can employ language in order to have access, via translation, to the cognitions and perceptions of the speakers and, ultimately, to the states of affairs that they talk about. This mechanism literally *extends* our own perceptual system (see Millikan, 1984, pp. 304–5) and has as a consequence that there is no difference between seeing that p and being told that p. In both cases we have a *perceptual* access to the state of affairs that p (Millikan, 2004, p. 122).

There are other ways for processes of utterance understanding to be non-inferential, besides being translational in Millikan's privileged sense. Recanati (2002b) considers cases in which a sentence's schematic meaning is 'fleshed out' so as to be made propositional; he observes that the meanings that are subject to these processes of 'free enrichment' or 'completion' are too abstract and schematic in order to be considered conceptual representations. He then surmises that these mechanisms of supplementation, since they manipulate non-conceptual (or non-*fully* conceptual) contents, are not inferential. Suppose John utters 'It's raining', meaning that it is raining in Paris. This sentence expresses the content *that it's raining*, which exhibits a conceptual gap – corresponding to the locational aspect. The mechanism of completion by which the content gets 'fleshed out' is considered by Recanati as non-inferential to the extent that it takes as its starting point a content which is not (fully) conceptual.

A second set of processes he considers are what he calls 'transfer'. Semantic transfer is involved in non-literal talk, and it is typically non-truth-preserving. Consider for example the transfer involved in understanding an utterance of 'The ham sandwich is getting restless': it brings the hearer from the false proposition *that the ham sandwich is getting restless* to the true proposition *that the ham-sandwich-orderer is getting restless*. In these cases what connects the first, semantically expressed, proposition to the second, intended one, is an 'associative' link which is by no means truth-preserving, and that is surely not a logical entailment.

To sum up, in this section we reviewed three ways in which utterance understanding could be regarded as non-inferential: one could claim, like Millikan, that understanding an utterance involves merely *translational* processes, but also, like Recanati, that it involves *free-enriching* and *associative* processes. Free-enriching processes count as non-inferential to the extent that they manipulate non-(fully) conceptual material, while associative processes are not inferential insofar as they may not preserve truth.

5.3 Inferences, after all

The aim of this section is to counter the idea that the comprehension of semantically under-determined sentences such as 'It's raining', 'Jill is ready', 'The leaves are green' and so on, is a non-inferential process like those envisaged by Millikan or Recanati.

First of all, regarding the translational model proposed by Millikan, even though it would seem to work fine as far as understanding sentences that suffer from no semantic defectiveness is concerned, it is not at all clear how utterance comprehension would proceed in cases where the sentences at issue suffer from semantic under-determinacy or involve some form of context-sensitivity. To illustrate the point, suppose Charles hears an utterance of 'It's raining': in Millikan's view – who by the way uses exactly the sentence 'It's raining' as an example (Millikan, 2004, p. 122) – through this act of utterance Charles gains direct access to the state of affairs that it is raining, so that being told that it is raining and seeing that it is raining end up as entirely equivalent processes. Yet Millikan seems to be a little too quick on the example, in that she neglects that, in order fully to understand that utterance in the sense of accessing the particular state of affairs talked about (that it is raining in Paris, say), one cannot merely translate one linguistic representation into a mental representation, but needs also to figure out a number of other aspects, such as what place is salient. That is, one must *integrate* the information one acquires linguistically with information one acquires from context – perhaps perceptually, or through other utterances, or even through reasoning. Integration of this information cannot be accomplished simply with the help of translation, because it involves pieces of information coming from different sources (language comprehension, perception, reasoning) that must first be put into a single format and then dealt with in such a way that the contextual information is used together with the linguistically gained information so as to obtain a representation of, and access to, a *specific* state of affairs (it is raining in Paris, say). Going back to Charles witnessing an utterance of 'It's raining': in order to arrive at any specific state of affairs, he will need to figure out *where* it is raining; this information may be acquired in many non-linguistic ways, for instance through perception (seeing the rain outside or feeling it on one's skin), or through some kind of reasoning. Ultimately, he will combine the information obtained though language comprehension (that it is raining) with the information obtained though these other channels (that it is raining in *l*, where *l* is a specific place) so as to conclude that what the speaker said is that it is raining in *l*. I do not see how this information could be put together and employed fruitfully if not by means of some inferential process, no matter how implicit or subpersonal: for instance, an inference to the best explanation to the effect that if it was said that it is raining, and it is raining in *l*, then the utterance must be true iff it is raining in *l*. So, perhaps Millikan's translational model works as long as understanding utterances of context-*insensitive* sentences is concerned, but it seems to me it has to admit some form of inference whenever the comprehension of context-*sensitive* sentences in a particular conversational setting is at stake.

As to Recanati, he emphasises that a process can be said to be 'inferential' only if it takes as its input a conceptual content. Some sentences express contents that are very 'abstract' or 'schematic'. This may make these contents not conceptually structured enough to enter an inference (see Recanati, 2002b, p. 122). The conclusion would be that, since they involve non-conceptual contents, processes of enrichment of the content of certain sentences are non-inferential. In the case of 'It's raining', Recanati would say that, since the content *that it's raining* is too abstract or schematic, it is non-conceptual, and hence there can be no account in which the enriched content *that it's raining in Paris* is the result of an inference.

I do not agree with Recanati's point. The fact that a content is 'abstract' or 'schematic' may make it under-determined, that is incapable of expressing a truth-condition in a context of utterance, but it does not entail that it lacks a conceptual structure. In the case of 'It's raining', it seems to me evident that the content expressed by the sentence is a fully conceptually structured content. The conceptual structure of the predicate 'to rain' may not appear in the sentence's surface representation, however the lexical concept TO RAIN arguably is associated with at least a slot for a locational component even though this may remain silent in the sentence's articulation. As a result, the sentence fails to express a proposition, but it does have a conceptual structure. So, it seems to me that Recanati is here labelling as non-conceptuality what is simply lack of propositional status (non-propositionality).

Moreover, the fact that the locational component is not explicitly articulated in the sentence may result in the sentence's content being non-propositional, yet this by no means prevents *using the sentence as a premise in an inferential reasoning*. As far as I can see, the following is a perfectly acceptable inference, in which it is sensible and safe to use a sentence like 'It's raining' although this does not strictly speaking express a proposition. One may reconstruct the reasoning as follows: the first premise tells us that it is true that it's raining – it doesn't matter whether we are capable of determining *whether* it is in fact true, and what place is involved in this process of verification; the second premise tells us that if it is true that it is raining, then it is true that the weather is not good (that it cannot be the case that it is raining and not be the case that the weather is not good). This implies that one is in a position to apply *modus ponens*, thus validly inferring the conclusion that the weather is not good from the two previous premises.

[1] It's raining.
[2] If it's raining, the weather is not good.
[3] The weather is not good.

This example shows that the non-propositional status of the semantic content of a sentence like 'It's raining' does not stand in the way of its participating in a valid inference.

In sum, it seems that the translational model promoted by Millikan should make room for inferential utterance comprehension when utterances of semantically under-determined sentences are at play; while Recanati's contention that comprehension of semantically under-determined utterances cannot be inferential because these express non-conceptual contents is ill-advised, first because it conflates non-conceptuality with non-propositionality, and second because the latter does not hinder participation in an inference.

5.4 Reconsidering the role of meta-representation

As we saw in section 5.1, Grice's working-out schema for implicatures has been criticised on the account that it could be interpreted as requiring too complex, personal-level inferences and too pervasive a role for meta-representation. The account put forth by Sperber, by contrast, admits subpersonal, not explicitly meta-representational, processes which however do deliver meta-representational results as their final step. In this section, I wish to argue against the idea that inferential processes of comprehension like those posited by Sperber imply reaching a meta-representational conclusion.

The idea that comprehension of, for instance, semantically under-determined sentences need not result in any meta-representation seems to be suggested by our intuitions. A test could help to show this point more clearly. The basic idea underlying the test is that of asking subjects to report what they understand, after having read or heard a brief story which culminates with an utterance of a semantically under-determined sentence such as 'It's raining'. For instance, subjects may be asked to read/hear the following story:

> Suppose you have a friend who lives in Paris. You often call each other on Skype, and you often begin the conversation by exchanging information about the weather in each of your locations of residence. Suppose you are on one of these Skype calls and you ask your friend: 'So, what's the weather in Paris?' She answers: 'Not very good. It's raining'. What have you understood from her answer?

The most immediate answer to the final question seems to be something like 'That it's raining in Paris', but also 'That the weather isn't very good, since it's raining in Paris'. The point is that in this scenario, if one were asked a generic and neutral question as to what one has understood of a speaker's utterance, one's most spontaneous response would not, I submit, involve a meta-representation. If Sperber's account were on the right track – that is, if comprehension processes had a meta-representation *as their conclusion*, the result would have to be different: the most spontaneous response to the question 'What have you understood?' would have to be 'That she means that it's raining in Paris'.

This example seems to pose a challenge for Sperber's account. The case just presented illustrates that our primary and most natural intuitions as to 'what we have understood' of a given utterance do not involve meta-representational contents of the form 'X believes that p', 'X means that q'. Note that the same result obtains, though perhaps less interestingly, if we change the final question into 'What did your friend say?' or also 'What did your friend mean?' To these questions as well, the most natural answer seems to be a non-meta-representational one, such as

'That it's raining in Paris', and not 'That she means that it's raining in Paris'. (It could be objected that these answers are good as far as they go, for they could be elliptical, leaving the possible meta-representational component unspoken only because it was already articulated in the question. But even if they were elliptical, I do not believe this would speak unequivocally in favour of the proponent of meta-representation: after all, the meta-representational component may even be articulated, but it would appear as a way of 'echoing' the earlier question, and not as a way of spontaneously reporting what one has understood.)

Be these intuitions as they may, there are at least two ways in which I could grant that meta-representation plays a role in comprehension. The first way has to do with the fact that, even though in the case just presented the speaker is interested in the proposition *that it's raining in Paris*, and not in the proposition *that the speaker means that it's raining in Paris*, in some other cases one may be interested precisely in the latter, meta-representational proposition. I expect that, when this happens, there needs to be a particular reason for being interested in entertaining the content *that the speaker means that p*. Perhaps the speaker has expressed herself in a particularly indirect, convoluted or cryptic way. Indeed there may be contexts in which the point is exactly that of entertaining a meta-representation as the result of a process of interpretation, for instance when dealing with the exegesis of literary, poetic, legal or other very technical texts. In these cases, it may be interesting for the interpreter to entertain a proposition of the form 'X means that p', especially if the piece of exegesis has to be explained or anyway transmitted to another individual. Cases of conversational implicature may give rise to the same phenomenon: suppose you read a recommendation letter in which it were stated that the student in question has good handwriting and regularly attends seminars. When reporting the content of the letter to a third party, it may be useful to do it in meta-representational terms, for instance by saying 'He implied that the student is not very good'.

Comprehension processes that culminate with meta-representational conclusions are certainly part of our cognitive life and linguistic practices, however they seem to be confined to special contexts, in which the communicative intentions of the speaker are not completely clear for various reasons, ranging from the kind of language or jargon used, to intentions to suggest rather than state some content, but even (I suppose) slips of the tongue or malapropisms. To suppose that all utterance comprehension leads invariably to entertain a meta-representation as its outcome is to conflate it with this more specific cognitive enterprise, which we may call 'hermeneutics'. Hermeneutics may be defined as the task of interpreting an utterance with the aim of settling the question of what the speaker/writer means; in other words, *it is an interpretive enterprise whose final goal is entertaining a meta-representation 'X means that φ'*. By contrast, comprehension may involve working out, on certain grounds, a simple 'object-level' representation φ. This is the first way in which I admit that meta-representation could have a role in utterance comprehension (broadly construed).

Secondly, I am ready to grant that the *concept* of utterance comprehension necessarily involves meta-representation, that is, that the following is a conceptual, a priori truth: necessarily, understanding that an utterance *u* has the content that *p* implies understanding what the speaker of *u* means. That is, understanding the content of an utterance is nothing but understanding what the utterer means. This requirement holds independently of whether subjects actually entertain a meta-representation as the result of a process of utterance interpretation; indeed whether or not this requirement is satisfied may not be *transparent* to a subject. Nevertheless, every instance of utterance comprehension should comply with this requirement in such a way that, if a speaker were to understand an utterance but fail to understand what the speaker means, that would not count as comprehension of *that* utterance. For instance, it seems that if one were to hear an utterance of 'It's cold here' (with the speaker referring to Paris) and understand the content that it is cold *in the place of utterance* – but without understanding that it is cold *in Paris*, one would not count as understanding *that* utterance, because one would have failed to fully understand what the speaker means.

Moreover, if a subject is competent about the concept 'comprehension' and is aware that she is engaged in utterance comprehension, I take it that she should cognise this truth at least at an *implicit* or *dispositional* level. This would also involve appreciating (at least at the implicit or dispositional level) the fact that, if the speaker uttered sentence *S*, then *she means something* by it, and it is the job of the hearer to find out. However, none of this entails that the subject needs to entertain any meta-representation at the cognitive level as the final result of the comprehension process. In fact, she may act *on the background assumption* that the speaker means something by her utterance *u* of *S* and focus directly on figuring out the content expressed by *u*, this implying that she will get a simple, object-level content *p* as the result of the comprehension process.

Moreover, if a subject is *not* competent about the concept of comprehension and she is not aware that she is running a comprehension task (for example, a very young child who nevertheless has some language competences), she will not be required to cognise this truth at either level, or to appreciate that if the speaker uttered S, she must mean something which is the job of the hearer to find out.

These reflections shed light on three distinct elements: (i) meta-representation plays a *conceptual–normative* role for (the concept of) comprehension; (ii) being competent on the concept of utterance comprehension and aware of one's being a comprehender requires that one cognises and appreciates this conceptual–normative role of meta-representation, at least at an implicit or dispositional level; (iii) appreciation of the conceptual–normative role of meta-representation in utterance comprehension *does not imply entertaining any meta-representations at the cognitive level*, as a result of one's running a comprehension process, because appreciating this role may imply holding some background assumptions.

These considerations lead to a way of clearly stating the difference between the account I am going to defend and Sperber's account: in the former, comprehension is *conceptually* meta-representational, but need not be cognitively meta-representational, while on Sperber's view, comprehension is *mainly cognitively* meta-representational. If the considerations presented so far are on the right track, Sperber's idea need not hold: utterance comprehension qua cognitive process may be non meta-representational or, at a minimum, the conclusion of such a comprehension process need not be meta-representational.

5.5 Conceptual constraints and non-meta-representational comprehension

In the previous chapter, I defended the view that the context-sensitivity of such sentences as 'It's raining', 'Jill is ready', 'The leaves are green' and so on is traceable to what I have called conceptual constraints. For example, the verb 'to rain' is associated with the conceptual constraint to the effect that if it rains, it rains somewhere. Conceptual constraints guide the supplementation of the content of semantically under-determined sentences. To the extent that such completions are effected in most cases by those who happen to read and hear occurrences of these sentences, and insofar as these individuals are engaged in the task of understanding what is being said with an utterance, we may claim that *conceptual constraints guide utterance comprehension*.

The guiding role of conceptual constraints is something that a proponent of the meta-representational model of utterance comprehension could perfectly well acknowledge. For instance, a Relevance Theorist could grant that, while engaged in reconstructing the content of an utterance of 'It's raining', the hearer could avail herself of some conceptual constraints in developing the 'logical form' of the sentence's semantic content, where the development of logical form consists in completing in various ways a schematic meaning (Sperber and Wilson, 1986, pp. 73, 181). Thus, a Relevance Theorist could grant that the logical form of 'It's raining' is expanded so as to create a slot for locations, which is to be filled with contextual information. Yet he or she will predictably maintain that this process is executed within the range of competence of a dedicated pragmatics module, which still delivers as its conclusion a meta-representation.

As we have seen, there are reasons to doubt that the conclusion of a comprehension process is a meta-representation, even though meta-representation certainly plays a conceptual–normative role in the notion of comprehension and that the speaker means something may be an implicit background assumption of the hearer.

In this section I would like to show that, once one recognises the role of conceptual constraints in the reconstruction of the content of an utterance, the role of meta-representation at the level of cognitive processes becomes secondary. Conceptual constraints may be sufficient, together with contextual clues, for the hearer to comprehend an utterance without resorting to meta-representation. The conceptual constraints proposal offers the means to overcome a model of utterance comprehension which relies heavily on meta-representation: using conceptual constraints plus contextual clues helps to run an inference whose premises and conclusion are non-meta-representational. Furthermore, even if the hearer may happen to employ meta-representational information in the inference, this does not imply that the conclusion of the inference has to be meta-representational. This contrasts not only with the Gricean model, in which meta-representation plays a massive role, but also with the Relevance-Theoretic view and especially Sperber's view as summarised in the quote at the end of section 5.1.

In what follows, I will illustrate a model for utterance comprehension that I will call the *Non-Meta model*. In showing how the model works, I will employ examples of semantically under-determined sentences and I will be relying on the conceptual constraints proposal I formulated in Chapter 4. Semantically under-determined sentences and the conceptual constraints account here provide a case study for the model and I do not rule out that a Non-Meta approach will also be applicable to other kinds of expressions. I will briefly illustrate some possible, further applications of it towards the end of the next section.

160 *Semantic Under-Determinacy and Communication*

In order to see the Non-Meta model at work, let us focus on an utterance of a semantically under-determined sentence like 'Jill is ready'. The hearer who endeavours to understand the content of this utterance may be viewed as going through an inferential process (albeit implicit or subpersonal), which could be reconstructed as follows: first, upon listening to that utterance of 'Jill is ready', the hearer may be viewed as presented with the semantic content <*Jill is ready*> (premise [1]). The hearer then exploits the conceptual constraints which she presumably masters to add premise [2] to the effect that being ready is being ready *for some purpose*. If, furthermore, the hearer has access to the particular context in which the utterance is performed and knows what activity is salient, she may add a further premise ([3]) introducing the activity for which Jill is ready, let us say skiing. By going through these three premises, the hearer may draw the conclusion to the effect that Jill is ready *for skiing*.

[1] Jill is ready.
[2] Being ready is being ready for some purpose.
[3] Skiing is the salient purpose.
[4] Jill is ready for skiing.

As one may have noted, the inference reproduced above does not involve any meta-representation, either in the form of an ascription of intention ('X intends that *p*') or belief ('X believes that *p*'), or even speech report ('X said that *p*').

It seems that, if the inference in [1]–[4] is a good reconstruction of a process really followed by hearers, then carrying out such an inference does not, *by itself*, require the use of any meta-representations of the form 'X believes/intends that *p*', or even 'X said that *p*', and so on. The interpretation of utterances of semantically under-determined sentences such as 'Jill is ready', 'It's raining', 'The leaves are green' and so on is therefore, *by itself*, not a task that requires the use of a hearer's mind-reading capacities.[2] We could instead describe the inference in [1]–[4] as the application on sentence meaning of predetermined constraints for organising thought and discourse, *plus* some independently and collaterally held information as to what is salient in context.

Yet, as anticipated some paragraphs ago, hearers may well be interested in, and therefore entertain, information about the attitudes of speakers, and there is no reason why this information should not figure in the inference, especially if the subject who performs the inference is perfectly capable of entertaining meta-representations. Though it is certainly true that some meta-representational premises may be used by a hearer, this by no means implies that the conclusion need be meta-representational as well. I will now illustrate a way in which meta-representations may play a role in a comprehension inference, without necessarily leading to a meta-representational conclusion.

It seems to me that meta-representation could help to *provide adequate grounds for one or more steps in the inference*. To illustrate, consider the implicit reasoning that a hearer has to perform when interpreting an utterance of 'It's raining'. In certain contexts, interpreting an utterance of 'It's raining' may require that one identifies what place the hearer is referring to, or talking about, or presupposing as relevant. In general, I shall regard the task of figuring out what a speaker is referring to, what a speaker is talking about, what a speaker is presupposing, and so on, as a mind-reading task, and therefore as a *meta-representational* task. If this is so, then in certain specific cases, one or more meta-representations may have to be entertained as one goes through the interpretive inference.

So suppose that, in the context of utterance at interest, the speaker intends to talk about the weather in Paris. On the view I propose, the hearer will run two tasks in parallel: the first is the interpretive process consisting in the application of the conceptual constraint to the effect that to rain is to rain somewhere. By means of this, the semantic/conceptual structure of the sentence may be 'expanded', thereby opening, as it were, a new conceptual/semantic slot to be filled in with an appropriate locational value. The second task is aimed at figuring out *what location the speaker is talking about*: this process should be regarded as meta-representational.

My proposal is that the meta-representational process delivers a proposition that provides *evidential support* for one of the passages in the conceptually constrained inference. This passage will concern what is going on in the context of the conversation, namely what is salient or relevant, and may be identified with premise [3] in the inference schema reported in what follows. I propose that the relation between premise [3] (or the like) and the meta-representation as to what the speaker is talking about will be such that the latter *epistemically supports* the former (it *justifies* it). In the case at hand, that the speaker is talking about Paris shall support epistemically premise [3] (rewritten as premise [3´]), to the effect that Paris is salient in context. The relation between the meta-representation and the premise is as follows:

[1] *It's raining.*
[2] To rain is to rain somewhere.

([3] The speaker is talking about Paris).
[3´] Paris is salient in context.
[4] *It's raining in Paris.*

This proposal allows us to integrate the idea that utterance interpretation could employ meta-representations (as to what the speaker is talking about, as to what she is referring to, and so on) with the idea that the conclusion of a comprehension process need not be meta-representational as well.

To sum up what I have proposed so far: the interpretation of utterances of semantically under-determined sentences is an inferential, conceptually constrained process which, *by itself*, does not seemingly require that hearers employ any meta-representational skill. Nevertheless, this inferential process may interact with meta-representations, namely in all those cases in which the hearer has to figure out what the speaker is referring to, talking about, or presupposing. In these cases, meta-representations may provide *epistemic support* for some of its steps, but by no means requires that a meta-representational conclusion is drawn.

The resulting model is one where the role of meta-representation is significantly reconsidered, if compared with the role assigned to meta-capacities by rival accounts. For example, in the Gricean schema, meta-representation had a pervasive role, since both the inference's premises and its conclusion were meta-representations. In the Relevance-Theoretic framework, processes delivering meta-representations were carried out by modular components: the reasoning's premises did not need to be explicitly meta-representational; nevertheless, it was maintained that the inference's conclusion is a meta-representation. The model I have proposed differs from both Grice's and the Relevance-Theorists' models in that it envisages inferences whose premises and conclusions may be wholly non-meta-representational and in which, in any case, at least the conclusion of the inference need not be meta-representational. If this is so, then *the role of meta-representation is to be largely reconsidered*. The differences between the three inferential accounts are illustrated in Table 5.1.

Note that the Non-Meta model is represented in the table as having it that language comprehension starts from *non*-meta-representational premises and ends with a *non*-meta-representational conclusion, thus being *wholly* meta-representation-free. However, what is truly crucial about the view, and distinguishes it from both the Gricean and the Relevance-Theoretic accounts, is *the thesis that utterance comprehension need not give rise to a meta-representational conclusion*. As already mentioned, it is not incompatible with my view that some of the premises in the inference

Semantic Under-Determinacy, Comprehension and Meta-Representation 163

Table 5.1 Comparing the Gricean, Relevance-Theoretic and Non-Meta accounts

Grice	Relevance Theory	Non-Meta
Meta-representational premises; Meta-representational conclusion	Non-meta-representational premises; Meta-representational conclusion	(Non)-meta-representational premises; Non-meta-representational conclusion; Meta-representations justify premises

may be meta-representational, as long as it is acknowledged that this does not entail that the conclusion is going to be meta-representational.

A small digression: actually, the theory could go even more radical and claim that even the information concerning what the speaker knows, what she is talking about, what she is referring to, which I have admitted as meta-representational and which provides epistemic support for some premises of the interpretive inference, *could be entertained non-meta-representationally*. How could this be possible? According to some theories of developmental psychology, attribution of attitudes to other subjects can and is typically non-meta-representational. Non-meta-representational attitude attribution may be achieved, according to Perner (1991, pp. 115–18) by enacting a 'Situation approach'. This implies picturing a subject who, say, wants that *p*, not as representing the state of affairs that *p* and being related with that representation, but as aiming directly at the situation that *p* (skipping the representational stage, so to speak). Suppose for instance that Polly wants to go to the movies; we can represent Polly as 'aiming' at the situation in which she is at the movies, without representing her as representing herself at the movies and being related with that representation. The same may go for attitudes like 'meaning', 'referring to', 'talking about'. Suppose that with her utterance of 'I got married and had a kid' Polly means that she got married and *then* had a kid: we could represent her meaning that content as her pointing to the situation in which she gets married first, and then has a kid. Or, suppose that Polly utters 'I like that' while staring at a statue. Again we may represent her as simply 'pointing at' or 'focusing attention on' or 'being concerned with' the statue as a physical object, with no need to represent her representing the statue in her mind. In all these cases, although we represent a relationship between the speaker and the environment, this relation is not one of representation (see also

Evans, 1982 and Proust, 2007). As a result, meta-representation is avoided and it could be avoided even in the Non-Meta inference described above. The picture seems attractive, however it cannot be an account of how a fully developed adult copes with utterance comprehension, since, as Perner himself admits, non-meta-representational attitude attribution has serious limitations. One of them is, for instance, that the thinker does not have a grasp of the fact that another subject may have a different perspective on the situation than the one she has, because she lacks the resources to conceive of mental representations. Indeed a non-meta-representational model of attitude attribution serves to explain how young children (under four years old) who allegedly lack a theory of mind can go about dealing with ascribing mental contents. The account has been extended to adults as well (Perner, 1991, pp. 250–1), insofar as they plausibly retain this approach as a *default*, effort-saving method for performing attitude attributions, reserving resorting to meta-representation for scenarios where error-fixing is required. However, the 'Situation approach' cannot be the whole story concerning our capacity to attribute mental contents to others. As a consequence, although the Non-Meta model should be open to the prospect that even background information may be entertained non-meta-representationally, it should avoid any expectation that this is so in general, or that this is an account of how psychologically mature individuals reason.

5.6 Advantages and objections

The Non-Meta model I have proposed brings some benefits with it. First of all, it sits nicely with the fact that speakers who lack access to any meta-representational information can nevertheless, in appropriate circumstances, be *reliable* in their working out the content of an utterance, because they can exploit conceptual constraints and *schemata* in general, plus contextual information which they need not either formulate or justify by means of a meta-representation.

A case in point could be that of a person whose meta-representational capacities are absent or impaired (a young child or a person with a specific mental impairment). According to the Non-Meta model, these subjects could – in appropriate circumstances – get at the content meant by the speaker with an utterance of, for instance, 'It's raining', because the process they would have to follow does not require them to entertain any meta-representations. It is sufficient that they master the language, that they are able to apply the relevant conceptual constraints and that they possess appropriate contextual information. For example, suppose

Charles, who lives in Paris, cannot meta-represent the intentions and beliefs of others, but knows that the speaker's utterance of 'It's raining' means that it is raining, *plus* that if it is raining, it is raining in some place. Suppose he also assumed (veridically, let us say), that every time someone says 'It's raining', that is because it is raining in Paris. From these elements he could conclude that it is raining in Paris, which would (let us say) be exactly what the speaker means. It seems that in these circumstances Charles can reliably infer what the speaker means even though he does not entertain any meta-representation.

It could be pointed out that, because of his incapacity to meta-represent, Charles cannot formulate the thought that that content is *what the speaker means*; or that he cannot entertain a background assumption to the effect that, when an individual utters a sentence, *she means something* (and *that* is what has to be found out by an interpreter). Therefore, what he carries out is not a process of comprehension, because by hypothesis the subject lacks the capacity to even grasp or appreciate the conceptual–normative role of meta-representation in utterance comprehension. I do not think this consequence is acceptable: in particular, I do not believe that *grasping or appreciating* the conceptual–normative role of meta-representation in utterance comprehension is required for utterance comprehension, although I deem it a conceptual truth that comprehension of an utterance is comprehension of what the speaker means. If this were a genuine requirement, we could not grant utterance comprehension to all those subjects who cannot perform mind-reading tasks (young children, people with mental impairments), while it seems to me clear that, as long as these subjects can reliably get at what the speaker means by employing their linguistic competences and contextual clues, they can be regarded as understanding in the full sense of the term.

The Non-Meta model has a good application potential, over and beyond the case study presented here, centred on semantic under-determinacy and conceptual constraints. The idea, in general, is that utterance comprehension can do without meta-representation because in a variety of cases hearers do not inquire into the beliefs and intentions of speakers in order to figure out what they mean, but they rather use rough-and-ready *schemata*, frames or representations of the world in order to reconstruct the content of certain utterances, reserving recourse to meta-representation to cases when a flaw in the communicative process occurs. One possible example pertains to the resolution of anaphoras and reference assignment to pronouns. To borrow an example from Recanati (1993, p. 265 cited in Recanati, 2004): suppose you hear an utterance of 'The policemen arrested Edgar. He had just stolen a wallet'. Here it is quite straightforward to presume that 'he' has the same reference as 'Edgar'. Recanati argues that this is due to our activating a stealing-and-getting-arrested frame, which affects reference assignment to the pronoun. In the case at hand, it seems plausible to suppose that the comprehension process does not require any meta-representation to be entertained, in that the activation of the relevant schema would seem to overthrow any potential appeal to what the speaker might mean with her utterance of 'He had just stolen a wallet'. This example illustrates that the Non-Meta model of utterance comprehension could be applied over and beyond semantically under-determined sentences and independently of the conceptual constraints proposal that I outlined in Chapter 4.

The model may also raise some objections, which I will confront in the remainder of this section. The first is an objection that may be called 'of the hasty acceptance'. If, the objection goes, the conclusion of the interpretive process is not a meta-representation of the form 'X means that p', but it is simply the proposition that p, assuming the hearer accepts the prior steps of the inference, understanding the utterance requires accepting its content p. Yet it seems this cannot be right, since one can understand what a speaker says/means without accepting it (one may understand many utterances one thinks false).

The objection is well taken, however it seems to me to work with an excessively strong conception of acceptance. Certainly, if one accepts all the prior steps of a comprehension inference, one is bound to accept the conclusion as well, however this may not be a robust, final or definitive kind of acceptance. In the case of interpretive inferences like those illustrated in this chapter, the acceptance of the conclusion may be just a matter of having accepted a certain train of reasoning, but not a matter of *trusting* what the speaker means, in the sense of believing it true. Perhaps, independent and genuinely *epistemic assumptions* should be in place in order for the hearer fully to accept (that is, regard as true) what the speaker says on a particular occasion (see Fricker, 1987, 1994), or the hearer must be warranted in some other way – for example, by a simple absence of defeaters – in endorsing the word of the interlocutor. Interpretive inferences may give rise to a purely 'formal' kind of acceptance, which is however only preliminary and needs that some extra, genuinely epistemic, requirements are met in order to become acceptance in the robust sense of the term. Consequently, the fact that the hearer comes to accept that p after having drawn an interpretive inference does not seem to be a harmful implication of the theory.

A second perplexity could be voiced as follows: how could a hearer who fully understands the content of an utterance as being p come to the conclusion that p without also coming to the conclusion that *what the speaker means (says) is p*? That is, if the hearer is carrying out a comprehension task, it seems that she could not derive the object-level conclusion that p without also entertaining the meta-representational conclusion that the speaker means that p. For, one may point out, for p to be the content of the utterance one arrives at is just for p to be what the speaker means (says). The objection states something that I regard as a conceptual truth, namely that understanding the content of an utterance as being p is nothing but understanding what the speaker means (says). Every case of utterance comprehension should comply with this requirement, however, to repeat, that need not imply that, at the cognitive level, the hearer entertains a meta-representation, or even that she is able to grasp the conceptual–normative import of meta-representation in the notion of comprehension, for reasons already mentioned pertaining to the unacceptable implication that so-called 'non-mentalising' subjects would lack utterance comprehension in the full sense (although they would master a language and be able to deploy contextual clues). The question of the conditions in which we have utterance comprehension is, it seems to me, independent of the question whether the interpreter has access to any meta-representations or appreciates the conceptual–normative import of meta-representation for the concept of comprehension.

5.7 Egocentric communicators

In this chapter, I have defended an account according to which utterance comprehension, at a minimum, *need not eventuate in a meta-representational conclusion*. It is worth mentioning that a far more radical account exists in the literature, according to which communication (and, consequently, comprehension) *is generally not a question of meta-representation*, that is, it is not structured so as to take the other subject's mental states into account. Thus, as Keysar (2008) has it, speakers do not rely on their addressees' beliefs and knowledge in order to design what to say; and conversely, addressees do not take account of the beliefs and knowledge of speakers when interpreting what the latter say. Needless to say, they may want to do this sometimes, but this by no means happens systematically (see also Keysar, 2007; Barr and Keysar, 2005).

Speakers and hearers are described as *egocentric*, where acting egocentrically here means that one plans what to say or interprets the utterance of another by relying on information that one holds privately, so to speak, and which is not shared between speaker and hearer. The egocentric tendency is explained, according to Keysar, by its alleged cognitive advantages: first of all, one's own perspective is usually dominant and provides interpretations of what the others say that appear more compelling to the hearer; secondly, considering one's own point of view is more automatic, and it takes less cognitive effort than considering the other's point of view, which is instead a costly and easily disruptible enterprise.

With respect to the Non-Meta view, Keysar's proposal is more radical in that it assigns no role to meta-representation in utterance comprehension, not even as a possible intermediate step of the interpretive process, and regards the whole process as meta-representation free. Engaging in meta-representation happens only when something in the conversation goes wrong – either on the speaker's or hearer's part – and needs fixing.

Keysar's deeply egocentricist view of communication and comprehension seems to me exposed to the following difficulty, which could be expressed as a dilemma: either the subjects are confined in their egocentric perspectives and the success of communication is nothing but a *felicitous accident*, or the fact that subjects often fall back upon information as to the beliefs and intentions of speakers means that *communication failures are omnipresent*. Let me detail the dilemma.

The view posits that, in communication, speakers and hearers do not generally entertain any meta-representation and only work with information they privately entertain. If the information one of the parties works with matches the information of the other party, then communication can succeed, but note that this would happen by sheer accident. Neither the speaker nor the hearer have any guarantee that the information each of them individually retains is the same that the other retains, so each instance of speech production or speech interpretation is a 'leap in the dark'. Consequently, if things go well and the message formulated by the speaker reaches the hearer, this constitutes nothing but a happy accident, not the result of a process responsibly either monitored or controlled by the participants. But this picture of communication is unacceptable. (One could object that even meta-representational assumptions concerning the other's beliefs and intentions are a 'leap in the dark': if each participant makes the right assumptions and communication succeeds, then this is a sheer accident too. I grant that meta-representational comprehension and production also involve an amount of chance, yet they seem the most *responsible* way of running a communication task, to an extent that even if success were the result of sheer chance, the parties would be excusable by having performed in the most responsible way possible.)

On the other hand, if Keysar admits that speakers or hearers rely on information about what the conversant believes or intends, this would be tantamount to admitting that a failure of communication is occurring; but since it seems that appeal to the beliefs and intentions of speakers is enormously common, this would imply seeing communication failures almost everywhere. Yet, presumably most of these would not be categorised as failures at all – they would be ordinary cases of communication where speculation concerning the mental contents of the interlocutor aids speech production and interpretation. In sum, Keysar's view is conflicted between two equally unacceptable consequences: that communication is generally a happy coincidence or that communication failures are ubiquitous.

To be fair, proponents of the egocentricist view do have an account available of how communication could be non-miraculously successful. In their view, the solution lies in the idea of conventionality, that is, the sharing of representations and processes for building meaning out of perceived communicative acts. On these views, a hearer manages to understand what a speaker says not so much by representing her mental states, but by interacting with her, trying to align one's own use of language with the use of one's interlocutor, thus ultimately reaching a situation of (optimal) matching between the mental representations of each participant. The interaction that brings about such an 'alignment' does not require any of the conversationalists to model the mental states of the other, since the adjustment of each mental representation (where needed) is achieved solely on the basis of what feedback one gets from the interlocutor, which causes effects of priming, imitation and ultimately mutual alignment. The whole process is described as automatic and indeed 'mechanical', fast and effortless (cf. Pickering and Garrod, 2004, but also Barr and Keysar, 2005; Barr, 2004). This model could help the proponent of egocentricism to explain how successful communication is not a mere accident, in that speaker and hearer could monitor and control the flow of information being conveyed through communication by paying attention to the way each of them uses language and adjusting their use of language and mental representation accordingly.

As appealing as it may be, this view has some limitations. As one may have noticed, the conventionalist account is exclusively suited to dialogue situations, where speaker and hearer can easily interact – and not to 'monologue' situations, where the hearer typically listens to or reads a text without the possibility of responding. In monologue situations it seems difficult for the hearer not to take account of the speaker's (putative) mental states and indeed conventionalists concede that in these circumstances resorting to meta-representation is fairly normal (Pickering and Garrod, 2004, p. 177).

The view I have defended shows that, even in monologue situations, meta-representation may not be so central to comprehension as to deliver meta-representational conclusions. Recipients may interpret the utterances of speakers by relying on rough-and-ready frames, such as those characterised as 'conceptual constraints' in the previous chapter, or frames organising encyclopedia information (for instance, the stealing-and-getting-arrested schema); they could deploy contextual clues that they need not picture in a meta-representational way. At the same time, they may use meta-representation, but as a way of depicting aspects of the utterance's background, such as what the speaker is talking about, what she is referring to and so on. Even in this case, that they entertain a meta-representation need not entail that the conclusion of the interpretive process they operate is in turn a meta-representation.

Overall, the Non-Meta view is less radical than the egocentricist view propounded by Keysar and other authors, in that, by assigning a role to meta-representation, it avoids the highly problematic dilemma that communication is either miraculous or studded with failures; moreover, it does better than the conventionalist solution that egocentricists seem to have at their disposal, because it offers a new account that significantly revises the role of meta-representation in monologue situations, whereas defenders of egocentricism have no strategy to implement and need to bite the bullet on the issue.

Conclusion

In this chapter, I have argued that the comprehension of utterances of semantically under-determined sentences need not follow a meta-representational path, and in any case it need not result in a meta-representation of the form 'X means that φ' or 'X believes that φ'.

- I first presented two Inferential approaches to utterance comprehension: on the approach initiated by Grice, meta-representation plays a pervasive role in inferences aimed at the reconstruction of (particularised) conversational implicatures; on the approach defended by Relevance Theorists and in particular by Sperber, meta-representation figures as the conclusion of an inference aimed at

utterance comprehension, even though the inference's premises need not be meta-representational (since they are processed by a dedicated module).
- I then presented two non-Inferential approaches to utterance comprehension: Millikan promotes a translational model while Recanati regards enrichment and associative processes as key.
- Against the considerations offered by Millikan, I argued that the model she proposes has to admit that inference plays some role in the comprehension of semantically under-determined sentences in particular conversational settings, especially with regard to integrating information coming from different sources; against Recanati, I argued that his argument that comprehension of some utterances cannot be inferential because the sentences used express non-conceptual contents rests on a wrong assumption: in the case of 'It's raining' for instance, the content is conceptual even though it is non-propositional, and inference is indeed possible.
- Against the Inferential approach defended by Sperber, I argued that our intuitions about what we have understood of certain utterances are not distinctively meta-representational. Nevertheless, I maintained that some interpretive enterprises may have a meta-representation as their final aim and I have for convenience referred to them as 'hermeneutics'; furthermore, I granted that meta-representation may play a conceptual–normative role in utterance comprehension. It seems a conceptual truth that understanding that the content of an utterance u is p is understanding what the speaker means with u. Some appreciation of this must be present, at least at the implicit or dispositional level, in those who are competent with the concept of comprehension, but it may nevertheless remain a background assumption which need not give rise to a meta-representational conclusion at the end of an interpretive process.
- I then proposed a Non-Meta model of how utterance comprehension may work in the case of semantically under-determined expressions: when a speaker listens to an utterance of, for instance, 'Jill is ready', she is presented with the content *that Jill is ready*; she then uses conceptual constraints (see Chapter 4) in order to expand the adicity of the predicate 'ready' and then fills the resulting free gap with contextual information. This process need not, by itself, involve any meta-representation. However, meta-representations may interact with some of the passages of the process: in particular, meta-representations concerning what the speaker is talking about, what she refers to and so on may provide support for premises concerning

what is salient in context. This, however, does not entail that the final result needs to be a meta-representation itself.
- I then compared the present model with an 'egocentricist' approach to utterance comprehension. I argued that it faces a dilemma: either it regards communication as miraculous or it has to admit ubiquitous communicative breakdowns. Even though proponents of the egocentricist model have at their disposal a 'conventionalist' account of utterance comprehension, this is appropriate only for dialogue situations, while in monologue situations the egocentricist has to bite the bullet on meta-representation; as opposed to this, the Non-Meta model leads to significant reconsideration of the role of meta-representation in both dialogue and monologue situations.

Notes

1 Arguing for Semantic Under-Determinacy

1. Predicates like 'tall', 'big', 'small', but also 'green', 'cold' and so on, are also known for being vague. Their vagueness should not be conflated with their semantic under-determinacy, though, as we shall see in greater detail in Chapter 2.
2. One could observe that, in some cases, a sentence like 'It's raining' is not generic at all. Take a scenario (like that pictured by Recanati, 2002a, 2004, 2010) in which it has not rained on Earth for quite some time. A rain detector signals rain on the Earth's surface, so the weatherman in charge of the device utters: 'It's raining'. In this case, one could observe that there is no genericity and the sentence does not exhibit any semantic under-determinacy. I do not think this account is correct. The sentence 'It's raining' *does* express a generic truth-condition, a condition that could not correspond to a state of affairs in any possible world – for, whenever it is raining, it is raining in some specific location. Only, it seems OK to utter such a sentence with no further completion because, even though it is clear that for its utterance to be true, it has to rain in some specific place, the conversation does not require such specification, either because there is no way of knowing where exactly it is raining, or because it does not matter. So, that 'It's raining' could be felicitously used in this scenario does not show that the sentence may not have generic truth-conditions, but it shows that in some conversational settings it could be OK to use sentences that express generic truth-conditions.
3. Of course, the postulation of context-sensitivity should not be 'cheap' and unmotivated (see Szabó, 2006). The very bulk of these theorists' proposals lies in their displaying arguments to substantiate a well-justified case for context-sensitivity.
4. What intuitions are exactly is debated and authors are divided between a doxastic approach, in which intuitions are either beliefs (see Lewis, 1983 among others) or dispositions to believe (see Van Inwagen, 1997; Sosa, 1998 among others), and an approach in which intuitions are considered along perceptual lines, as 'intellectual seemings' (see Bealer, 1998 among others).
5. See Stanley (2000) and Stanley and Szabó (2000) for the idea that there are free variables in the sentence's logical form. The idea of lexically (sub-syntactically) articulated parameters is defended on many occasions by Taylor, who tries to block Cappelen and Lepore's slippery slope by emphasising the importance of sub-syntactic completions for the Moderate Contextualist. Taylor (2007) distinguishes between context-sensitivity, typically represented by indexicality, and speech-situation sensitivity, typically instantiated as suppressed arguments in the sub-syntactic lexical structure of a word: these two phenomena contribute to the *narrow content* of an assertion. He then distinguishes the narrow content of an assertion and the total content of an assertion, where the former arises from semantic/

174 Notes

syntactic features plus the resolution of context- and speech-situation sensitivities and the latter is obtained once pragmatic externalities (for instance, implicatures) are added. His suggestion might be taken to be that, in order to resist Cappelen and Lepore's charge that Moderate Contextualism collapses into Radical Contextualism, the Moderate Contextualist need only determine whether some expression is speech-situation sensitive or whether it determines a pragmatic externality, and he seems pretty sanguine about the feasibility of such a distinction.

6. Recanati faces the threat of a slippery slope from a different angle. He argues (Recanati, 2006, p. 24) that there is no threat of a slippery slope here, because according to Radical Contextualists the kind of context-sensitivity that generalises to all language is not of the same kind as the context-sensitivity Cappelen and Lepore have in mind. Cappelen and Lepore seem to identify context-sensitivity with processes of semantically driven *saturation* (whereby predicates like 'green', 'ready' or 'know' are completed), while Radical Contextualists contend that what generalises is *modulation*, which is conceived as a pragmatically guided process of meaning enrichment, strengthening, loosening or refinement. Since these two kinds of context-sensitivity can be kept apart, the risk of a slippery slope can be avoided. See also Pagin and Pelletier (2007, pp. 50–4) for a very similar strategy. Ezcurdia (2009) adopts yet another strategy: she resists the collapse into Radical Contextualism by appealing to some features of our intuitions – stability and clarity; the intuition that if context were *not* to intervene, truth-value would change; and the plausibility that a covert context-sensitivity has arisen in use.

7. Clapp (2009, pp. 92–3) has two explanations for why it seems much more difficult to construct a Real Context-Shifting Argument for expressions that are not obviously indexical. The first is that these expressions are context-sensitive in 'slippery' ways – that is, their interpretation could vary *along many lines* in such a way that it is not easy to determine along which axis one should envisage the contextual shift. A second reason is that the context in which the word is used tends to 'absorb' the contexts of the mentionings, in such a way that the semantic value or enrichment of the context of use 'leaks into' the context of mentioning.

8. Clapp (2009, pp. 94–6) argues for the same idea with a slightly more indirect strategy. He first replicates the schema of 'Real' Context-Shifting Arguments for an obviously context-sensitive expression like 'home', then he invites the hearer to compare his mimicked argument with a 'Real' Context-Shifting Argument for 'rich'. The result, he claims, is that the 'rich' story is no more plausible than the 'home' story; if it is, and since the context-sensitivity of 'home' is not negotiable, then 'rich' is context-sensitive just like 'home'.

9. Bezuidenhout (2006, p. 8) emphasises the importance of making it clear that the second context (of mention) has to be *differentiated* from the first context (of use) – implying that Cappelen and Lepore disingenuously fail to do so in order to bend the cases in their favour; once this is accomplished, she explains, it becomes apparent that 'Real' Context-Shifting cases could be run for expressions like 'red', 'green', 'ready' and 'know' as well, and not just for Kaplanian indexicals.

10. This of course does not exclude that, were it to come out that the arguments for the Minimalist's meta-semantic views are better than the arguments for

the Contextualist's ones, this would legitimise the Minimalist approach to semantic under-determinacy and context-sensitivity. My point is that, at the meta-semantic level, it may not be easy to adjudicate which arguments are better, because the considerations each disputant might adduce may have equal weight, or, even worse, because it may be difficult to identify a common metric to evaluate the goodness of each party's arguments.
11. Similar considerations can be read in Szabó (2001, p. 125), who notes that arguing for the semantic under-determinacy of 'This is a novel' by pointing at borderline cases of novelhood is a way of trivially generalising arguments from semantic under-determinacy.

2 The Peculiarity of Semantic Under-Determinacy

1. I assume that lexical ambiguity carries over to phrases and sentences that contain the ambiguous word: thus a phrase that contains an ambiguous lexical item will be ambiguous, and a sentence that contains an ambiguous lexical item will be ambiguous.
2. A finer-grained distinction should be traced, between *homonymy* and *polysemy* (Lyons, 1977). Homonymy obtains whenever two different lexemes have the same phonetic and graphic realisation. As the reader may note, 'bank' is precisely a case of homonymy because two different lexical entries (the former indicating river sides and the latter indicating financial institutions) share a common lexeme and phoneme. Polysemy obtains whenever one and the same lexical entry has multiple, albeit related meanings. For instance, the word 'newspaper' means either a specific token of a newspaper issue, or the newspaper issue type; it also may mean the newspaper publisher, or even the newspaper's editorial committee. This distinction will not be essential for our purposes.
3. Without invoking cognitive considerations, Bezuidenhout points out something similar, to the effect that words like 'ready' have indefinitely many senses depending on context, while ambiguous words have definitely many senses, independently of the context in which they are used (Bezuidenhout, 2002, pp. 107–8).
4. See also Stanley's (2000, pp. 405–6) discussion on 'discourse initial' utterances.
5. I take it that even the occurrence of verbs like 'is' or 'has' cannot afford an insight into the proposition meant by the speaker, because a bare utterance of 'Grace has' or 'Seven is' does not allow us to decide whether 'has' and 'is' act as auxiliary or non-auxiliary verbs.

3 Semantic Under-Determinacy and the Debate on Context-Sensitivity

1. The difference between a particularised and a generalised conversational implicature is spelled out by Levinson (2000, p. 16) as follows: an implicature is particularised iff an utterance implicates it only by virtue of specific contextual assumptions, that would not ordinarily or invariably obtain; an implicature is generalized iff an utterance implicates it in ordinary circumstances, unless there are unusual specific circumstances which defeat it. It may be

contended that embeddings do not count as 'unusual' circumstances which could block the implicature, so according to this definition the generalised conversational implicature could indeed arise.
2. It could be pointed out that, at this stage, all these notions collapse into each other; yet they have been characterised very differently in the literature, and I suspect that it is ultimately an empirical question whether they all come down to the same phenomenon at the linguistic and cognitive level. Generalised conversational implicatures have been described as the result of heuristics that are applied in a context-independent manner (unless defeating assumptions become salient), plus they operate globally, that is, on whole sentences and not on individual constituents or sub-sentences (see Levinson, 2000). Standardised uses generate contents in a default manner, where reasoning is short-circuited or compressed due to routinisation, plus they operate globally (see Bach, 1995, 1998; Bach and Harnish, 1979). Finally, free enrichment operates in a strict context-dependent way, taking account of specific contextual features, plus it operates locally (see Recanati, 2004, 2010).
3. For arguments from overgeneration, see Cappelen and Lepore (2002, 2005), Recanati (2002a), Breheney (2003), Hall (2008) and the attendant discussions in Cohen and Rickless (2007), Sennet (2008), Pagin (2005), Stanley (2005a), Cappelen and Hawthorne (2007).
4. For more on methodological objections, see also section 4.2.1.
5. This argument would not be subscribed by Cappelen and Lepore, who would maintain that the proposition that Chiara is tall is true iff (in all the worlds where) Chiara has the property of being tall, *full stop*. However, there seems to be nothing as being tall *tout court*. So, either we admit that there exist properties like being tall *tout court* (and also being green *tout court*, being ready *tout court*), something which seems hard to swallow unless one reduces being tall *tout court* to some other property (cf. Travis, 2006, p. 44); or we have to admit that predicates like 'being tall', 'being green' and 'being ready' are syntactically or lexically more complex than may appear at first sight.
6. Though Bach's Ultra-Minimalism will be the privileged focus of the present section, two views that can also fall under the same heading deserve mention. The first is Soames' theory, while the second is Korta and Perry's 'Radical' Minimalism. Soames' proposal is devised to address some classic problems in the theory of reference, such as Frege-style identity statements. In order to cope with these problems, Soames (2002, 2004) traces a distinction between the semantic content of a sentence, which is common to all assertions performed with that sentence, and the content or information which a speaker intends to convey with an assertion of a sentence. Thus, the semantic content of 'Peter Hempel is Carl Hempel' is a Russellian proposition that assigns the identity function to the same individual (Mr Hempel). Yet almost everyone would assert 'Peter Hempel is Carl Hempel' meaning something more specific, for instance that Peter Hempel, *the guy sitting over there*, is Carl Hempel, *the famous philosopher*. By appealing to this enhanced content Soames is able to capture the cognitive significance of Frege-style identity statements involving co-referential proper names by at the same time maintaining the idea that they express a common content or 'matrix', cashed out as a Russellian proposition. Notice that Soames depicts such contents as often non-propositional – and this squarely identifies this position as an example of Ultra-Minimalism.

Korta and Perry (2006, 2007) propose what they dub a 'Radical' Minimalism in which they distinguish: (i) the proposition that all utterances of a sentence S have in common, which they call utterance-bound content. For instance, the sentence 'I am tired' expresses the utterance-bound content to the effect that the utterer of u is tired at the time of utterance of u; (ii) what is said, identified as the content-in-context of an utterance of S, where indexicality, ambiguity and vagueness have been resolved: for example, that Delia is tired at 6 pm on 3 November 2013; (iii) the plurality of propositions that are more or less indirectly conveyed by an utterance of S: for example, that Delia is so tired as to be unable to go to the movies; that Delia does not feel like going to the movies, and so on. Tracing this distinction is motivated by the need to work out a more consistent Minimalism than that defended by Cappelen and Lepore, who identify minimal propositions with (ii) but at the same time expect that these are what all utterances of S have in common – which is clearly false, since (ii) might contain context-dependent elements (such as the referent of 'I'). What all utterances of a sentence S have in common is something like (i), namely *reflexive* or *utterance-bound* content. At the same time, utterance-bound content is not 'said' in any interesting sense; and neither the plurality of contents that can be derived from an utterance of S can sensibly be called 'what is said'. Korta and Perry ultimately wish to restore a notion like (ii), that could be useful for semantic theorising and can return a canonical conception of 'what is said'.

7. The view importantly departs from Relativist accounts of the semantics of 'know' such as that elaborated by MacFarlane (2005). He endorses the idea that the truth value of 'A knows that P' changes relative to an epistemic parameter e, but claims that the value of such a parameter is fixed by a *context of assessment*, that is, a context in which a proposition is evaluated – which might not coincide with the context of utterance.

8. The Relativist who wishes to point to such epistemic operators may be tempted to refer to the work of Ludlow (2005). Here, Ludlow defends a Contextualist position about the semantics of knowledge ascriptions by noting that there are felicitous utterances of, for instance, 'She doesn't know that p, by the standards of chemistry'. Here the expression 'by the standards of chemistry' is supposed to make the epistemic standards for 'know' explicit. If this is so, then this suggests that there is room for such epistemic standards at the level of the truth-conditions of knowledge ascriptions, even when speakers do not explicitly articulate them. The Relativist could take advantage of Ludlow's results and claim that expressions such as 'by the standards of chemistry', 'according to John' and so on ought to be regarded as epistemic operators. Stanley (2005b, p. 164) opposes this move (whether or not advanced by the Relativist), and argues that these expressions do not have any special epistemic import, though they can be felicitously appended to knowledge ascriptions. This is easily demonstrated by the fact that the same expressions can be appended to sentences that do not contain any epistemic terminology, and therefore cannot be used to make knowledge ascriptions. For example: 'By the standards of chemistry, what is in the Hudson river is not water'; 'According to John, the bus will arrive soon'.

9. The notion of an Austinian proposition stems from Austin's (1950) idea that statements consist in the utterance of a sentence performed while referring

178   Notes

to a situation in the world. The sentence has a certain descriptive content which, by itself, is neither true nor false; a situation is needed to support this content, thus making it true or false. Later, theorists such as Barwise and Perry (1983), and Barwise and Etchemendy (1989), drew from Austin in elaborating what they have called a Situation Semantics. Here a statement expresses an *infon*, that is, a content which is neutral with respect to situations; infons are true only in a situation if the situation at issue supports them. The combination of infon and situation is an *Austinian proposition*: unlike the infon, which is not evaluable as it stands, the Austinian proposition is evaluable, because it incorporates both the infon's descriptive information and the situation in which it should be taken to hold. If the infon holds in the situation, then the Austinian proposition is true. The term 'infon' has been replaced by Recanati (2007) with 'lekton', and situations with circumstances of evaluation, but the substance remains the same: the combination of lekton and circumstances of evaluation makes up an Austinian proposition. For a formal introduction to these issues, see Van Benthem and Ter Meulen (2011).

4 Semantic Under-Determinacy and Conceptual Constraints

1. This formulation follows the standard way of conceiving the workings of indexicals and demonstratives mainly due to Kaplan (1989). Alternative ways of spelling out the semantics of indexicals have been proposed, and some seem to question the idea that their reference assignment is semantic in that they attack the idea that their reference is fixed 'automatically' and by default in the context of utterance (see among others Nunberg, 1993; Predelli, 1998a, b; Schlenker, 2003; Santorio, 2012; Mount, 2008; Parsons, 2011; Rabern, 2013). These authors tend to give an account of indexicals and demonstratives in terms of what Kaplan would have called 'monsters'. However, even in this alternative conception, it is arguable that the contextual contribution of the term is *still* semantically controlled, in that the term's meaning would still put *some* (even minimal) constraints on what referent is assigned to the term's occurrence.
2. Recanati (2002a, pp. 326–7) opposes this take on 'It's raining' in which the location argument is existentially quantified over – a solution which he calls *Existential Closure By Default (ECBD)*. He argues that whatever plausibility this account has, it depends on a comparison between overt indexicals ('he') and covert ones. Since, as he rightly notes, overt indexicals never undergo ECBD, it is doubtful that covert indexicals will do. I agree about this difference – see section 2.1.3 – but I reject the contention that the plausibility of ECBD in 'It's raining' depends on any such comparison. As will become clear later on, ECBD in 'It's raining' might obtain because some fundamental conceptual constraints on To Rain have to be followed, and *not* because the sentence contains some indexical form. This proposal rules out that ECBD in 'It's raining' depends on a comparison between overt indexicals like 'he' and any alleged covert indexical in the logical form of the sentence. Later on (2010, pp. 104–5), Recanati additionally argues that readings of 'It's raining' that posit existential quantification give rise to problems when it comes

to negation, in that they exhibit no interaction between the negation and the existential quantification, to the point that it is impossible to provide a wide-scope reading of 'It is not raining', to the effect that *there is some place x and it's not raining in x*. His criticism is directed to a view which he extracts from Partee, according to which 'It's not raining' contains a syntactically articulated variable. Yet, as we will see in the next section, there is no need to postulate such a variable; it follows that 'It's raining' means simply that a rain event is not taking place. Semantically, this is equivalent to the narrow-scope reading to the effect that *it is not the case that there is a place x and it is raining in x*. Thus, in the syntactically simplified account I am going to propose, the wide-scope reading does not arise, although the account allows for 'It's raining' (as well as 'It's not raining') to take an existentially quantified reading. This eschews Recanati's criticism.
3. A node α c-commands another node β in a parse-tree if α and β are not hierarchically related, that is, they do not 'dominate' each other, and the first branching that dominates α also dominates β.
4. Adjunction is a relation that obtains between a node α and a node β when node β is combined with node α without this causing any change in the category of α, for instance the phrase category.
5. The notion of conceptual truth here should be understood as being as philosophically innocuous as it could be: here conceptual truths will be considered as *truisms or platitudes* that reveal the way speakers understand some concepts (see Pietroski, 2005, p. 17). The epistemological issue whether the grasping of any of these propositions (for instance, that being ready is being ready for something) entails *knowing/believing/being justified to take* them to be true (Williamson, 2006) plays no distinctive role in the proposal I am about to make; conceptual truths need only be propositions that, in being grasped, are judged 'obvious', 'risk-free' or 'sure'. Moreover, I will make no commitments over whether conceptual truths exhaust what there is to the semantics of a concept or word.
6. Fillmore traces a distinction between *Definite* Null Instantiation (DNI) and *Indefinite* Null Instantiation (INI). In DNI, while the conceptual argument is omitted, the element that fills that slot is recoverable in context; thus, when one says 'I understand', even though the object-argument is omitted, it is understood that it is a particular element that the hearer can retrieve in context (perhaps in previous discourse). In INI, the omitted conceptual argument does not have a contextually retrievable counterpart and it is existentially quantified over instead. So for instance, in 'Clark is eating', there need be no salient food in the conversational context and the sentence could be interpreted as stating that Clark is eating *something or other*. Put in Fillmore's terms, my main claim here is that all of (10)–(13) undergo INI (and whether they undergo DNI is a matter of how these sentences are used in particular contexts, as I explain shortly after in the text).
7. It should be mentioned in passing that this view contrasts with the one according to which, for instance, 'being ready' is dyadic at the syntactic level but the argument corresponding to the activity or purpose for which one is ready can go *implicit* (Haegeman, 1994). I believe my account allows us more sharply to match, on the one hand, arguments with constraints that are both conceptual and syntactic and, on the other hand, adjuncts with

constraints that are conceptual but *not* syntactic. Haegeman's account does not accomplish such a nice match, in that it has to admit arguments that are nevertheless syntactically optional (instead of being simple conceptual slots corresponding to adjuncts). Plus, my account still complies with Haegeman's characterisation of 'argument' as the 'minimally required participant', only with a *less inclusive* conception of minimally required participants.
8. But see also the following references from introductory articles and books on the matter: Karttunen and Peters (1979), Levinson (1983, p. 127), Horn (2003, p. 383).
9. It may be objected that which slots are to be filled is a matter of what information is relevant to the conversation, so *pragmatics is key* in the process of truth-condition elaboration after all. This however does not disprove that the processes at issue are semantic in nature. The reason is that, since the relevant slots respond to conceptual truths or 'truisms', all slots have to be filled on pain of incoherence, absurdity, nonsense and so on. So *there is* a semantically mandated process of completion. Contextual factors and hence pragmatic considerations will help determine which slots need to be filled with contextual information rather than with default elements or existential closure. But in general, slot-filling is mandated by semantic or conceptual requirements, and there is no way in which pragmatic considerations could block these requirements – they could just make them more or less relevant relative to the conversation's goals.

5 Semantic Under-Determinacy, Comprehension and Meta-Representation

1. Even though note that Grice himself seemed to think that these processes need not be implemented at the conscious, explicit level and that an intuitive grasp of what the speaker means was sufficient on the part of the hearer (see Grice, 1967/1989, p. 31).
2. After all, one may know that skiing is salient in context for reasons independent of one's meta-representing the beliefs and intentions of the interlocutor. Not to mention the fact that the hearer may employ non-meta-representational strategies in order to establish what is salient in context. For an account of how hearers may gain knowledge of the salient aspects of context while not taking the (putative) intentions of the speaker into consideration, see Gauker (2008).

Bibliography

Atlas J. (1977) 'Negation, Ambiguity and Presuppositions', *Linguistics and Philosophy*, 1, 321–36.
Austin J. L. (1950) 'Truth', *Proceedings of the Aristotelian Society*, Suppl. Vol. 24, 111–28.
Austin J. L. (1962) *How to Do Things with Words* (Oxford: Clarendon Press).
Bach K. (1994a) 'Conversational Impliciture', *Mind & Language*, 9, 124–62.
Bach K. (1994b) 'Semantic Slack' in Tsohatzidis S. L. (ed.) *Foundations of Speech Act Theory* (London: Routledge), pp. 267–91.
Bach K. (1995) 'Standardization vs. Conventionalization', *Linguistics and Philosophy*, 18, 677–86.
Bach K. (1998) 'Standardisation Revisited' in Kasher A. (ed.) *Pragmatics: Critical Assessment* (London: Routledge).
Bach K. (2005) 'Context ex machina' in Szabó Z. G. (ed.) *Semantics vs. Pragmatics* (Oxford University Press), pp. 15–44.
Bach K. (2006) 'The Excluded Middle: Semantic Minimalism without Minimal Propositions', *Philosophy and Phenomenological Research*, 73(2), 435–442.
Bach K. (2007) 'Regressions in Pragmatics (and Semantics)' in Burton-Roberts, N. (ed.) *Advances in Pragmatics* (New York and Basingstoke: Palgrave Macmillan).
Bach K. (2010) 'Impliciture vs Explicature: What is the Difference?' in Soria B. and Romero E. (eds) *Explicit Communication: Robyn Carston's Pragmatics* (Basingstoke: Palgrave Macmillan), pp. 126–37.
Bach K. (2012) 'Context–Dependence (such as it is)' in García-Carpintero M. and Kölbel M. (eds) *The Continuum Companion to the Philosophy of Language* (London: Continuum), pp. 153–84.
Bach K. and Harnish R. M. (1979) *Linguistic Communication and Speech Acts* (Cambridge, Mass.: MIT Press).
Barba J. (2007) 'Formal Semantics in the Age of Pragmatics', *Linguistics and Philosophy*, 30, 637–68.
Barr D. J. (2004) 'Establishing Conventional Communication Systems: Is Common Knowledge Necessary?', *Cognitive Science*, 28, 937–62.
Barr D. J. and Keysar B. (2005) 'Making Sense of How We Make Sense: the Paradox of Egocentrism in Language Use' in Colston H. L. and Katz A. N. (eds) *Figurative Language Comprehension* (Mahwah, NJ: Lawrence Erlbaum), pp. 21–43.
Barwise J. and Etchemendy J. (1989) *The Liar: an Essay on Truth and Circularity* (New York: Oxford University Press).
Barwise J. and Perry J. (1983) *Situations and Attitudes* (Cambridge, Mass.: The MIT Press).
Bealer G. (1998) 'Intuitions and the Autonomy of Philosophy' in DePaul M. R. and Ramsey W. (eds) *Rethinking Intuition* (Lanham, Md: Rowman & Littlefield), pp. 201–39.
Behne T., Liszkowski U., Carpenter M. and Tomasello M. (2011) 'Twelve-month-olds' Comprehension and Production of Pointing', *British Journal of Developmental Psychology*, 30 (3), 359–75.

182 Bibliography

Bezuidenhout A. (2002) 'Truth-conditional Pragmatics', *Philosophical Perspectives*, 16, 105–34.
Bezuidenhout A. (2006) 'The Coherence of Contextualism', *Mind & Language*, 21(1), 1–10.
Bierwisch M. (1983) 'Formal and Lexical Semantics', *Linguistische Studien*, 114, 56–79.
Boghossian P. (1994) 'Inferential Role Semantics and the Analytic/Synthetic Distinction', *Philosophical Studies*, 73, 109–22.
Borg E. (2004) *Minimal Semantics* (Oxford: Clarendon Press).
Borg E. (2009) 'Must a Semantic Minimalist be a Semantic Internalist?', *Proceedings of the Aristotelian Society Supplementary*, LXXXIII, 31–51.
Borg E. (2012a) *Pursuing Meaning* (Oxford: Oxford University Press).
Borg E. (2012b) 'Semantics without Pragmatics' in Allen K. and Jaszczolt K. (eds) *The Cambridge Handbook of Pragmatics* (Cambridge: Cambridge University Press), pp. 513–28.
Brandom R. (2000) *Articulating Reasons: an Introduction to Inferentialism* (Harvard: Harvard University Press).
Breheney R. (2003) 'A Lexical Account of Implicit (Bound) Contextual Dependence' in *Semantics and Linguistic Theory (SALT)*, 13 (Ithaca, USA: CLC Publications, Cornell University), pp. 55–73.
Bretherton I. (1991) 'Intentional Communication and the Development of an Understanding of Mind' in Frye D. and Moore C. (eds) *Children's Theories of Mind: Mental States and Social Understanding* (Mahwah, NJ: Lawrence Erlbaum), pp. 49–75.
Brogaard B. (2008) 'In Defence of a Perspectival Semantics for *know*', *Australasian Journal of Philosophy*, 86(3), 439–59.
Burge T. (1977) 'Belief de re', *Journal of Philosophy*, 74, 338–62.
Cappelen H. (2008) 'Content Relativism and Semantic Blindness' in García-Carpintero M. and Kölbel M. (eds) *Relative Truth* (New York: Oxford University Press), pp. 256–86.
Cappelen H. and Hawthorne J. (2007) 'Locations and Binding', *Analysis*, 67, 95–105.
Cappelen H. and Hawthorne J. (2009) *Relativism and Monadic Truth* (New York: Oxford University Press).
Cappelen H. and Lepore E. (1997) 'On an Alleged Connection between Indirect Quotation and Semantic Theory', *Mind & Language*, 12, 278–96.
Cappelen H. and Lepore E. (2002) 'Indexicality, Binding, Anaphora and a Priori Truth', *Analysis*, 62 (276), 271–81.
Cappelen H. and Lepore E. (2003) 'Context-Shifting Arguments', *Philosophical Perspectives*, 17, 25–50.
Cappelen H. and Lepore E. (2005) *Insensitive Semantics: a Defense of Semantic Minimalism and Speech Act Pluralism* (Oxford: Blackwell).
Cappelen H. and Lepore E. (2006) 'Shared Content' in Lepore E. and Smith B. C. (eds) *The Oxford Handbook of Philosophy of Language* (New York: Oxford University Press), pp. 1020–55.
Carston R. (1988) 'Implicature, Explicature, and Truth-Theoretic Semantics' in Kempson R. (ed.) *Mental Representations: the Interface between Language and Reality* (Cambridge: Cambridge University Press), pp. 155–81.
Carston R. (2002a) *Thoughts and Utterances: the Pragmatics of Explicit Communication* (Oxford: Blackwell).

Carston R. (2002b) 'Linguistic Meaning, Communicated Meaning and Cognitive Pragmatics', *Mind & Language*, 17, 127–48.
Carston R. (2004) 'Explicature and Semantics' in Davis S. and Gillon B. (eds) *Semantics: a Reader* (Oxford: Oxford University Press), pp. 817–45.
Carston R. and Hall A. (2011) 'Implicature and Explicature' in Schmid H-J. and Geeraerts D. (eds) *Cognitive Pragmatics*, vol. 4 of Handbooks in Pragmatics (Berlin: Mouton de Gruyter).
Chalmers D. J. (2011) 'Verbal Disputes', *Philosophical Review*, 120 (4), 515–66.
Clapp L. (2009) 'In Defense of Context-Shifting Arguments' in Viger C. and Stainton R. (eds) *Compositionality, Context and Semantic Values. Essays in Honour of Ernie Lepore* (New York: Springer), pp. 79–105.
Cohen B. and Murphy G. (1984) 'Models of Concepts', *Cognitive Science*, 8, 27–58.
Cohen J. and Rickless S. (2007) 'Binding Arguments and Hidden Variables', *Analysis*, 67, 65–71.
Cohen L. J. (1971) 'Some Remarks on Grice's Views about the Logical Particles of Natural Language' in Bar-Hillel Y. (ed.) *Pragmatics of Natural Languages* (Dordrecht: Riedel), pp. 50–60.
Cohen S. (2000) 'Contextualism and Skepticism', *Philosophical Topics*, 10, 94–107.
Collins J. (2007) 'Syntax, More or Less', *Mind*, 116 (464), 805–50.
Corazza E. and Dokic J. (2007) 'Sense and Insensibility, or where Minimalism Meets Contextualism' in Preyer G. and Peter G. (eds) *Context-Sensitivity and Semantic Minimalism* (New York: Oxford University Press), pp. 169–93.
Corazza E. and Dokic J. (2010) 'Situated Minimalism', *Synthese*, 184 (2), 179–98.
Crimmins M. (1992) *Talk about Beliefs* (Cambridge, Mass.: Bradford/MIT).
Crimmins M. and Perry J. (1989) 'The Prince and the Phone Booth: Reporting Puzzling Beliefs', *Journal of Philosophy*, 86, 685–711.
DeRose K. (1995) 'Solving the Skeptical Problem', *Philosophical Review*, 104, 1–52.
Dreier J. (1990) 'Internalism and Speaker Relativism', *Ethics*, 101, 6–26.
Dummett M. (1973) *Frege: Philosophy of Language* (London: Duckworth).
Dummett M. (1991) *The Logical Basis of Metaphysics* (Harvard: Harvard University Press).
Dummett M. (1993) 'What is a Theory of Meaning? (II)' in *The Seas of Language* (Oxford: Clarendon Press), pp. 34–94.
Egan A. (2007) 'Epistemic Modals, Relativism and Assertion', *Philosophical Studies*, 133, 1–22.
Egan A. (2011) 'Relativism about Epistemic Modals' in Hales S. (ed.) *A Companion to Relativism* (London: Blackwell), pp. 219–41.
Egan A., Hawthorne J. and Weatherson B. (2005) 'Epistemic Modals in Context' in Preyer G. and Peter G. (eds) *Contextualism in Philosophy: Knowledge, Meaning, and Truth* (New York: Oxford University Press), pp. 131–69.
Evans G. (1982) *The Varieties of Reference* (Oxford: Oxford University Press).
Ezcurdia M. (2009) 'Motivating Moderate Contextualism', *Manuscrito*, 32 (1), 153–99.
Fauconnier G. (1985) *Mental Spaces: Aspects of Meaning Construction in Natural Language* (Cambridge, Mass. and London: The MIT Press).
Fillmore C. J. (1982) 'Frame Semantics' in *Linguistics in the Morning Calm* (Seoul: Hanshin Publishing Co.), pp. 111–37.
Fillmore C. J. (1985) 'Frames and the Semantics of Understanding', *Quaderni di Semantica*, 6(2), 222–54.

Bibliography

Fillmore C. J. (1986) 'Pragmatically Controlled Zero Anaphora', *Proceedings of the 12th Annual Meeting of the Berkeley Linguistics Society*, 95–107.
Fillmore C. J. (2003) *Language Form, Meaning, and Practice* (Stanford: CSLI Publications).
Fillmore C. J. and Baker C. (2010) 'A Frames Approach to Semantic Analysis' in Heine B. and Narrog H. (eds) *The Oxford Handbook of Linguistic Analysis* (Oxford: Oxford University Press), pp. 313–39.
Fodor J. (1998) *Concepts. Where Cognitive Science Went Wrong* (Oxford: Oxford University Press).
Fodor J. (2001) 'Language, Thought and Compositionality', *Mind & Language*, 16, 1–15.
Fodor J. and Lepore E. (1992) *Holism: a Shopper Guide* (New York: Wiley-Blackwell).
Frege G. (1918/1956) 'The Thought', *Mind*, 65, No. 259, 289–311.
Fricker E. (1987) 'The Epistemology of Testimony', *Proceedings of the Aristotelian Society Supplementary Vol.*, 61, 57–83.
Fricker E. (1994) 'Against Gullibility' in Matilal B. K. and Chakrabarti A. (eds) *Knowing from Words* (Alphen aan den Rijn: Kluwer), pp. 125–61.
García-Carpintero M. (2001) 'Gricean Rational Reconstructions and the Semantics/Pragmatics Distinction', *Synthese*, 128, 93–131.
Gauker C. (2008) 'Zero Tolerance for Pragmatics', *Synthese*, 165, Issue 3, 359–71.
Gauker C. (2012) 'What Tipper is Ready for: a Semantics for Incomplete Predicates', *Noûs*, 46 (1), 61–85.
Gibbs R. W. and Moise J. F. (1997) 'Pragmatics in Understanding What Is Said', *Cognition*, 62, 51–74.
Gillon B. (1990) 'Ambiguity, Generality and Indeterminacy: Tests and Definitions', *Synthese*, 85, 391–406.
Glanzberg (2007) 'Context, Content, and Relativism', *Philosophical Studies*, 136 (1), 1–29.
Grassmann S., Stracke M. and Tomasello M. (2009) 'Two-year-olds Exclude Novel Objects as Potential Referents of Novel Words Based on Pragmatics', *Cognition*, 112, 488–93.
Grice H. P. (1967/1989) 'Logic and Conversation' in *Studies in the Ways of Words* (Cambridge, Mass.: Harvard University Press), pp. 22–41.
Grice H. P. (1969/1989) 'Utterer's Meaning and Intentions' in *Studies in the Ways of Words* (Cambridge, Mass.: Harvard University Press), pp. 86–117.
Haegeman L. (1994) *Introduction to Government and Binding Theory*, 2nd edn (Oxford: Blackwell).
Hall A. (2008) 'Free Enrichment or Hidden Indexicals?', *Mind & Language*, 23 (4), 426–56.
Harman G. (1978) 'What is Moral Relativism?' in Goldman A. I. and Kim J. (eds) *Values and Morals* (Dordrecht, Holland: Reidel), pp. 143–61.
Heim I. and Kratzer A. (1998) *Semantics in Generative Grammar* (Oxford: Blackwell Publishing).
Horn L. (2003) 'Pragmatics: Implicature' in Frawley W. J. (ed.) *International Encyclopedia of Linguistics*, 2nd edn (Oxford: Oxford University Press), pp. 381–4.
Hornstein N. et al. (2005) *Understanding Minimalism* (New York: Cambridge University Press).
Horwich P. (1998) *Meaning* (Oxford: Oxford University Press).
Jackendoff R. (1990) *Semantic Structures* (Cambridge, Mass.: MIT Press).

Kaplan D. (1989) 'Demonstratives' in Almog J. et al. (eds) *Themes from Kaplan* (Oxford: Oxford University Press.), pp. 481–563.
Karttunen L. and Peters S. (1979) 'Conversational Implicature' in Oh C. and Dinneen D. (eds) *Syntax and Semantics, 11: Presupposition* (New York: Academic Press), pp. 1–56.
Katz J. (1972) *Semantic Theory* (New York: Harper & Row).
Katz J. and Fodor J. (1963) 'The Structure of a Semantic Theory', *Language*, 2, 170–210.
Kempson R. (1975) *Presupposition and the Delimitation of Semantics* (Cambridge: Cambridge University Press).
Kennedy C. and McNally L. (2010) 'Color, Context, and Compositionality', *Synthese*, 174, 79–98.
Keysar B. (2007) 'Communication and Miscommunication: the Role of Egocentric Processes', *Intercultural Pragmatics*, 4 (1), 71–84.
Keysar B. (2008) 'Egocentric Processes in Communication and Miscommunication?' in Kecskes I. and Mey J. L. (eds) *Intention, Common Ground and the Egocentric Speaker-Hearer* (Berlin and New York: Mouton de Gruyter), pp. 277–97.
King J. (2003) 'Tense, Modality, and Semantic Values', *Philosophical Perspectives*, 17 (1), 195–246.
King J. and Stanley J. (2005) 'Semantics, Pragmatics, and the Role of Semantic Content' in Szabó Z. G. (ed.) *Semantics vs. Pragmatics* (New York: Oxford University Press), pp. 111–64.
Kompa N. (2002) 'The Context-Sensitivity of Knowledge Ascriptions', *Grazer Philosophische Studien*, 64, 1–18.
Korta K. and Perry J. (2006) 'Varieties of Minimalist Semantics', *Philosophy and Phenomenological Research*, LXXIII (2), 451–9.
Korta K. and Perry J. (2007) 'Radical Minimalism, Moderate Contextualism' in Preyer G. and Peter G. (eds) *Content and Context. Essays on Semantics and Pragmatics* (Oxford: Oxford University Press), pp. 94–111.
Korta K. and Perry J. (2011) *Critical Pragmatics. An Inquiry into Reference and Communication* (New York: Cambridge University Press).
Lahav R. (1989) 'Against Compositionality: the Case of Adjectives', *Philosophical Studies*, 57, 261–79.
Lasersohn P. (2005) 'Context Dependence, Disagreement, and Predicates of Personal Taste', *Linguistics and Philosophy*, 28(4), 643–86.
Levinson S. (1983) *Pragmatics* (Cambridge: Cambridge University Press).
Levinson S. (2000) *Presumptive Meanings: the Theory of Generalized Conversational Implicatures* (Cambridge, Mass.: MIT Press).
Lewis D. (1979) 'Attitudes de dicto and de se', *Philosophical Review*, 88, 513–43.
Lewis D. (1980) 'Index, Context, and Content' in Kanger S. and Öhman S. (eds) *Philosophy and Grammar* (Dordrecht: Reidel), pp. 79–100.
Lewis D. (1983) 'Introduction', *Philosophical Papers*, Vol. I (Oxford: Oxford University Press).
Lewis D. (1996) 'Elusive Knowledge', *Australasian Journal of Philosophy*, 74, 549–67.
Lopez de Sa D. (2008) 'Presuppositions of Commonality' in García-Carpintero M. and Kölbel M. (eds) *Relative Truth* (New York: Oxford University Press), pp. 297–310.
Ludlow P. (2005) 'Contextualism and the New Linguistic Turn in Epistemology' in Preyer G. and Peter G. (eds) *Contextualism in Philosophy: Knowledge, Meaning and Truth* (New York: Oxford University Press).

Bibliography

Lyons J. (1977) *Semantics*, Vol. 2 (Cambridge, UK: Cambridge University Press).
MacFarlane J. (2005) 'The Assessment Sensitivity of Knowledge Attributions', *Oxford Studies in Epistemology*, 1, 197–233.
MacFarlane J. (2007) 'Semantic Minimalism and Nonindexical Contextualism' in Preyer G. and Peter G. (eds) *Context-Sensitivity and Semantic Minimalism: New Essays on Semantics and Pragmatics* (Oxford: Oxford University Press), pp. 240–50.
MacFarlane J. (2009) 'Nonindexical Contextualism', *Synthese*, 166, 231–50.
Marconi D. (1997) *Lexical Competence* (Cambridge, Mass.: MIT Press).
Martí L. (2006) 'Unarticulated Constituents Revisited', *Linguistics and Philosophy*, 29 (2), 135–66.
Millikan R. G. (1984) *Language, Thought, and Other Biological Categories: New Foundations for Realism* (Cambridge, Mass.: The MIT Press).
Millikan R. G. (2004) *Varieties of Meaning: the Jean-Nicod Lectures 2002* (Cambridge, Mass.: MIT Press).
Minsky M. (1975) 'A Framework for Representing Knowledge' in Winston P. (ed.) *The Psychology of Computer Vision* (New York: McGraw-Hill), pp. 211–77.
Montminy M. (2010) 'Two Contextualist Fallacies', *Synthese*, 173, 317–33.
Mount A. (2008) 'The Impurity of "Pure" Indexicals', *Philosophical Studies*, 138, 193–209.
Neale S. (1990) *Descriptions* (Cambridge, Mass.: MIT Press).
Neale S. (2004) 'This, That and the Other' in Reimer M. and Bezuidenhout A. (eds) *Descriptions and Beyond* (Oxford: Oxford University Press), pp. 68–183.
Neale S. (2007) 'On Location' in O'Rourke M. and Washington C. (ed.) *Situating Semantics: Essays on the Philosophy of John Perry* (Cambridge, Mass.: MIT Press), pp. 251–393.
Noveck I. (2004) 'Pragmatic Inferences Related to Logical Terms' in Noveck I. and Sperber D. (eds) *Experimental Pragmatics* (Basingstoke: Palgrave Macmillan), pp. 301–21.
Nunberg G. (1978) *The Pragmatics of Reference* (Bloomington: Indiana University Linguistics Club).
Nunberg G. (1993) 'Indexicality and Deixis', *Linguistics and Philosophy*, 16, 1–43.
Pagin P. (2005) 'Compositionality and Context' in Preyer G. and Peter G. (eds) *Contextualism in Philosophy* (New York: Oxford University Press), pp. 303–48.
Pagin P. and Pelletier J. (2007) 'Content, Context and Composition' in Preyer G. and Peter G. (eds) *Context-Sensitivity and Semantic Minimalism: New Essays on Semantics and Pragmatics* (New York: Oxford University Press), pp. 25–62.
Parsons J. (2011) 'Assessment-Contextual Indexicals', *Australasian Journal of Philosophy*, 89 (1), 1–17.
Partee B. (1973) 'Some Structural Analogies between Tenses and Pronouns in English', *Journal of Philosophy*, 70(18), 501–9.
Partee B. (1989) 'Binding Implicit Variables in Quantified Contexts', *Proceedings of the Chicago Linguistics Society*, 25 (Chicago: University of Chicago Press), pp. 342–65.
Perner J. (1991) *Understanding the Representational Mind* (Cambridge, Mass.: MIT Press).
Perry J. (1979) 'The Problem of the Essential Indexical', *Noûs*, 13(1), 3–21.
Perry J. (1986) 'Thought without Representation', *Supplementary Proceedings of the Aristotelian Society*, 60, 137–52.

Perry J. (1994) 'Fodor and Lepore on Holism', *Philosophical Studies*, 73 (2–3), 123–38.
Perry J. (1998) 'Indexicals, Contexts and Unarticulated Constituents' in Aliseda-Llera A., Van Glabbeek R. and Westerståhl D. (eds) *Computing Natural Language* (Stanford: CSLI Publications), pp. 1–12.
Petruck M. R. L. (1996) 'Frame Semantics' in Versucheren J. et al. (eds) *Handbook of Pragmatics* (Amsterdam: John Benjamins).
Pickering M. J. and Garrod S. (2004) 'Toward a Mechanistic Psychology of Dialogue', *Behavioural and Brain Science*, 27, 169–226.
Pietroski P. (2005) *Events and Semantic Architecture* (New York: Oxford University Press).
Pinker S. (2007) *The Stuff of Thought: Language as a Window into Human Nature* (London: Allen Lane).
Predelli S. (1998a) 'I Am Not Here Now', *Analysis*, 58(2), 107–15.
Predelli S. (1998b) 'Utterance Interpretation and the Logic of Indexicals', *Mind & Language*, 13(3), 400–14.
Predelli S. (2005a) *Contexts: Meaning, Truth, and the Use of Language* (Oxford: Oxford University Press).
Predelli S. (2005b) 'Painted Leaves, Context, and Semantic Analysis', *Linguistics and Philosophy*, 28(3), 351–74.
Prior A. N. (1968) 'Now', *Noûs*, 2 (2), 101–19.
Proust J. (2007) 'Metacognition and Metarepresentation: Is a Self-Directed Theory of Mind a Precondition for Metacognition?', *Synthese*, 159, 271–95.
Pupa F. and Troseth E. (2011) 'Syntax and Interpretation', *Mind & Language*, 26 (2), 185–209.
Pustejovsky J. (1995) *The Generative Lexicon* (Cambridge, Mass.: MIT Press).
Quine W.v.O. (1940) *Mathematical Logic* (Harvard: Harvard University Press).
Quine W.v.O. (1960) *Word and Object* (Cambridge, Mass.: MIT Press).
Rabern B. (2013) 'Monsters in Kaplan's Logic of Demonstratives', *Philosophical Studies*, 164 (2), 393–404.
Recanati F. (1989) 'The Pragmatics of What Is Said', *Mind & Language*, 4, 295–329.
Recanati F. (1993) *Direct Reference: from Language to Thought* (Oxford: Blackwell).
Recanati F. (1994) 'Contextualism and Anti-Contextualism in the Philosophy of Language' in Tsohatzidis S. (ed.) *Foundations of Speech-Act Theory: Philosophical and Linguistic Perspectives* (London: Routledge), pp. 156–66.
Recanati F. (2001) 'What Is Said', *Synthese*, 128, 75–91.
Recanati F. (2002a) 'Unarticulated Constituents', *Linguistics and Philosophy*, 25, 299–345.
Recanati F. (2002b) 'Does Linguistic Communication Rest on Inference?', *Mind & Language*, 17, 105–26.
Recanati F. (2004) *Literal Meaning* (Cambridge: Cambridge University Press).
Recanati F. (2006) 'Crazy Minimalism', *Mind & Language*, 21(1), 21–30.
Recanati F. (2007) *Perspectival Thought* (New York: Oxford University Press).
Recanati F. (2010) *Truth-Conditional Pragmatics* (New York: Oxford University Press).
Richard M. (2004) 'Contextualism and Relativism', *Philosophical Studies*, 119 (1–2), 215–42.
Richard M. (2008) *When Truth Gives Out* (New York: Oxford University Press).
Rothschild D. and Segal G. (2009) 'Indexical Predicates', *Mind & Language*, 24 (4), 467–93.

Bibliography

Rumelhart D. E. (1980) 'Schemata: the Building Blocks of Cognition' in Spiro R. J. et al. (eds) *Theoretical Issues in Reading Comprehension* (Hillsdale, NJ: Erlbaum), pp. 33–58.

Rumelhart D. E. and Ortony A. (1977) 'The Representation of Knowledge in Memory' in Anderson R. C., Spiro R. J. and Montague W. E. (eds) *Schooling in the Acquisition of Knowledge* (Hillsdale, NJ: Erlbaum), pp. 99–137.

Santorio P. (2012) 'Reference and Monstrosity', *Philosophical Review*, 121(3), 359–406.

Saul J. (2002) 'What Is Said and Psychological Reality; Grice's Project and Relevance Theorists' Criticisms', *Linguistics and Philosophy*, 25, 347–72.

Schlenker P. (2003) 'A Plea for Monsters', *Linguistics and Philosophy*, 26 (1), 29–120.

Searle J. (1978) 'Literal Meaning', *Erkenntnis*, 13, 207–24.

Searle J. (1980) 'The Background of Meaning' in Searle J., Kiefer F. and Bierwisch M. (eds) *Speech Act Theory and Pragmatics* (Dordrecht: Riedel), pp. 221–32.

Sellars W. (1954) 'Presupposing', *The Philosophical Review*, 63(2), 197–215.

Sennet A. (2008) 'The Binding Argument and Pragmatic Enrichment, or, Why Philosophers Care Even More than Weathermen about "Raining"', *Philosophy Compass*, 3(1), 135–57.

Soames S. (2002) *Beyond Rigidity: the Unfinished Semantic Agenda of Naming and Necessity* (New York: Oxford University Press).

Soames S. (2004) 'Naming and Asserting' in Szabó Z. G. (ed.) *Semantics vs. Pragmatics* (Oxford: Oxford University Press), pp. 356–82.

Sosa E. (1998) 'Minimal Intuition' in DePaul M. R. and Ramsey W. (eds) *Rethinking Intuition* (Lanham, Md: Rowman and Littlefield), pp. 257–69.

Sperber D. (1995) 'How do We Communicate?' in Brockman J. and Matson K. (eds) *How Things Are: a Science Toolkit for the Mind* (New York: Morrow), pp. 191–9.

Sperber D. (2000) 'Metarepresentation in an evolutionary perspective' in Sperber D. (ed.) *Metarepresentation: a Multi-Disciplinary Perspective* (Oxford University Press), pp. 115–37.

Sperber D. and Wilson D. (1986) *Relevance: Communication and Cognition* (Cambridge: Harvard University Press).

Sperber D. and Wilson D. (1998) 'The Mapping between the Mental and Public Lexicon' in Carruthers P. and Bouchers J. (eds) *Language and Thought: Interdisciplinary Themes* (Cambridge: Cambridge University Press), pp. 184–200.

Sperber D. and Wilson D. (2002) 'Pragmatics, Modularity and Mind-Reading', *Mind & Language*, 17, 3–23.

Stalnaker R. (1970) 'Pragmatics', *Synthese*, 22 (1–2), 272–89.

Stanley J. (2000) 'Context and Logical Form', *Linguistics and Philosophy*, 23, 391–424.

Stanley J. (2002a) 'Making it Articulated', *Mind & Language*, 17 (1–2), 149–68, reprinted in Stanley (2007) (page references from the latter).

Stanley J. (2002b) 'Nominal Restriction' in Peter G. and Preyer G. (eds) *Logical Form and Language* (Oxford: Oxford University Press), reprinted in Stanley (2007), pp. 365–90.

Stanley J. (2005a) 'Semantics in Context' in Preyer G. and Peter G. (eds) *Contextualism in Philosophy: Knowledge, Meaning, and Truth* (New York: Oxford University Press) pp. 221–54.

Stanley J. (2005b) *Knowledge and Practical Interests* (Oxford: Oxford University Press).
Stanley J. (2007) *Language in Context* (New York: Oxford University Press).
Stanley J. and Szabó Z. G. (2000) 'On Quantifier Domain Restriction', *Mind & Language*, 15, 219–61.
Stojanovic I. (2007) 'Talking about Taste: Disagreement, Implicit Arguments, and Relative Truth', *Linguistics and Philosophy*, 30, 691–706.
Sundell T. (2011) 'Disagreements about Taste', *Philosophical Studies*, 155 (2), 267–88.
Szabó Z. G. (2001) 'Adjectives in Context' in Harrish R. and Kenesei I. (eds) *Perspectives on Semantics, Pragmatics, and Discourse* (Amsterdam: John Benjamins Publishing Company), pp. 119–47.
Szabó Z. G. (2006) 'Sensitivity Training', *Mind & Language*, 21 (1), 31–8.
Taylor K. (2001) 'Sex, Breakfast, and Descriptus Interruptus', *Synthese*, 128, 45–61.
Taylor K. (2003) *Reference and the Rational Mind* (Stanford, Calif.: CSLI Publications).
Taylor K. (2007) 'A Little Sensitivity Goes a Long Way' in Preyer G. and Peter G. (eds) *Context-Sensitivity and Semantic Minimalism: New Essays on Semantics and Pragmatics* (New York: Oxford University Press), pp. 63–93.
Tomasello M. (2001) 'Perceiving Intentions and Learning Words' in Bowerman M. and Levinson L. (eds) *Language Acquisition and Conceptual Development* (Cambridge: Cambridge University Press), pp. 132–58.
Travis C. (1975) *Saying and Understanding* (Oxford: Blackwell).
Travis C. (1985) 'On What Is Strictly Speaking True', *Canadian Journal of Philosophy*, 15, 187–229, reprinted in Travis (2008).
Travis C. (1996) 'Meaning's Role in Truth', *Mind*, 100, 451–66.
Travis C. (1997) 'Pragmatics' in Hale B. and Wright C. (eds) *A Companion to the Philosophy of Language* (Oxford: Blackwell), pp. 87–107.
Travis C. (2002) *The Uses of Sense. Wittgenstein's Philosophy of Language* (New York: Oxford University Press).
Travis C. (2006) 'Insensitive Semantics', *Mind & Language*, 21(1), 39–49.
Travis C. (2008) *Occasion Sensitivity* (New York: Oxford University Press).
Unger P. (1995) 'Contextual Analysis in Ethics', *Philosophy and Phenomenological Research*, 55, 1–26.
Van Benthem J. and Ter Meulen A. (2011) *Handbook of Logic and Language* (Frankfurt: Elsevier).
van Craenenbroeck J. and Merchant J. (2013) 'Ellipsis Phenomena' in den Dikken M. (ed.) *The Cambridge Handbook of Generative Syntax* (Cambridge: Cambridge University Press), pp. 701–45.
Van Inwagen P. (1997) 'Materialism and the Psychological-Continuity Account of Personal Identity', *Philosophical Perspectives*, 11, 305–19.
von Fintel K. and Gillies A. (2008) 'CIA Leaks', *The Philosophical Review*, 117(1), 77–98.
Waismann F. (1951) 'Verifiability' in Flew A. (ed.) *Logic and Language* (London: Blackwell), pp. 119–23.
Wettstein H. (1979) 'Indexical Reference and Propositional Content', *Philosophical Studies*, 36 (1), 91–100.
Wettstein H. (1981) 'Demonstrative Reference and Definite Descriptions', *Philosophical Studies*, 40 (2), 241–57.
Williamson T. (1994) *Vagueness* (London: Routledge).

Williamson T. (2006) 'Conceptual Truth', *Aristotelian Society Supplementary Volume*, 80 (1), 1–41.

Wilson D. (2000) 'Metarepresentation in Linguistic Communication' in Sperber D. (ed.) *Metarepresentation: a Multi-Disciplinary Perspective* (New York: Oxford University Press), pp. 410–45.

Wittgenstein L. (1953) *Philosophical Investigations*, translated by Anscombe G. E. M. (Oxford: Blackwell).

Zwicky A. M. and Sadock J. M. (1975) 'Ambiguity Tests and How to Fail Them', *Syntax and Semantics*, 4, 1–36.

Index

adjectives 14, 34, 54, 91, 106
adjective–noun phrases 2
ambiguity 9, 38, 41, 53–5, 76, 175
argument/adjunct distinction 129–31, 138, 146
attitude attribution 20, 148, 150, 163, 164

Binding Argument 14, 18, 93–4
Binding Assumption 18, 92, 94, 121–4

cancellability 134–6, 146
circumstances of evaluation 15–16, 62–3, 96, 105–10, 178
 and counts-as parameter 16, 107, 109
Conceptual Constraints 16–21, 95, 112, 113, 119, 124–39, 145–7, 158–60, 164–6, 170, 171, 178
conceptual truths (or truisms) 129, 131, 137, 179, 180
Context-Shifting Arguments 8–9, 25, 36–51, 55, 97, 174
 and completive context-shifts 9, 41–2, 51
 meaning-manipulative context-shifts 9, 42, 51
Contextualism
 Extreme 12, 81–3
 Indexical 14, 16, 18–19, 90–6, 109, 111, 113
 Moderate 33, 40, 173
 Non-Indexical 15–16, 81, 96, 104–10, 111–12
 Radical 13–18, 33–5, 40–1, 83–90, 102–4, 109–10, 111–12, 113, 117–18, 174

definite descriptions 2, 11, 65, 68, 70
detachability 134, 136, 146
divide and conquer strategy 13–15, 85–6, 90, 104, 111

effable mental contents 68–9, 72–6
ellipsis
 semantic ellipsis (*see* under-articulation)
 syntactic ellipsis 11, 52, 63–5, 66, 77
 under-articulation 11, 52, 65–9, 77–8
essential indexicals 70
eternal sentences 68, 70
eternal thoughts 69, 71, 72
explicature 85, 88–90, 102, 111

frames (or schemata) 17, 127–8, 131, 138, 146, 165, 170
free enrichment 13–14, 85–6, 91, 194, 109, 118, 151, 176
free variables in logical form 41, 91, 173

gappy picture 69, 72, 74
genericity 8, 29–36, 51, 71, 99–10, 173

hidden indexicals 10, 57, 59, 63, 77

implicature
 conventional implicature 133–4, 136
 conversational implicature 5, 19, 85–90, 102–4, 111, 118, 148–9, 154, 156, 170, 174
 generalised conversational implicature 14, 118, 133–6, 174
impliciture 15, 101–4, 111, 117
incompleteness 7, 16, 25–36, 47–8, 50–1, 68–9, 83, 98, 104, 109–10, 114–15, 129–31, 142
indexicality
 and anaphoric relations 10, 59
 and a priori truths 10, 59–60
 and free enrichment 83–4
 and indefinite readings 10, 60–1

indexicality – *continued*
  and perspectivity 10, 57–9
  and rigidity effects 10, 61–3
  semantic under-determinacy not reducible to 10, 38, 52, 56–63, 77
Ineffability 52, 69–71
intuitions 7, 16, 26, 28–9, 33–6, 41, 45–50, 86–90, 97, 101, 109–12, 119–20, 124, 129–32, 141–2, 144, 155–6, 171, 173, 174

lack of qualification 3
lexical meaning 19, 95, 139, 141, 144
logical form 14, 18, 41, 57, 77, 91–5, 111, 119, 124–5, 173, 178
  development of 159

mental modules 20, 159, 171
meta-representation 20–1, 147–50, 154–70
  the epistemic role of 162–3
meta-representational conclusion 150, 155–6, 161–3, 167, 171–1
Minimalism 12, 14–16, 19, 47, 81, 96–101, 107, 112, 174–5, 176–7

negation 2, 88, 179
Non-Meta model 21, 159–60, 162–4, 165–6, 170, 171

pragmatic processes 13–14, 84, 86–8, 90, 94, 103, 109, 111, 117
pragmatics
  mind-reading 4, 116, 159, 160–1, 165
  speaker's intentions 4, 15, 97, 101, 103, 109, 116, 148, 156, 165, 168–9
  what the speaker means 5, 20, 47, 83, 103, 115, 147, 156, 165, 167, 171
propositions
  at-which-worlds challenge 15, 98–101
  granularity of propositions 7, 100
  minimal proposition 14–15, 97–101, 107, 112, 177

propositional radical 6, 15, 101, 102

quantification 2, 21, 70–1, 91–4, 115, 120–4, 137, 178, 179

reference 59, 61–3, 68, 70–1, 103, 117, 136, 166, 176, 178
  Atomism and 141, 142, 144
  mental 73, 76
Relevance Theory 20–1, 85, 148–9, 158–9, 63, 179

scalar implicature 86
Semantic Atomism 19, 113, 139, 141–5, 146
semantic binding 92, 121–2
semantic content 5–7, 15, 18, 26–31, 83–4, 87, 89, 97, 101–4, 107, 154, 160, 176
  see also sentence content
Semantic Holism 19, 113, 139–41, 144, 146
Semantic Molecularism 19, 113, 139, 146
semantic under-determinacy
  and conceptual truncation 1, 11, 50, 115, 129
  and context-sensitivity 12, 81
  serious and less serious 3
  as a *sui generis* phenomenon 9, 52, 76
semantically controlled processes 13, 17, 61, 83, 91, 101, 178
semantics
  and compositionality 4, 14, 25, 47, 95–5, 112, 117, 133, 145–6
  and convention 4, 93, 103, 117, 145
  literal meaning 3–5, 11, 66, 77, 87–8, 115
sentence content 13, 81, 84–5, 101, 103, 111
syntactic binding 18, 92, 121–2
syntactically articulated elements 9, 14, 18, 51, 92, 94, 119, 125, 179
syntax 14, 18–19, 42, 58, 61, 84–5, 90–6, 111–12, 119, 121–2, 125–6, 131, 133, 145, 150

Index   193

truth-relativism   15–16, 105, 111, 177

Ultra-Minimalism   15, 81, 96, 101–4, 111, 117–18, 176
unarticulated constituents   25, 26, 84
unspecificity   48
utterance comprehension   16, 19–21, 110, 112, 128, 138, 147–50, 152–72
    Anti-Inferentialism on   150–3
    Inferentialism on   19–21, 147, 148–50

utterance content   5, 14, 85, 88, 94–5, 117, 135

vagueness   10, 38–9, 41, 42, 50, 55–6, 71, 76–7

weather predicates   14, 34, 58, 60, 115, 133, 154–5, 161
weatherman case   60, 115, 130, 173
what is said   5, 85–90, 102–3, 111, 133, 146, 177

Printed and Bound in the United States of America.